TOP TRAILS OF
COLORADO AND NEW MEXICO

INCLUDES MESA VERDE, CHACO, COLORADO
NATIONAL MONUMENT, GREAT SAND DUNES AND
BLACK CANYON OF THE GUNNISON NATIONAL PARKS

by Eric Henze

Gone Beyond Guides
Publisher

General Information

What is the Grand Circle?

So you've been done an Arizona vacation, maybe even Colorado and Utah, but have you done the Grand Circle? You may have heard of the term and likely know it well if you live within it. For those that don't know what the Grand Circle means, you aren't alone. It is, in a nutshell, one of the "must do" vacation destinations in North America.

The Grand Circle encompasses five southwestern states but more importantly, is so named because it contains the highest concentration of national and state parks in the United States. Within this 500-mile diameter area, there are almost 80 parks and hundreds of other attractions. Simply put, the Grand Circle is a bounty of fun and adventure. This isn't about going to Zion or the Grand Canyon, it's about going on a once in a lifetime vacation, something so incredible that it becomes one of the top things you have ever done.

Within the Grand Circle are attractions found nowhere else in the world. Some of these seem to defy the laws of physics while others defy the boundaries of what you thought was possible. I've taken folks into areas where nobody spoke a word because they simply had never seen land like this before. They were in speechless awe and it's true, the journey can be beyond words, the land can be that striking. Within it are timeless monoliths, thousands of arches, delicately balanced rocks, some of the wildest rapids in the world and the deepest canyons. It contains the darkest nighttime skies in North America and the brightest colors during the day. The land is a symphony, at times thunderous and deafening, at other times a single soft note trailing into the silence of a deep blue sky. Here there are hoodoos, goblins, fins, tall alpine peaks and slot canyon so narrow there is barely room for one person. There are red rock cliffs, sheer vertical walls of rock so high that they are the emotional equal in sandstone what Yosemite is in granite.

This is a place that resets a person. One can't help but slow to the pace of the land. A visit here is a mixture of relaxation and wonder. You will find yourself returning to the pace of nature as you venture farther from the pace of man. It brings with it a connectedness reminding the visitor the things that are truly important in life.

This is a land carved by water and wind over millions of years and the results are astounding natural works of art. It is no wonder that this area contains the largest concentration of national parks and national monuments in the United States. Sure, the circle contains the internationally known Grand Canyon and Zion, but these are just two of its twelve national parks. Add to this list another 30 national monuments, 3 national recreation areas, several tribal parks and 29 more state parks. Moreover, these are just the lands formally set aside.

By the numbers, most of the parks that make up the Grand Circle are within Utah and Arizona, but the full magnitude of the circle encompasses lands within Nevada, New Mexico, and Colorado as well. The imaginary circle is about 500 miles in diameter or roughly 126 million acres of land. As daunting as that sounds, one can comfortably visit 7-8 of the most popular national parks (and several other parks along the way) in 10 days. Of course, the more one is able to slow down and spend here, the more one will see, but the point is, if you are looking for a vacation where every day is different, you can experience a large and varied amount of places in a relatively short amount of time here.

Historically, the Grand Circle was a term created when the Southwest National Parks were just beginning. The NPS worked with the Union Pacific

Parks Covered in This Book

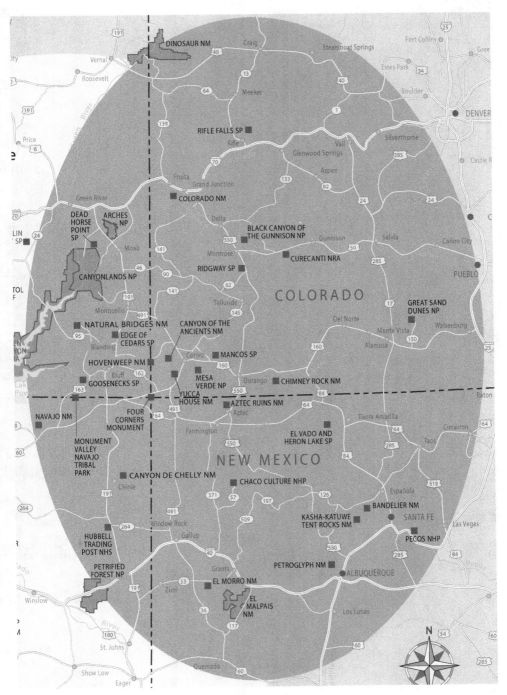

5

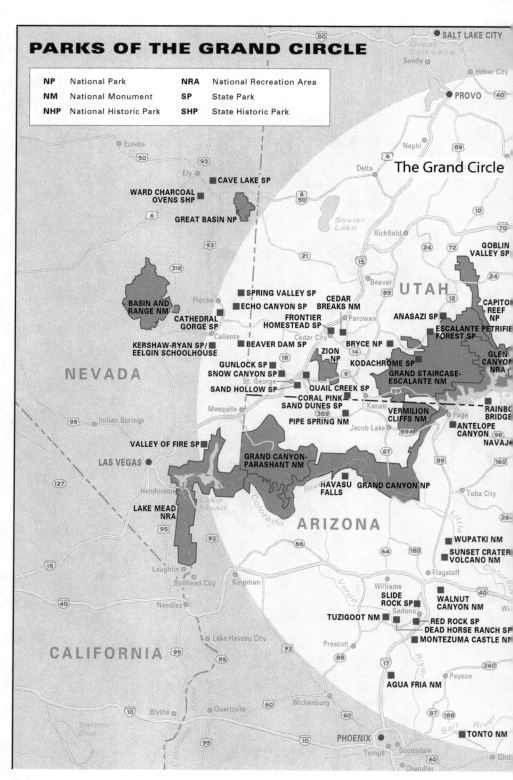

PARKS OF THE GRAND CIRCLE

NP	National Park	**NRA**	National Recreation Area
NM	National Monument	**SP**	State Park
NHP	National Historic Park	**SHP**	State Historic Park

The Grand Circle

SALT LAKE CITY

Great Salt Lake

Sandy

Heber City

PROVO

Eureka

Nephi

Delta

Ely

CAVE LAKE SP

WARD CHARCOAL OVENS SHP

GREAT BASIN NP

Sevier Lake

Richfield

UTAH

GOBLIN VALLEY SP

BASIN AND RANGE NM

Pioche

SPRING VALLEY SP

ECHO CANYON SP

CEDAR BREAKS NM

Beaver

Parowan

ANASAZI SP

CAPITOL REEF NP

CATHEDRAL GORGE SP

FRONTIER HOMESTEAD SP

ESCALANTE PETRIFIED FOREST SP

KERSHAW-RYAN SP/ EELGIN SCHOOLHOUSE

Caliente

Cedar City

BEAVER DAM SP

BRYCE NP

GLEN CANYON NRA

GUNLOCK SP

ZION NP

KODACHROME SP

NEVADA

SNOW CANYON SP

St. George

GRAND STAIRCASE-ESCALANTE NM

QUAIL CREEK SP

SAND HOLLOW SP

CORAL PINK SAND DUNES SP

Mesquite

Kanab

VERMILION CLIFFS NM

RAINBOW BRIDGE

PIPE SPRING NM

Page

ANTELOPE CANYON

Indian Springs

Jacob Lake

NAVAJO

VALLEY OF FIRE SP

LAS VEGAS

GRAND CANYON-PARASHANT NM

Henderson

Tuba City

Lake Mead

HAVASU FALLS

GRAND CANYON NP

LAKE MEAD NRA

Colorado

ARIZONA

Little Colorado

Laughlin

WUPATKI NM

SUNSET CRATER VOLCANO NM

Bullhead City

Kingman

Flagstaff

Needles

Williams

SLIDE ROCK SP

WALNUT CANYON NM

Lake Havasu City

Sedona

TUZIGOOT NM

RED ROCK SP

DEAD HORSE RANCH SP

CALIFORNIA

Prescott

MONTEZUMA CASTLE NM

Verde River

AGUA FRIA NM

Payson

Blythe

Quartzsite

Wickenburg

Salt River

TONTO NM

Salton Sea

Colorado River

PHOENIX

Tempe

Scottsdale

Chandler

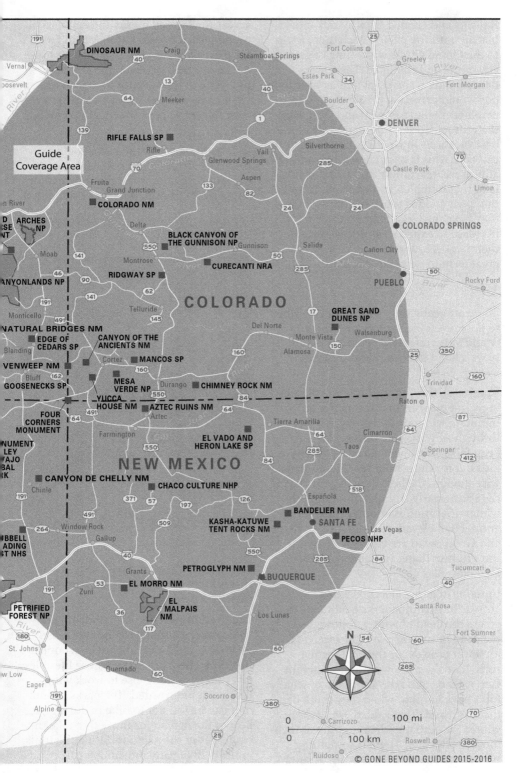

Guide
Coverage Area

DINOSAUR NM
Vernal
oosevelt
Craig
Steamboat Springs
Fort Collins
Greeley
Fort Morgan
191
40
34
Estes Park
Boulder
Meeker
DENVER
64
13
139
Silverthorne
RIFLE FALLS SP
285
Castle Rock
70
Rifle
Vail
Glenwood Springs
Fruita
Aspen
70
Grand Junction
133
Limon
COLORADO NM
n River
82
24
24
COLORADO SPRINGS
D
ARCHES
SE
NP
NT
Delta
BLACK CANYON OF
THE GUNNISON NP
Gunnison
Salida
Cañon City
Moab
550
50
PUEBLO
50
Rocky Ford
141
Montrose
ANYONLANDS NP
RIDGWAY SP
CURECANTI NRA
285
90
62
141
191
Telluride
COLORADO
GREAT SAND
DUNES NP
Monticello
145
17
Walsenburg
NATURAL BRIDGES NM
Del Norte
Monte Vista
150
350
EDGE OF
CEDARS SP
CANYON OF THE
ANCIENTS NM
Alamosa
25
Blanding
160
VENWEEP NM
Cortez
MANCOS SP
160
Trinidad
160
Bluff
162
GOOSENECKS SP
MESA
VERDE NP
Durango
CHIMNEY ROCK NM
Raton
87
YUCCA
HOUSE NM
AZTEC RUINS NM
84
FOUR
CORNERS
MONUMENT
491
Aztec
64
Tierra Amarilla
Cimarron
64
64
NUMENT
LEY
AJO
BAL
K
Farmington
EL VADO AND
HERON LAKE SP
64
Taos
Springer
412
550
285
84
NEW MEXICO
518
CANYON DE CHELLY NM
CHACO CULTURE NHP
Española
Chinle
191
BANDELIER NM
371
57
197
126
KASHA-KATUWE
TENT ROCKS NM
SANTA FE
Las Vegas
264
Window Rock
509
PECOS NHP
BBELL
ADING
T NHS
Gallup
285
84
Tucumcari
40
550
PETROGLYPH NM
LBUQUERQUE
Grants
EL MORRO NM
53
Santa Rosa
Zuni
36
EL
MALPAIS
NM
Los Lunas
PETRIFIED
FOREST NP
191
117
180
60
St. Johns
Fort Sumner
w Low
54
N
Quemado
60
285
Eager
191
Socorro
380
70
Alpine
100 mi
Carrizozo
0
0
100 km
Roswell
380
25
Ruidoso
© GONE BEYOND GUIDES 2015-2016

7

Railway and created trips by rail and bus up until the 1970's. Back then, a trip to the Grand Circle was a time of great adventure and romance. There were dance bands at the stops and as your tour bus would drive away from the lodge, employees would line up and "sing away" the visitors. Today, it remains one of the best vacations in North America that one can take. This is a vacation destination of adventure, relaxation, and wonder. It is a land that humbles, inspires, and refreshes the spirit and for those that know of it, they have the Grand Circle as a bucket list place to experience at least once in their lives. The term Grand Circle is a great term to describe this land.

When to Go

There are really only two factors on when to go, do you like temperate climates or would you prefer less people. Weather plays a hand in both but in different ways.

In general, the Grand Circle is a blisteringly hot place in the summer, starting in mid to late June and going full force through August. That doesn't seem to keep folks away, particularly if you have kids out for the school year. Temperature wise though, the best time to go is during the spring/early summer and fall/early winter. Elevation is another consideration. High elevation parks such as Bryce and Great Basin are typically cooler in the summer than say Canyonlands or Lake Powell.

In terms of going at a time when the crowds have thinned, the best times to go are the dead of winter, followed by the dead of summer. Winter receives a lot fewer crowds for the obvious reasons. It's colder, snowier, and wetter. In fact, it tends to be the antithesis of what folks have in mind when they think of the southwest. That said, these parks in winter are perhaps when they are at their most spectacular. There is something transformative about a dusting of snow

across the layered mesas and canyons or topping each hoodoo of Bryce. In fact, for places like Bryce, which receive tons of visitors each summer, the arguably best time to go is winter. I've been out on trails covered in snow on a crisp clear day with the entire park practically to myself.

Winter at any of the parks can be magical, but it does run the risk of being miserable. In fact, you could be snowed in, which isn't the worst thing that could happen to a person, but can be difficult if

View from Dinosaur National Monument

your boss is expecting you back at work. In addition, some of the parks are simply closed in the winter.

The dead of summer is a good second choice as it is usually too hot for most. That said, given kids are out of school at this time, there are many whose lifestyles gives them nothing else to work with, so it can still be crowded. The parks in summer can be too hot to hike in during the heat of the day, so for those that take this tactic, get in the habit of hitting the trails in the cool of early morning.

Where to Go

If you think about it, there is a fair amount of irony in guidebooks that tell you the best places to go to avoid crowds. They are basically saying, we've learned all these secret cool places that no one goes to and we are now publishing this information in a globally available guidebook for anyone to read. If you see one of these sections, don't believe it, the word is already out on all these "secret places". In fact, places such as Havasu Falls are so impacted, it is nearly impossible to get a permit to hike the trail.

That said, there are some general tips to getting an otherwise crowded national park or monument to yourself. Take the Grand Canyon for example. This park receives some 4.5 million visitors to the South Rim alone. The vast majority of these folks don't hike any farther than to the overlooks. So simply getting out on any trail cuts the population of the park down by about 90%. If you've purchased this book, that means you like to hike, so you are on good footing right from the start.

There are other tips to share. In general, I've found that the more strenuous the hike is, the harder the trail is to get to, and the longer the trail's length, the greater the chances you will have the trail to yourself. If the trail is a short little paved walkway with interpretive signs, be prepared to share it. If it is one of the routes described in these guides, so rugged there isn't even a trail, be prepared to survive on your own because you are likely the only one out that way.

The same can be said about weather. Heat, rain, snow, and cold tend to filter out a fair amount of people. What's amazing about this is sometimes inclement weather will bring out the most unique views of a trail you will likely ever see. Now keep you in mind that you should add in a large degree of common sense. You don't want to have a slot canyon "all to yourself" in a thunderstorm or hike in the direct heat of a summer's day unless you are fully prepared and acclimated. Don't be stupid in your quest to have the place to yourself. The point here is, in general I've found a rather obvious truth. If a guidebook says it's secret, it isn't. The more remote a place is, the longer the hike, the steeper the inclines, the more extreme the journey, these all act as filters to minimizing the crowd factor.

Being Prepared

Hiking in the Grand Circle can be highly rewarding. However, don't let the desert fool you. This is an extreme environment, and one shouldn't just venture out without some forethought and preparation. This section seems straightforward, but as the rangers at the Grand Canyon can attest to, there are literally dozens of people that venture out into the wilderness with nothing more than enthusiasm. Since enthusiasm alone can really put a damper on your hike, here are some tips to make your hikes safer and more enjoyable.

Water

Rule of thumb; bring three quarts per person per day. Some folks prefer two 1.5-liter bottles; some find they can balance their day or backpacks out better with three 1.0-liter bottles. Make sure the bottles do not leak by turning them upside down to see if water comes out. If it's only a drip, it's still a problem.

Water is pretty heavy, but bringing more rather than less keeps you hydrated and allows you to go farther.

If you are traveling with small children, you will likely need to carry their water for them beyond one quart. Keep this in mind as you are packing.

Clothing

Bring layers as appropriate for the hike. This means if the temperatures are cooler when you are at rest; bring a layer or two to keep you warm. Windbreakers are great allies in keeping warmth in and cold out and are also lightweight. In really cold temps a good beanie helps as well as some 15% of your body temperature is lost through your head. If it looks like rain, bring a waterproof version of that windbreaker.

In the heat, most folks go with the t-shirt and shorts, which is fine, but definitely bring a hat. The heat can be oppressing, especially with no shade and that hat will definitely help. I also recommend a full brimmed hat over a baseball cap. This will provide more shade and definitely helps keep the back of your neck from getting sunburned.

In either hot or cold weather, bring another warm layer if you can. This is your emergency backup layer should you find yourself having to spend the night in the wilderness for whatever reason. A windbreaker that can be rolled up or a long sleeve shirt can make a big difference if you find yourself facing the setting sun with nothing but a t-shirt and shorts on a summer trip. I've also found it to be a good thing to have on hand for others that may need some warmth when you don't.

Boots, Tennis and Water Shoes

Most people will tend to go for their tennis shoes because they are comfortable and easier to lace up. That said, boots are preferred because they offer a lot more protection, especially around the ankles. Tennis shoes are great for flat surfaces, but boots are made for uneven terrain. It's like taking a sedan tire on a 4WD road instead of an all-terrain tire. You wouldn't do it to your car, don't do it to your feet. Where a good boot and also, be the boot. Wear it in before you start your hiking adventures so you don't get blisters.

If the trail involves some hiking in water, it really helps to have a pair of water shoes. They are lightweight and keep your boots dry. A dry boot makes for a happy hiker, whereas a wet boot can destroy your feet in short order.

Daypack

A decent no nonsense day back to hold everything is essential. At the end of the day, you just want something that will last a long time. The more parts the pack has, the more parts that can fail. Zipper quality is number one. Most otherwise solid daypacks fail because of the zipper.

Also, a little tip on the daypack. If you get one that zips like an upside down U, put the zippers on one side or the other, not at the top. I have seen and personally had a branch find its way between the two zippers at top and open the entire contents of the pack onto the trail. In my case, it opened on brushy 30-degree incline I was scrambling up and I watched my lunch and water roll downhill out of sight forever.

Other Gear

At this point, you have three quarts of water, a bunch of layers, some food, and no room for anything else right. Well, it can seem that way. What to bring is a balancing act. On the one hand, you want to be lightweight. The more stuff you have on your back, the more burdensome it will feel. On the other hand, you do want to be prepared. In the excellent book, Climbing Ice by Yvon Chouinard, he says something that is about as true a piece of advice I've ever heard in this context.

If you bring it, you will use it.

What this means is if you bring a sleeping bag, you will likely spend the night in it. If you bring rope, you will likely use that rope. So start with packing only what you need for the hike.

Essentials include:

- Water and some food
- A hat
- Extra clothing as appropriate
- Sunscreen
- A map and possibly this trail guide (if you feel you will need it to navigate the trail)

On top of this, I would seriously consider also bringing:

- Some form of fire, a lighter, or fire starter of some kind
- Compass
- Small first aid kit, a whistle, and reflector mirror (for emergencies)
- A sharp knife
- Moleskin (for blisters)
- Ibuprofen (to help if you aren't acclimated to the heat)
- Water purification tablets
- Small flashlight
- Cell phone
- GPS device

It's hard to come up with a list that works under all conditions and the above list is more geared towards summer hiking than winter, so adjust what you bring for cold, rain, or snow. Also, be sure to bring something fun, a little treat goes a long way and is much better appreciated on the trail. This falls under "being kind to yourself" which is described below.

Know Yourself

Gung Ho-ness

Many of these trails are steep and long. Add in that you are at high elevations and the temperatures are hot means many of the hikes in this book can be

The tent rocks of Kasha-Katuwe

challenging. With that in mind, choose a hike that is appropriate for you. You will enjoy the hike more and plus; you will be able to go on another hike the next day. Know your physical limitations and don't test them to the point that you will need to be rescued.

Find Your Pace

Great hiking partners are not only experienced; they are great for each other because they both travel at the same pace. Start by finding your own pace and ask others to share that pace with you. If you are the faster traveler, slow down to the pace of the other person or group.

Take Breaks, Eat Snacks

Taking a ten-minute break every hour actually improves your stamina, allowing you to enjoy the hike more and go longer. Resting helps remove metabolic waste products such as lactic acid and gives your body time to flush them out. Eating snacks and drinking fluids helps refuel your body so you can continue onwards happy and content.

Black Canyon of the Gunnison

Time Flies

Being stuck on the trail after the sun sets isn't much fun, well unless there's a full moon out and no canopy to block the light. That can actually be a lot of fun and is highly recommended. Wait, the point I'm trying to make here is if you are out in the wilderness, watch your time and be aware of how long it took you to get to your turn around point. If the trail starts as a major descent, some of the steeper trails require twice as much time for returning up then it took getting down. The Grand Canyon is a good example of this. Being stuck in areas where the temperature drops dramatically at night is also a concern. Here, the The Narrows hike in Zion is a great example. Also, if you think you might be caught out in the dark, having a little flashlight, per person, can be a lifesaver.

Don't Be Afraid to Abort the Trip

If you or another hiker is showing signs of exhaustion, heat stroke, hypothermia or if the weather doesn't look like its adding up right, don't hesitate to turn back. Typically, these trips are planned far in advance and there is plenty of anticipation and excitement, but nothing is worth serious health issues or worse from not making the right decision. If someone doesn't feel they are up to a hike or someone in the group feels they may be putting themselves in danger, take their concerns seriously. Heat stroke and hypothermia can get serious and can lead to death.

Hypothermia, altitude sickness, and heat exhaustion have nothing to do with physical ability. I've seen firsthand the symptoms of each of these health issues and everyone that experienced them started out in terrific shape. It can hit hard and quickly. The typical "first signs" that I've seen are loss of mental sharpness and generally just out of it. The victim appears drunk and off, but otherwise may seem "themselves" at times. Don't second-guess here, if your buddy isn't acting like his or her normal self; stop, assess and remediate the issue. Don't keep pressing on.

The Hazardous H's + Altitude Sickness

The below is put out by the National Park Service and gives a good overview of some of the health issues to look out for while hiking. Since some of the trails within the Grand Circle are at altitude, a description of altitude sickness or acute mountain sickness (AMS) is also included.

Heat Exhaustion

The result of dehydration due to intense sweating. Hikers can lose one or two quarts (liters) of water per hour.

Symptoms: pale face, nausea, vomiting, cool and moist skin, headache, cramps.

Treatment: drink water with electrolytes, eat high-energy foods (with fats and sugars), rest in the shade for 30-45 minutes, and cool the body by getting wet.

Heatstroke

A life-threatening emergency where the body's heat regulating mechanisms become overwhelmed by a combination of internal heat production and environmental demands. Your body loses its ability to cool itself. Grand Canyon has two to three cases of heatstroke a year. Untreated heat exhaustion can lead to heatstroke.

Symptoms: flushed face, dry skin, weak and rapid pulse, high core body temperature, confusion, poor judgment or inability to cope, unconsciousness, seizures.

Treatment: the heatstroke victim must be cooled immediately! Continuously pour water on the victim's head and torso, fan to create an evaporative cooling effect. Immerse the victim in cold water if possible. Move the victim to shade and remove excess clothing. The victim needs evacuation to a hospital. Someone should go for help while attempts to cool the victim continue.

Hyponatremia (water intoxication)

An illness that mimics the early symptoms of heat exhaustion. It is the result of low sodium in the blood caused by drinking too much water and losing too much salt through sweating.

Symptoms: nausea, vomiting, altered mental states, confusion, frequent urination. The victim may appear intoxicated. In extreme cases seizures may occur.

Treatment: have the victim eat salty foods, slowly drink sports drinks with electrolytes, and rest in the shade. If mental alertness decreases, seek immediate help!

Hypothermia

A life-threatening emergency where the body cannot keep itself warm, due to exhaustion and exposure to cold, wet, windy weather.

Symptoms: uncontrolled shivering, poor muscle control, careless attitude. Look for signs of the "umbles" - stumbling, mumbling, fumbling, grumbling.

Treatment: remove wet clothing and put on dry clothing, drink warm sugary liquids, warm victim by body contact with another person, protect from wind, rain, and cold.

Altitude Sickness

Altitude sickness is your body not being able to acclimate to altitude. If untreated, it can lead to high altitude pulmonary oedema (HAPE) which is a life threatening condition where your lungs fill with fluid, making it difficult to breath. It can also lead to high altitude cerebral oedema (HACE), which is a buildup of fluid in your brain. Both can cause death within hours if not treated.

Symptoms: The most common symptom is typically a headache similar to that felt with a hangover. Some folks will feel nausea and may vomit as well as a general malaise feeling, and dizziness.

Treatment: If you are experiencing AMS, the best and only treatment is descending. Altitude sickness is not uncommon, especially if you have ascended in elevation too fast, starting at elevations of 8200 feet (2500 m). While it is common, some people are only slightly affected, while others feel so bad they have to turn around. For all, even those slightly affected, be self-aware as it can lead to pulmonary and cerebral oedema, which are very serious conditions.

If You Get Lost

Daniel Boone once said, "I have never been lost, but I will admit to being confused for several weeks." If you do get lost, you will quickly realize you aren't Daniel Boone and wished you had of paid more attention to all those nifty tricks you might have seen on those survival shows. Never fear, this book might just save you. Read the following tips if you happen to get lost.

- Stay calm. The sun's setting and you still haven't found the trail, let alone your car. This is not a time to freak out. Take some deep breaths and stay calm. You will get through this. I realize if you are freaking out, reading this won't help one bit. I recommend rereading the first sentence in this bullet point until it makes sense. Once you are thinking rationally, continue to the next bullet.

- Ration water and food. Stay hungry, ration your water, don't eat and drink everything at once.

- Readjust your schedule to maximize for hydration. Water loss has

Cliff Palace at Mesa Verde National Park

now become your biggest enemy. This means hiking during the cool of the morning and evening, while hunkering down at mid-day. Aim for shade and stay put during the heat of the day. Remember, the power of threes when it comes to survival. Though you will be incredibly hungry, you can survive three weeks without food. For water, that time period is only three days (and for air, three minutes). Water loss is the biggest barrier to you surviving or not if you are lost in the desert.

- Make a plan. If you have a compass, see a landmark, can get a sense of direction from the sun, use all these things to help make a plan of action. This starts by staying calm. With calmness, you can think. In thought, you can assess what you know (and what you don't know). From this catalog of observations, you can make a plan. Try to remain rational and fact based in your observations, its okay to make an assumption, but assess how confident you are of these assumptions.

- Stay at an even calm pace, pick your path. Look ahead to where you want to go, aim for paths of least resistance and effort versus paths that are harder to get through, if possible. Don't rush your walking, stay calm.

- Follow a road, a trail, or a route. If you see a road or a trail, take it. You have greatly increased your chances of being found or finding a way out yourself.

- Stay off the ground during the day. Finding shade is important when resting as the ground temperature can by 30 degrees hotter than the air temperature.

- Hike together at the pace of the slowest member and only separate if someone is injured.

- Stay with your car. If you are near your car, stay with it. It will make finding you easier and will provide shade, shelter and hopefully some food.

Southwest Colorado

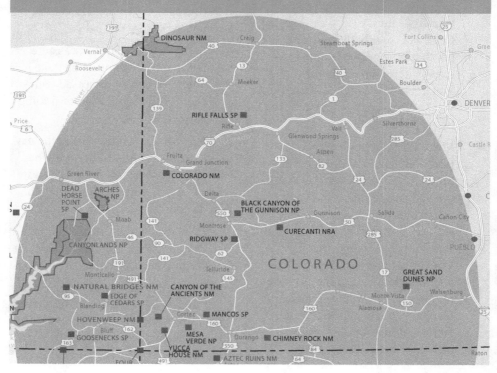

Mesa Verde National Park

Quick Facts

Official Park Website: http://www.nps.gov/meve

Visitor Center: (970) 529-4465

Park Accessibility:
- Okay for 2WD and RVs
- Day and Overnight Use

Experience Level:
- Family Friendly – Casual Hiker

Camping in Park:
- Morefield Campground: 267 T/RV sites restrooms, drinking water, showers, hookups, and a dump station. Some sites can be reserved at (800) 449-2288. Campground rarely fills up.

Lodging in Park:
- Far View Lodge, reservations by phone: (800) 449-2288 or online at http://www.visitmesaverde.com/accommodations/far-view-lodge.aspx

Dining in Park:
- Metate Room and Far View Terrace Restaurant

Nearest Town with Amenities:
- Cortez, CO is 10 mi / 16 km from park

Getting There:
- From Cortez, CO: Take US-160 E 10 mi / 16 km to park entrance

Cliff Palace

MESA VERDE NATIONAL PARK

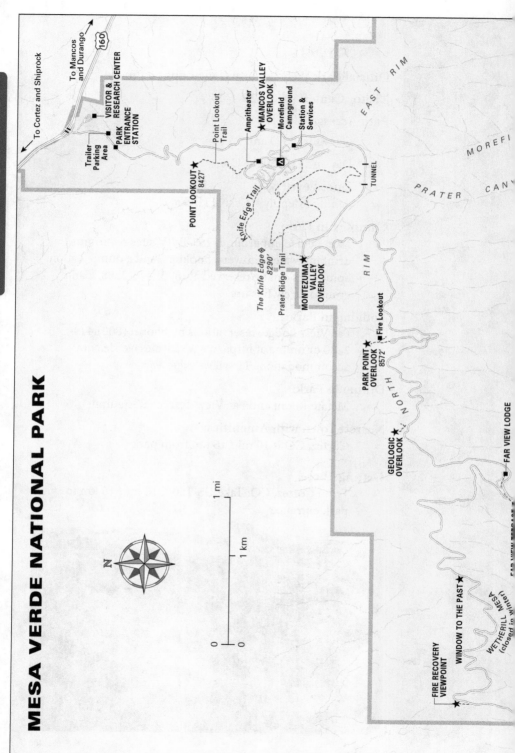

N

1 mi

1 km

To Cortez and Shiprock

To Mancos and Durango

160

VISITOR & RESEARCH CENTER

PARK ENTRANCE STATION

Trailer Parking Area

POINT LOOKOUT 8427'

Point Lookout Trail

Ampitheater

MANCOS VALLEY OVERLOOK

Morefield Campground

Station & Services

Knife Edge Trail

The Knife Edge ⬦ 8290'

Prater Ridge Trail

MONTEZUMA VALLEY OVERLOOK

TUNNEL

EAST RIM

MOREFI

PRATER   CANY

NORTH   RIM

Fire Lookout

PARK POINT OVERLOOK 8572'

GEOLOGIC OVERLOOK

FAR VIEW LODGE

WINDOW TO THE PAST

WETHERILL MESA (closed in winter)

FIRE RECOVERY VIEWPOINT

FAR VIEW MESAS

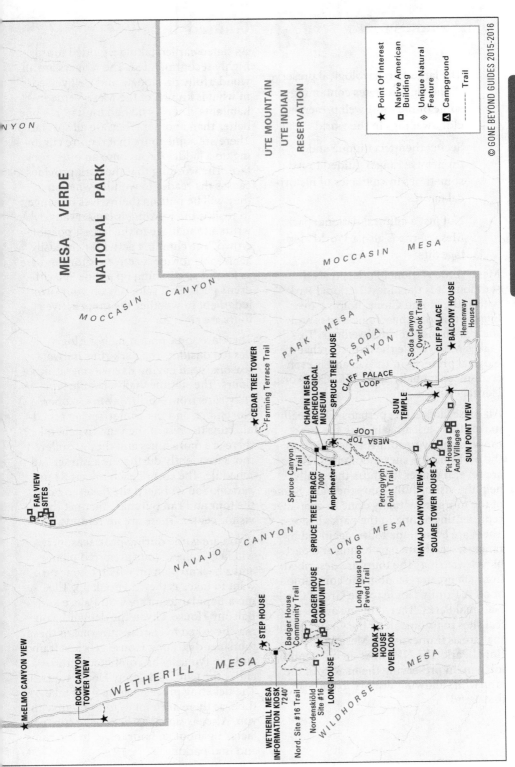

© GONE BEYOND GUIDES 2015-2016

Legend

★ Point Of Interest
□ Native American Building
◆ Unique Natural Feature
▲ Campground
------ Trail

MESA VERDE NATIONAL PARK

UTE MOUNTAIN
UTE INDIAN
RESERVATION

MOCCASIN MESA

MOCCASIN CANYON

PARK MESA

SODA CANYON

CEDAR TREE TOWER
Farming Terrace Trail

CHAPIN MESA ARCHEOLOGICAL MUSEUM
SPRUCE TREE HOUSE

CLIFF PALACE LOOP

Soda Canyon Overlook Trail

CLIFF PALACE

SUN TEMPLE

Hemenway House

BALCONY HOUSE

MESA TOP LOOP

Spruce Canyon Trail

SPRUCE TREE TERRACE 7000'
Ampitheater

Petroglyph Point Trail

Pit Houses And Villages

NAVAJO CANYON VIEW
SUN POINT VIEW
SQUARE TOWER HOUSE

FAR VIEW SITES

NAVAJO CANYON

LONG MESA

McELMO CANYON VIEW

ROCK CANYON TOWER VIEW

WETHERILL MESA

STEP HOUSE

Badger House Community Trail

BADGER HOUSE COMMUNITY

Long House Loop Paved Trail

WETHERILL MESA INFORMATION KIOSK 7240'

Nord. Site #16 Trail

Nordenskiöld Site #16

LONG HOUSE

KODAK HOUSE OVERLOOK

MESA

WILDHORSE

N Y O N

What Makes Mesa Verde Special

- The largest archaeological preserve in the United States containing some of the most well preserved cliff dwellings in the world

- Seeing them via unique and immersive ranger guided tours, sometimes in character of historical figures

- Not just a cultural national park, Mesa Verde is also a World Heritage Site

Mesa Verde National Park is truly a standout. It is the oldest National Park within the Grand Circle, holding over five thousand archaeological sites and some six hundred cliff dwellings. This makes Mesa Verde the largest archaeological preserve in the US and is even recognized globally as a UNESCO World Heritage Site.

All these facts aside, perhaps what really makes this park amazing are the park ranger's ability to connect the visitor to the park and the sites themselves. There are several ranger led tours that really help the visitor fully enjoy the park. Some of the tours are actually done in character representing a time in the park's history. There are even some tours, again led by rangers, which are part hiking and part bicycle touring. The tours are described in much greater detail in the companion book A Family Guide to the Grand Circle National Parks. There are few archaeological sites in or outside of the Grand Circle that are as immersive as Mesa Verde National Park. The NPS does an outstanding job here in preserving the history of the area while allowing visitors to enjoy it first-hand.

Guided Tours

As stated earlier, taking a guided tour is highly recommended. The rangers are all wonderfully passionate and well versed in what is known of the Mesa Verde inhabitants. There is no bad tour, nor is one better than another. They are all special. There are some tours that require climbing up a ladder or out onto an open rock face. The wording that the park provides causes the reader to wonder whether they will be putting themselves in danger. In reality, the wording is conservatively written to manage to the largest possible crowd. The climbing activities are easily achievable for most active visitors and are as fearful as climbing up a slide at a children's park. That said, rely on your own judgment in whether the more active tours are right for you.

There are some operating hour logistics to consider. The park runs in two seasons, each having its own operating hours. The summer/fall schedule typically runs from April/May to October/November, and the winter/spring schedule runs the rest of the year. In general, there are more tours and they are offered more frequently during the summer/fall schedule. The cost of each tour is $4 per person. You will need the ticket to take the tour and can purchase them at the visitor center. There are no refunds.

If you are going during peak season, it will help to have your preferred plan and a backup plan on which tours you want to take, as they do book up. The most popular tours are Cliff Palace and Balcony House. Given the demand, you may be asked to choose only one of these tours per day. Long House gets less traffic and can typically be combined with either the Cliff or Balcony House tours. The ticketing process can in itself take time, as there are a lot of folks there with you. Also, as stated earlier, make sure you factor in about an hour to get to the ruins and find parking.

During the summer/fall schedule, the rangers also offer Cliff Palace Twilight tours. These tours are limited to groups of twenty, last 90 minutes and—as the name suggests—are led in the early evening between 6:30 and 7:15 pm. This is a chance for the ranger to educate in a character that is a historical representative of the park's past. The ranger will stay in character the entire time, which is quite magical given the setting and the early evening hour. For many this is the highlight of their stay. Tickets for the Cliff Palace Twilight tours are $20 per person for all ages.

Tickets can be picked up at the following locations:

- Mesa Verde Visitor and Research Center: (main visitor center near entrance, seasonal hours, but typically 8 am to 5 pm)

- Morefield Ranger Station (near Morefield campground, open during peak season only, limited hours, 7 am to 11 am)

- Colorado Welcome Center (in Cortez at 928 E. Main St., Cortez, CO 81321, Phone: (970) 565 4048. Seasonal hours typically from 8 AM to 5 PM)

One more tip before discussing the tours themselves: Water is the only food item that is allowed on the tours. Food, beverages, candy and gum are not permitted. Tours are an hour long, so fill up prior to your arrival.

Cliff Palace Tour

Cliff Palace is the largest cliff dwelling in the park and in the United States. It is also the most popular tour. Visitors will get a close look at what is considered the former social center of the Mesa Verde communities. The ranger-guided tour lasts one hour and does involve some hiking on uneven stone pathways and steps. There are small 8–10 foot (2.6 -3m) ladders that one needs to ascend a 100-foot (30m) climb. At the visitor center there are somber warnings about these ladders; however, for most people they are similar to climbing a playground slide. The total walking distance is a short quarter-mile (400m) round trip.

There are 150 rooms that make up the dwelling along with 23 kivas, round ceremonial chambers. The dwelling is thought to have housed 100 people. This community was divided into smaller sub communities or polities. It is thought that each polity had its own kiva. The number of kivas in Cliff Palace suggests that this area was a highly social area as the ratio of rooms to kivas is much higher (nine rooms for each kiva built in Cliff Palace versus an average of 12 to 1 for the overall Mesa Verde community).

Cliff Palace Panorama

The structures are made of sandstone, mortar and wooden beams. Sandstone blocks were shaped using harder stones with mortar to seal and maintain structural integrity. In some places, small "chinking" stones were placed in larger gaps. Once finished, the walls were colored with earthen pigments. A sharp eye in Cliff Palace and in the other dwellings will note that the doorways are fairly small. The average man was 5'6" while the height of the average woman was around 5'.

One of the more prominent dwellings is a large square tower known as the Square Tower House. The Square Tower House was in ruins by the 1800s and has been restored by the National Park Service. It stands 26 feet tall and has four levels.

Balcony House Tour

This one-hour ranger-guided tour is a little more adventurous than the Cliff Palace tour and explores a cliff dwelling sitting on a high ledge facing east. The eastern view meant colder winters, but the tradeoff for those living here was increased security. The ledge was only accessible via a series of small footholds carved into the cliff by the early dwellers. This is believed to be the only way into and out of the dwelling and was thus easy to defend.

Modern visitors are faced with a similar challenge, although the National Park Service has done a good job of making the journey adventurous but safe. The visitor will need to climb up a 32-foot ladder at the beginning of the tour. To get back out, one will need to bend low through a 12-foot-long tunnel to climb two 10-foot ladders. As with all of these tours, you will need to feel comfortable that you and your party can climb the ladders.

The Balcony House is smaller than the Cliff Palace, with 45 rooms and two kivas. Don't let the smaller size fool you.

Kiva in Balcony House

Given the Balcony House was harder to get to, it was placed into the park's hands in better shape than some of the other dwellings. Many of the wooden beams can still be seen supporting roofs and sticking out of room walls. The Balcony House gives an intimate look at the Mesa Verde cliff dwellings. Besides the wooden beams and roofs, another favorite feature is a T- shaped doorway that can be seen during the tour.

Long House Tour

The Long House Tour is the longest, most in-depth and engaging tour offered. The tour is 90 minutes compared to the usual one-hour tours of Cliff Palace and Balcony House, includes a tram ride to and from the trailhead and is on the less traveled Wetherill Mesa. Unfortunately, it is also the hardest to get to for folks in an RV as vehicles over 25 feet are prohibited on the Wetherill Mesa Road. It is only open from Memorial Day to Labor Day each year. This tour is the most strenuous and requires a ¾-mile (1.2 km) hike round trip to access the dwellings.

The tour begins at the Wetherill Mesa information kiosk. Here you will board a tram that travels through a pinyon juniper forest undergoing recovery from a recent burn. Once at the Long House Trailhead, you follow a paved path downhill about 1/3 mile (0.54 km) to reach the ruins. At one point, there is a concrete staircase of 50 steps with railing.

The hike itself adds to the ambiance of discovery. The ruins are not in sight at first, only the tops of mesas and wide canyons. The hike descends through wonderful rock and pinyon juniper forests. In the summer, it is hot and dry and, while this leads to the strenuous aspects of the hike, it may give appreciation for what the early inhabitants faced. Once fully immersed in the surroundings, Long House comes into view.

After a short lecture near the ruins, the tour includes climbing two 15-foot (4.5m) ladders up into the site itself. No longer standing alongside the ruins, you are now inside them, bringing a personal aspect to experiencing the dwellings. The ruins themselves are fairly extensive, with more than 100 rooms, including multi-story buildings. Long House is the second largest cliff dwelling in the park. The ranger will point out some petroglyphs along the way as well. The tour ends by taking the same trail back, this time up-hill. On a hot day, the 50 concrete steps won't look as welcoming going up as they did going down. The tram will take you back to the Wetherill parking area.

Self-Guided Tours

Spruce Tree House (Chapin Mesa)

Note: Spruce Tree House has been closed for the foreseeable future due to concerns relating to rock falls.

During the winter months from November to early March, the Spruce Tree House is not only a ranger-led guided tour but is free. The tours last one hour and are given three times a day. The rest of the year, it is available as a self-guided tour.

Spruce Tree House is the third largest cliff dwelling (Cliff Palace and Long House are larger). It is also the best pre-served of the cliff dwellings. The walking distance of the tour is ½ mile (0.8 km) round trip and begins at the Chapin Mesa Archeological Museum. Visitors can meander at leisure along paths that encourage a more relaxed experience. There are around 130 rooms and 8 kivas, which were believed to have housed 60 to 80 people. There are many multistory buildings to view and a kiva that one can enter as part of the tour.

Far View Sites Complex (Chapin Mesa)

The Far View Sites are often overlooked on the drive to the more known sites at Chapin Mesa proper. The Far View Sites are unique in that these villages sit at the top of the mesa rather than in an alcove of a cliff. There were at one time 50 villages in the half square mile surrounding this area. The self-guided tour gives a nice walk among five of the villages plus a dry reservoir. The trail is unpaved but level and is ¾ mile (1.2km) long. These surface sites include Far View House, Pipe Shrine House, Coyote Village, Far View Reservoir, Megalithic House, and Far View Tower. This is a great hike if you want to round out the day's experience on your way back to the campground.

Badger House Trail (Wetherill Mesa)

The Badger House Community is a series of four sites on a paved and gravel trail. The sites include Modified Basketmaker Pithouse, Developmental Pueblo village, Badger House and Two Raven House. Like Far View Sites Complex, these sites sit on top of the mesa. The trail is 2.5 mile (4km) if started at the Wetherill Mesa Kiosk or 1.5 miles (2.41 km) if you take the tram to the Badger House tram stop. The tour is both educational and peaceful.

Step House (Wetherill Mesa)

The Step House is one of the more unique self-guided tours in that one can see clear distinctions pointing to two separate occupations of the site. The first inhabitants were the Modified Basketmakers, which dated to A.D. 626. Evidence of their habitation can be found between the old stone steps on the southern edge of the site and the large boulders to the north. The area was inhabited again in BCE 1226 as evidenced by the masonry structures seen within the rest of the site. Two standouts of the ruins are a pit house and the petroglyphs.

The trail is steep and ¾ mile (1.2 km) long along a winding path. Many visitors that come to Wetherill Mesa combine the Step House self-guided tour with the ranger-led Long House tour. Allow a good half day if you decide this is the right combination for you.

Hiking Mesa Verde

Point Lookout Trail

Strenuous – (2.2 mi / 3.5 km), round trip, elev. Δ: 510 ft / 155 m, trailhead at Morefield Campground

This is one of the three trails that start from the Morefield Campground. The trail does pass by some Ute structures and other ruins as it makes its way to a highpoint called Point Lookout. The point stands as a natural lookout tower for the entire Mesa Verde area. It was used by the United States Calvary to signal fellow mounted forces as well as earlier by the Utes.

There is an elevation gain of about 500 feet, most of it occurring in the first half mile as the trail winds on up via a series of switchbacks. The trail continues through Oak brush vegetation with a few more switchbacks and then more gently climbs the final half mile to the top. The trail here narrows to a knife ridge, but there is plenty of vegetation on either

side. Here there are remnants of Ute structure, inscriptions, initials and other interested artifacts as you reach the top and the great views of the Mancos and Montezuma Valley.

Knife Edge Trail

Easy – (2.0 mi / 3.2 km), round trip, elev. Δ: 59 ft / 18 m, trailhead at Morefield Campground

One of the other three hikes near the Morefield Campground, this short there and back trail gives some decent views of Montezuma Valley. The trail starts by passing between the Prater Ridge and an obvious little rock hillock called Lone Cone. There is a bit of elevation at first, but much of the trail is flat as it follows the old Knife Edge Road. The trail pretty much just ends at a sign that says, "STOP!! Trail End" indicating it's time to turn back. This short trail is nicely secluded on most days and provides a great place to take in a sunset.

Prater Ridge Trail

Strenuous – (7.8 mi / 12.6 km), round trip, elev. Δ: 710 ft / 216 m, trailhead at Morefield Campground

This loop is the longest of the three trails that start from the nearby Morefield Campground. The trail climbs until it reaches Prater Ridge and then follows

Wetherill Mesa

along the rim of the cuesta. Like all of the trails near the campground, it is light on ruins but big on nature. Prater Ridge gives expansive views of the Montezuma Valley. This is honestly one of the best of the longer hikes in the park. It makes a complete loop, giving a variety of views of the southern Colorado countryside. If you want to make it a smaller loop, there is an obviously marked cutoff trail that trims the loop by roughly half.

Farming Terrace Trail

Moderate – (0.5 mi / 0.8 km), round trip, allow 15 minutes, elev. Δ: 120 ft / 37 m, trailhead on Chapin Mesa

While the distance of this small loop trail isn't terribly long, it is fairly well exposed and can get hot. This trail gives a nice peak into how the Ancestral Puebloans farmed the land. At first glance, it just looks like a bunch of terraces, but one learns that they made good use of water runoff, diverting it as it made its way downhill to provide much needed moisture to their crops. The whole thing is quite ingenious to see unfold before the hiker. The trail is also close to the Cedar Tree Ruins, which is worth exploring. Make a right once you retrace the loop back to the road to see a kiva and a tower remnant.

Spruce Canyon Trail

Moderate – (2.4 mi / 3.9 km), round trip, elev. Δ: 529 ft / 161 m, trailhead on Chapin Mesa

Spruce Canyon Trail begins at the Spruce Tree House trail and gives the viewer a chance to experience the ecosystem of the canyon floor. The trail heads to the bottom of Spruce Tree Canyon and then back up along the mesa top in one nice loop. Like the Petroglyph Point Trail, the loop finishes at the Chapin Mesa Archeological Museum, which is well worth exploring in its own right.

Petroglyph Point Trail

Moderate – (2.4 mi / 3.9 km), round trip, elev. Δ: 196 ft / 60 m, trailhead on Chapin Mesa

This trail begins from the Spruce Tree House trail and is one of the more pleasant hikes in Mesa Verde. The loop starts down below the mesa top, following what feels like an ancient trail used years ago. One winds through narrow rock passages among pinyon juniper forests with views of Spruce and Navajo Canyons. The trail "ends" at the petroglyphs, which are impressive and worth the hike. From the rock art, the trailheads up to the top of the mesa for a level and easy walk back to the parking area. The hike drops you at the Chapin Mesa Archeological Museum, which is well worth a visit in its own right. Across the street is the Spruce Tree Terrace Café to finish off the hike with a well-deserved snack.

A trail guide is available and registration (at the museum) is required.

Soda Canyon Overlook Trail

Easy – (1.2 mi / 1.9 km), round trip, allow 30 minutes, elev. Δ: 72 ft / 22 m, trailhead on Chapin Mesa

This is an easy and flat hike that leads to three great overlooks from which several ruins can be viewed, including the Balcony House. There is a viewing scope installed at the canyon's edge at the middle overlook. The southernmost overlook gives the best views of Balcony House.

Nordenskiöld Site No. 16 Trail

Easy – (1.0 mi / 1.6 km), round trip, allow 30 minutes, elev. Δ: 228 ft / 69 m, trailhead on Wetherill Mesa

This trail found in the Wetherill Mesa section leads to an overlook of Nordenskiöld Site 16. The trail itself is flat and passes through a portion of the 2000 Pony Fire burn area. As a result, the land is a mixture of grasslands showing the wonder of recovery against a multitude of sentinel dead trees standing as silent evidence of the fire. The trail crosses a paved tram road occasionally. It is prohibited for hikers to walk the tram road, but okay to take the tram back if you want. The tram does make a stop at the Nordenskiöld site overlook, which is the end of the trail. The overlook gives a view into Site 16, a nice double alcove cliff dwelling. The site is named for Gustav Nordenskiöld, who made the first extensive excavations of the site back in 1891.

Badger House Community Trail

Moderate – (2.3 mi / 3.7 km), round trip, allow 1 hour, elev. Δ: 52 ft / 16 m, trailhead on Wetherhill Mesa

This is a rather flat but exposed trail which was hit by the 2000 Pony Fire. The trail is straightforward with a mixture of pea gravel and paved trail, offering some self-guided sections displaying various aspects of the Badger top site ruins. The top site ruins do have different qualities then the alcove ruins, so the Badger House trail helps make for a rounded experience.

Limited Backcountry Hikes

Each year, the Mesa Verde park rangers offer up exclusive and unique backcountry hikes and tours. The offerings are different each year and are definitely worth looking into. These hikes and guided ranger tours often go to areas that are not open or even publicized. The hikes typically require advance purchase of tickets and the number of tickets available each day is limited. Each hike is very special and even unprecedented in what the open up for visitors to see and experience.

For a list of the current year's hikes, check with the park for more information by going to the following link: http://www.nps.gov/meve/planyourvisit/backcountry_hikes.htm. Some of the hikes that seem to be perennial offerings are listed below. That said, each year they change them enough to warrant going to the website for current details.

Wetherill Mesa Bike and Hike Adventure

Strenuous – (9.0 mi / 14.5 km), round trip, allow 4.5 hours, not including driving time

Tickets are $18.00 for adults. Tours are limited to 15 people. Bike not included (you need to bring your own). There are rental bikes available, call (970) 529-4631 for information on local bike rental places.

Kokopelli Bike and Board offers bikes for rental in Cortez (130 W Main St, Cortez, CO 81321. (970) 565-4408). Also, tour times were limited to Wednesdays and Sundays as of this writing.

This is likely one of the coolest ranger led hikes in the entire Grand Circle. You get to hike with a ranger for four miles and bike alongside for another five miles. This isn't a tram stuffed full of people and some guy reciting into a megaphone, this is a full immersion bimodal journey into depths of Mesa Verde accompanied by an expert.

The entire trip is filled with great views of cliff dwellings with in depth trips to Nordenskiöld #12, Double House and even includes a short hike to Long House. Allow about six hours total for the hike and driving time to the starting point from the visitor center. The trip is okay for young adults able to travel 9 miles comfortably. Also, bring plenty of water, snacks, sunscreen, and a hat. Folks must be in good overall shape for this adventure.

Yucca House National Monument

Official Park Website: http://www.nps.gov/yuho

Visitor Center:

No visitor center at park. Park is administered by Mesa Verde NP: (970) 529-4465

Park Accessibility:

- Okay for 2WD and RVs

- Day Use Only

Experience Level:

- Family Friendly – Casual Hiker

Camping in Park:

- None

Lodging and Dining in Park:

- None

Nearest Town with Amenities:

- Cortez, CO is 12 mi / 19 km from the park

Yucca House NM Entrance

Getting There:

- From Cortez, CO: Take US-491 South turn right onto County Road B. After 0.8 miles, turn right onto County Road 20.5. Total distance is 12 mi / 19 km to park entrance

The park holds one of the larger Ancestral Puebloan sites, with hundreds of rooms. What makes Yucca House special however is what isn't there. There are no facilities, no visitor guides, no campsites, and no trails to be found. There is an easement access for a road to be built, but since its inception in 1919, there is no road. All that defines Yucca House is a lone-gated entrance. You walk up to it, you open the gate, and from here, you are on the same page as any other archaeologist and visitor. The place is yours to discover.

There are some paths created from use, follow these to find various mounds, some with bits of walls and other elements of ancient structures revealing themselves. The fascination is how quickly nature has taken back these lands. To walk around what is a 600 plus room complex and seeing more scrub and faint traces is a wonder in its own right.

Yucca House is a great place to stop as a side trip to Mesa Verde. It is a quick 20-minute drive from Cortez, Colorado via Highway 160E. The park is not well marked, but can be found easily with GPS navigation apps on most smartphones.

Canyons of the Ancients National Monument

Official Park Website: http://www.blm.gov/co/st/en/nm/canm.html

Visitor Center:

No visitor center at park. Park is administrated by BLM in conjunction with Canyons of the Ancients and Anasazi Heritage Center, 27501 Highway 184, Dolores, Colorado USA 81323, Phone: (970) 882-5600. Visitors are encouraged to stop here first for orientation before visiting the park.

Park Accessibility:

- High clearance 4WD

- Primarily Overnight Use

Experience Level:

- Experienced Hiker – Backcountry Hiker

Camping in Park:

- No developed campground, backcountry camping allowed with some limitations, see park website for details.

Lodging and Dining in Park:

- None

Nearest Town with Amenities:

- Cortez, CO is 18 mi / 29 km from the park

Getting There:

- From Cortez, CO: Take US-491 South turn right onto County Road G. Continue on Road G for about 14.4 miles. Total distance is 18 mi / 29 km to park entrance

The Canyons of the Ancients National Monument is unlike any other park set aside for the preservation of Ancestral Puebloan lands. It is in a very true sense an outdoor museum meant primarily to preserve the past. To date, more than 6,000-recorded sites have been discovered over the park's 176,056 acres (roughly half the size of Canyonlands National Park). The trails are more routes and even roads into the park are scarce. Many of the ruins in this park are not publicized.

To explore this monument, it is highly encouraged that the visitor first visits the Anasazi Heritage Center for orientation and current conditions. The center is located at 27501 Highway 184, Dolores, Colorado USA 81323, Phone: (970) 882-5600. Even before going to the center, it's a good idea to watch the video created by the park's stewards from the website link below.

Canyons of the Ancients is a very special place and any visit here carries with it a sense of responsibility for the visitor. One steward of the area stated it best; the only thing you can take is that which fills your heart. Enjoy the ruins with respect and ideally from a distance. Resist the urge to take a piece of pottery or a grinding stone home with you. Even resist the urge to move them for others to see. This is a sacred and spiritual area for many.

To get a much better idea of the park, take about 10 minutes to watch the below video by the stewards of this area. These are the words of the descendants of the people who lived here and are found on the park's home page. Besides giving a good idea of the landscape of some of the ruins in the area, their message is a strong one. Visit with respect. Take nothing. Say thank you when you leave. The video can be found here. www.youtube.com/watch?v=AvAuUeJoTIQ

Mancos State Park

Quick Facts

Official Park Website: http://cpw.state.co.us/placestogo/parks/Mancos

Visitor Center: (970) 533-7065

Park Accessibility:
- Okay for 2WD and RVs
- Day and Overnight Use

Experience Level:
- Family Friendly to Casual Hiker

Camping in Park:
- Main Campground: 24 T/RV, drinking water, vault toilets, no hookups
- West Campground: 9T, no drinking water, vault toilets

Lodging and Dining in Park:
- None

Nearest Town with Amenities:
- Mancos, CO is 5 mi / 8 km from the park

Getting There:
- From Durango, CO: Take US-160 West to CO-184 West (aka North Main Street in Mancos) to County Road 42 to County Road N. Total distance is 44 mi / 71 km to park

Mancos State Park

What Makes Mancos State Park Special

- The serenity of the Jackson Gulch Reservoir with the Rocky Mountains in the distance
- The grand views and peaceful hikes
- Being a great camping hub for nearby Durango and Mesa Verde National Park

Mancos State Park is a pleasant little camping spot located near Mesa Verde National Park. The park surrounds Jackson Gulch Reservoir and offers camping and two reservable yurts. Scenery here includes the always-amazing Rocky Mountains. Overall, this is a laid back little place, especially in the off-season. There are ample fishing opportunities as well as winter activities, such as snowshoeing and cross-country skiing.

Hiking Mancos State Park

Nature Trail

Easy – (0.2 mi / 0.3 km), round trip, allow 10 minutes

A very short nature trail near park entrance.

Horseshoe Trail

Easy – (0.8 mi / 1.3 km), one-way trip, allow 30 minutes

Horseshoe Trail winds from the park entrance around the lake to connect with Chicken Creek Trail. Great views along the way.

Mule Deer Trail

Easy – (1.9 mi / 3.1 km), round trip, allow 1 hour

This is a gentle walk along an old access road. Nice views of the lake can be found along this lazy trail as well as shoreline access. The trail ends at the quarry area.

Black Bear Trail

Moderate – (1.9 mi / 3.1 km), round trip, allow 1 hour

Black Bear is a loop trail that starts from the Chicken Creek Trailhead into the forest, where it ambles to a small watershed and back out connecting to where you started. If going clockwise, stay to the right at all trail junctions. This trail can be combined with others to create longer treks.

Mountain Lion Trail

Easy – (0.6 mi / 1.0 km), one way, allow 15 minutes

This is primarily a connector trail to Black Bear and Chicken Creek trails. Start near the quarry and head away from the reservoir to connect to Black Bear Trail. Some minor elevation gains.

Chicken Creek Trail

Moderate – (7.8 mi / 12.6 km), one-way, allow 4 – 5 hours

Chicken Creek Trail is a there and back hike popular with cross-country skiers in the winter. Mancos State Park is where the trail begins or ends, depending on which direction you start the hike. That said most folks start the trail from the Chicken Creek Trailhead off West Mancos Road (NFSR #561) to avoid the park's entrance fee.

The trail follows along the Chicken Creek watershed until merging with the Morrison Trail. The beginning parts located just outside the park's boundaries are definitely worth exploring. The last 1.5 miles (if coming from Mancos SP) is open to motorized visitors.

Chimney Rock National Monument

Quick Facts

Official Park Website: http://www.chimneyrockco.org/

Visitor Center: (970) 883-5359

Park Accessibility:
- Okay for 2WD and RVs
- Day Use Only

Experience Level:
- Family Friendly to Casual Hiker

Camping in Park:
- None

Lodging and Dining in Park:
- None

Nearest Town with Amenities:
- Piedra, CO is 9 mi / 14 km from park

Getting There:
- From Durango, CO: Take US-160 East to CO-151 West. Total distance is 47 mi / 76 km to park entrance

Chimney Rock National Park is close to Mesa Verde National Park and is worth visiting for an immersive experience into the Chaco culture. The park sits in the San Juan National Forest at an elevation of 6,600 to 7,400 feet. The park contains important ruins of the Chaco people sitting next to two natural stone towers from which the park gets its name.

This park was created in 2012 by President Barack Obama and is well known for providing a very personal experience. There are two ranger led tours given each day in season with one price allowing you to experience one or both of the tours. Each tour lasts about one hour.

Another bonus of Chimney Rock is its connection to theories that it was used for astronomical purposes. During the summer months there are full moon and night sky archaeoastronomy programs that tie in the Chacoan culture to astronomy. There are also annual cultural events where one can learn how to grind corn, create a pictograph, and even throw an atlatl hunting spear.

One rare event that is connected to Chimney Rock is the major lunar standstill. During the course of an 18.6-year cycle, the wobbly imperfections in the earth and moon's orbit cause the moon to rise at different points on the horizon. At the end of each cycle, the moon appears to rise in the same spot for about three years. This is known as a lunar standstill. If one stands in the center of the easternmost kiva in the northern section of the ruins, you can witness the moon rising between the two stone pillars that make up Chimney Rock. While that sounds pretty cool, a large amount of patience will be needed to view this event. The next standstill isn't until 2022.

The walking tours can be self-guided, however, like Mesa Verde National Park, taking the ranger led tour will provide a much more robust experience. The tours are available seasonally from May 15 through September 30. They currently run at $12 for adults and $5 for children ages 5 – 16. Tours are given three times daily at 9:30am-11:30am, 11:00am-1:00pm, and 1:00pm-3:00pm. If you opt to do the self-guided tours, note that access opens daily at 10:30am and closes at 3:00pm.

Great Sand Dunes National Park and Preserve

Quick Facts

Official Park Website: http://www.nps.gov/grsa

Visitor Center: (719) 378-6399

Park Accessibility:

- Okay for 2WD and RVs in main portion of park, 4WD needed on some backcountry roads to access select trails

- Day and Overnight Use

Experience Level:

- Family Friendly – Experienced Hiker

Camping in Park:

- Piñon Flats Campground: 44 T/RV sites + 3 group sites, open April through November, drinking water, flush toilets, no hookups, 22 sites are first come-first served, 22 are reservable at http://www.recreation.gov/

- Medano Road Primitive Campgrounds: 21 primitive tent sites accessible by 4WD along Medano Road. Go here for more information: http://www.nps.gov/grsa/planyourvisit/medano-pass-road.htm

Lodging in Park:

- None in park, there are several just outside the park. Details can be found here: http://www.nps.gov/grsa/planyourvisit/lodging.htm

Dining in Park:

- Oasis Restaurant and Store, located just outside of the park, open seasonally

Nearest Town with Amenities:

- Alamosa, CO is 34 mi / 55 km from the park

Getting There:

- From Denver, CO: Take US-285 South to CO-17 to Lane 6 North to CO-150 North. Total distance is 226 mi / 364 km to park entrance.

- From Albuquerque, NM: Take I-25 North to US-285 North to CO-150 North to CO-150 North. Total distance is 237 mi / 381 km to park entrance

On the Dunes

What Makes Great Sand Dunes NP Special

- Seeing and maybe even climbing the tallest sand dunes in North America, standing 750 feet high from their base

- More than a bunch of sand, there are also alpine lakes, 13,000 + foot mountains, wetlands, evergreen forests, and tundra-landscapes to be explored

- Building a sand castle on the banks of Medano Creek and getting in some sandboarding on the dunes

Great Sand Dunes National Park and Preserve is great for many reasons. First and foremost, the dunes here spread across an enormous area and there is no equal in terms of height in North America. The dunes definitely bring awe to anyone seeing them.

Nevertheless, the park holds a lot more for the visitor than the sand. Starting from the base of the dunes, there is Medano Creek, which flows during the spring and early summer. It carves against the base of the dunes, carrying sand with it and at times, portions of the creek become dams from the sand. At some point, the dams break, sending small waves downstream. These surges of flowing water can last from a few seconds to over a minute and at peak season can resemble small ocean waves as they travel down the streambed. Folks use the creek to build sand castles and to enjoy a bit of skim boarding.

The dunes sit at the base of Sangre de Cristo mountain range and a good portion of the range is within the park's boundaries. Here you can hike into thick pine, fir, and aspen forests, traveling up into the higher elevations with a creek typically by your side. You can climb above the tree line to alpine lakes and even to the top of one or more of six peaks above 13,000 feet.

Along with a number of other fauna, the park also hosts a large variety of mammals, including bighorn sheep, bison, beavers, pronghorn, black bears, and mountain lions. A good portion of the grasslands surrounding the park have been set aside as a preserve with the help of Nature Conservancy. It is also considered the quietest of all the parks in the contiguous United States. The setting of these dunes, with backdrops of towering mountains and lush green flora all around is a truly wonderful experience. All in, Great Sand Dunes National Park and Preserve holds one of widest variety of things to see and do of any park in the Grand Circle.

Hiking Great Sand Dunes National Park and Preserve

Great Sand Dunes and Medano Creek

As you can imagine, there are no established trails within the sand dunes. Most folks cross Medano Creek from the visitor center and start hiking. The tallest

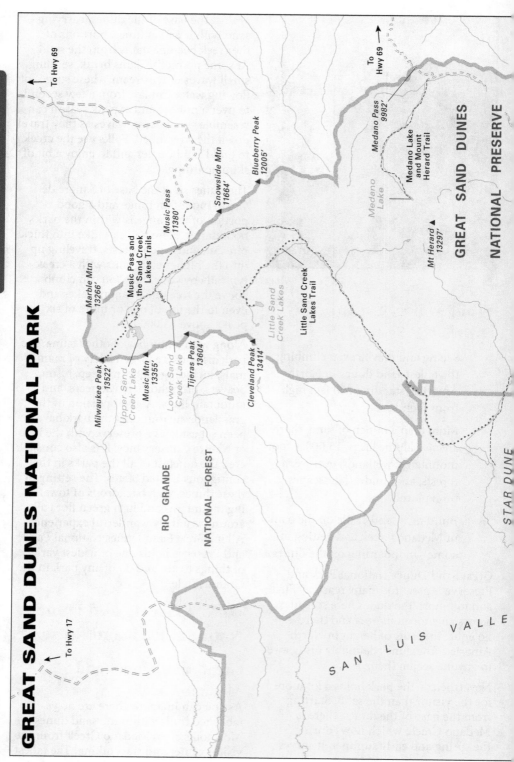

GREAT SAND DUNES NATIONAL PARK

To Hwy 69 →

To Hwy 69

Medano Pass
9982'

Medano Lake and Mount
Herard Trail

Medano Lake

Mt Herard ▲
13297'

GREAT SAND DUNES

NATIONAL PRESERVE

Blueberry Peak
▲ 12005'

Snowslide Mtn
▲ 11664'

Music Pass
11380'

Music Pass and
the Sand Creek
Lakes Trails

Little Sand
Creek Lakes

Little Sand Creek
Lakes Trail

Marble Mtn
▲ 13266'

Milwaukee Peak
▲ 13522'

Upper Sand
Creek Lake

Music Mtn
▲ 13355'

Lower Sand
Creek Lake

Tijeras Peak
▲ 13604'

Cleveland Peak
▲ 13414'

RIO GRANDE

NATIONAL FOREST

STAR DUNE

To Hwy 17 ←

SAN LUIS VALLE

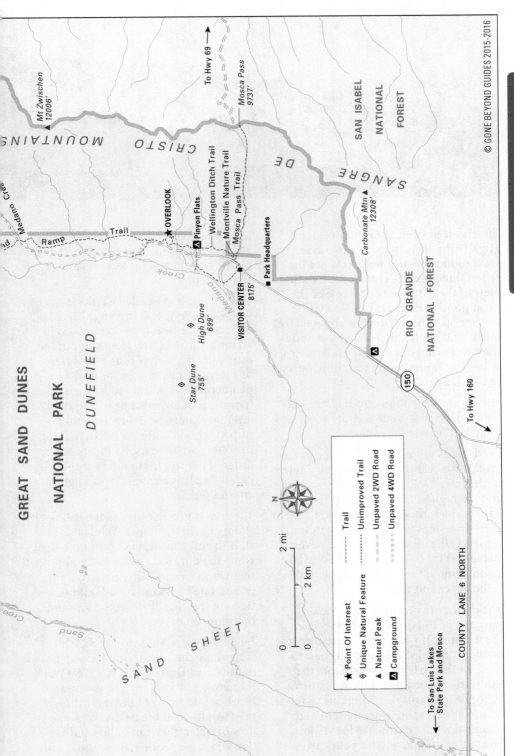

GREAT SAND DUNES
NATIONAL PARK

DUNEFIELD

SAND SHEET

Star Dune
755'

High Dune
699'

VISITOR CENTER
8175'

OVERLOOK

Pinyon Flats

Wellington Ditch Trail

Montville Nature Trail

Mosca Pass Trail

Park Headquarters

Trail

Ramp

Medano Creek

Medano Creek

Sand Creek

Mt Zwischen
12006'

SANGRE DE CRISTO MOUNTAINS

Mosca Pass
9737'

To Hwy 69

Carbonate Mtn
12308'

SAN ISABEL
NATIONAL
FOREST

RIO GRANDE
NATIONAL FOREST

150

To Hwy 160

To San Luis Lakes
State Park and Mosca

COUNTY LANE 6 NORTH

N

0   2 mi
0   2 km

★ Point Of Interest
◇ Unique Natural Feature
▲ Natural Peak
△ Campground

— — — — — Trail
.... Unimproved Trail
= = = = Unpaved 2WD Road
= = = = = Unpaved 4WD Road

Great Sand Dunes

SOUTHWEST COLORADO

dune as seen from the visitor center is High Dune. This is about a two-hour walk round trip and while it is not the tallest dune, it does give a commanding view of the entire area. It is one of the most popular dunes hiked. The tallest dune is Star Dune, which is about 50 feet taller than High Dune at 750 feet and is the tallest sand dune in North America. Allow five hours round trip for a journey to Star Dune.

Hiking amongst sand dunes is straight-forward in theory, but here are some tips to make the journey easier.

Sand dunes are a bit mischievous by na-ture. What seems close up is really much farther away. What seems easily scalable and the highest turns out to be twice as hard and not the highest one after all. For every two steps you go one step upwards. It's sand after all, always in flux, never stable and for this reason it's best to allow a good amount of time. Along with time, bring water and food.

The dunes can get quite hot, reaching upwards of 150 degrees Fahrenheit in the summer. If you are tempted to roam barefoot amongst the sands, its best to do so in the early morning before the sun starts beating down. Wind is also a factor. Wind is playing a big role in the reason all this sand is in one spot and it sadly doesn't take breaks for visitors. The grains of sand will hit your calves

at times and may even sting a bit. They also get everywhere, so be sure to bring plastic bags to seal up cameras and other fragile items.

One other piece of advice is don't go where everyone else is going. There is an incredible beauty in seeing sand in an undisturbed state. Here you can see miniature dune ripples as a top layer of a larger dune, the brushing of a lone plant creating natural sand art, and the footprints of an insect or rodent on some unknown journey. Being in an undis-turbed section of dunes is like walking in a Zen garden made by the monastic order of nature. That said, be mindful of fragile plant areas and tread lightly around them.

The area is popular for sandboarding or sliding down the dunes. While it is pos-sible to enjoy the dunes with snow sleds when the dunes are wet, most equipment that works in snow isn't advised for the dunes. Look for sand boards and slides that are specifically designed for sand for optimum enjoyment.

Finally, there is Medano Creek, which runs along the entire southwestern base of the Great Dunes. This is a great place for families as kids and the young at heart can do many of the same things they would do at the beach. With the flow of water, they can build sand cas-tles, shoot the gentle rapids, and splash

Happiness is digging your toes in the sand

around in the creek. If you have any engineers in the family, they can create their own dams, creek flows and cities made of sand. And yes, of course the dam will eventually break, especially if they have younger siblings. Medano Creek, when flowing, is a popular destination for this reason. The creek flows from early spring to early summer depending on the snowpack.

Mosca Pass Trail

Moderate to Strenuous – (6.8 mi / 10.9 km), round trip, allow 3 hours, elev. Δ: 1,453 ft / 443 m, trailheads at just north of visitor center and Montville trailhead

Mosca Pass Trail is a nice hike for immersion into the forest. The trail travels along Mosca Creek at a steady 13% incline until reaching Mosca Pass, a low pass in the Sangre de Cristo Mountains and a trailhead access point outside the park. The pass itself is at 9,737 feet (2,968 meters) and has been used by the original inhabitants and early explorers alike. It is unlikely that the trail was named by the first who walked it as "mosca" is Spanish for "fly".

The hike travels primarily through evergreen forests. Views become more frequent as the trail climbs in elevation towards the tree line. There are meadows, rocky outcroppings and of course Mosca Creek to be seen along the way. The journey of this there and back trail ends at the pass and parking lot of those venturing this trail from the other direction via CR-583.

Montville Nature Trail

Easy – (0.5 mi / 0.8 km), round trip, allow 30 minutes

This is a short little loop and is not only great for small kids, is also a smart way to escape the heat of the dunes in summer. The trail offers nice views of Mount Herard and the sand dunes.

Wellington Ditch Trail

Easy – (1.0 mi / 1.6 km), one way, allow 30 minutes, elev. Δ: 73 ft / 22 m, trailhead at Piñon Flats Campground

This is a short trail that connects the Montville Nature Trail to the campground. The hike offers some nice views of the dunes and surrounding area.

Sand Ramp Trail

Strenuous – (11.0 mi / 17.7 km), one way, allow 6 hours, elev. Δ: 400 ft / 122 m, trailhead at Piñon Flats Campground

Sand Ramp Trail makes for a great backpacking trail to the northern side of the dunes. The trail skirts between the dunes and the base of the Sangre de Cristos, passing by Medano and Cold Creeks before meeting up with Sand Creek. The nice aspect of this as a backpacking trip is to obtain a pristine sand dunes experience. Sand Creek runs along the northwest section of the dunes and is the fraternal twin to Medano Creek. Once at Sand Creek and along the way, there are more chances to see an untouched environment. In addition, here is the Star Dune Complex, which is a smaller and shorter segment of the dune field but again, its remoteness brings the gift of being pristine. That said, if you are looking for a more unspoiled experience and don't want to hike eleven miles to get there, consider backpacking a couple miles into the dunes from the visitor center. You'll need a permit for either trip. Sand Ramp Trail also is the starting point for the Sand Creek Lakes, described below

Little Sand Creek Lakes

Strenuous – (17 mi / 27.4 km), round trip, primarily for backpacking, 2 -3 days, elev. Δ: 1,045 ft / 319 m, trailhead at Music Pass Road

Follow the directions for Music Pass, turning right at the juncture towards the Sand Creek Trail. From here, follow

down Sand Creek until finding a juncture for Little Sand Creek Lakes. Hike another 2.5 miles to reach the larger of the two lakes. There is another much smaller lake a little higher up.

It is possible to reach these lakes from the main section of the park via Sand Creek Trail. This is a very long hike and Sand Creek may be impassable during the high water of early summer. Check in with the visitor center if this route looks enticing.

Music Pass and the Sand Creek Lakes

Moderate – (8.8 mi / 14.2 km), round trip, allow 6 hours, elev. Δ: 1,910 ft / 579 m, trailhead at Music Pass Road

Music Pass is a straightforward hike traveling primarily through a transitional ecosystem of forest and tundra. The trail leads to the Lower and Upper Sand Creek Lakes and overall, this is one heck of a nice trail, scenery wise. Both lakes are right at the tree line giving amphitheater views of the mountains that surround them. This is also a great area to summit

Great Sand Dunes NP has the tallest dunes in North America

a number of peaks in the area, including Music and Marble Mountains as well as Tijeras, Cleveland, Milwaukee and Blueberry Peaks.

The major consideration of this hike is its distance from the main visitor center area of the park. The trailhead is found by traveling some 137 miles from the visitor center to Westcliffe, CO. From there, turn right from Highway 69 onto CR 119 and continue for about 6 miles to a T intersection. At the T, things get mildly interesting. Turn right onto CR 120, which makes a sharp right shortly thereafter, becoming CR 119 again. Continue on another 5 miles to the 2WD parking lot or another 2.5 miles on a rough 4WD road to the Music Pass Trailhead proper. You will definitely want to have a 4WD vehicle if you drive the final distance.

From here, follow the trail to Lower and then Upper Sand Creek Lakes. Keep right at the junction as going left will take you down Sand Creek Trail (see Little Sand Creek Lakes Trail below). Lower Sand Creek Lake is found via a spur trail to the left. There is a fair amount of forest canopy that doesn't give way until you are close to the lake. The towering mountain behind the lake is Tijeras Peak. Upper Sand Creek Lake is another 1.2 miles. Avoid the faint spur trail on the right about 0.7 miles in that leads to Milwaukee Pass. This lake is only 50 feet higher than the lower lake and gives a nice view of Music Mountain. As an aside, the pass was so named because it is said music can be heard from the surrounding mountaintops. If you yourself don't hear music, sing loudly so that others will hear your tune and carry on the legend.

Medano Lake and Mount Herard

Strenuous – (10.0 mi / 16.1 km), round trip, full day trip, elev. Δ: 3,700 ft / 1,128 m, trailhead at Medano Pass Road

If the group you are with is looking at the massive dunes but you are looking at the even more massive mountains behind these dunes, this trail is for you. The good news is during the summer months; sturdy hiking boots, plenty of food, water, and grit will get you to the top. The thing to consider is the trail starts at 10,000 feet from a 4WD high clearance road and the elevation gain is 3,700 feet over the duration of the hike. If you are still interested, keep reading this is an amazing hike with simply commanding views and one that climbs above the tree line into the always intriguing ecology of alpine tundra.

Take the Medano Pass Primitive Road to the trailhead, crossing Medano Creek nine times. A high-clearance 4-wheel drive, full-size SUV, truck, or Jeep is required. The road is sandy near the dunes for about four miles and rocky near the pass. There are few place to turn around, especially in the first five miles. It is recommended to drop the air pressure to about 20 psi for the sandy parts, which means having a portable air compressor for the tires is a plus afterwards, (go slow if you don't have one). The turnoff for the trail is well marked and about a half mile before the pass.

Once on the trail, it will climb moderately at first, passing through an impressively large stand of aspens. The trail steepens as you get closer to Medano Lake, about 3.5 miles from the trailhead. Medano Lake is at 11,500 feet and there are plenty of spots to camp for the night. Otherwise, to continue to the summit, connect with a faint trail to the upper bowl above the lake and head left up a moderately steep ramp to the summit. The final ascent to the very top is more gently sloped, which will be a welcome reprieve. From here, enjoy the views, the curvature of the earth and a couple of victory fist bumps. You are at standing at 13,340 feet (4,066 m)!

Ridgway State Park

Quick Facts

Official Park Website: http://cpw.state.co.us/placestogo/parks/Ridgway

Visitor Center: (970) 626-5822

Park Accessibility:

- Okay for 2WD and RVs
- Day and Overnight Use

Experience Level:

- Family Friendly to Casual Hiker

Camping in Park:

- 4 campgrounds in park, sites available vary by season, 258 T/RV + 25 walk-in tent sites, drinking water, restrooms, showers and laundromat, no hookups, reservable online or at (800) 678-2267, go here for full details: http://cpw.state.co.us/placestogo/parks/Ridgway/Pages/Camping.aspx

Lodging and Dining in Park:

- None

Nearest Town with Amenities:

- Placerville, CO is 38 mi / 61 km from the park

Ridgway State Park

Getting There:

- From Durango, CO: Take US-550 North for 87 mi / 140 km to park entrance

What Makes Ridgway State Park Special

- Breathtaking mountain scenery as the backdrop of an emerald blue lake
- Being nicknamed the "Switzerland of America"
- Cooling off in the lake after a long hike

This is one of the more popular parks in Colorado, giving locals and visitors a chance to swim, fish, water-ski and hike. The Ridgway Reservoir itself is a deep blue and most non-winter months the surrounding area is a blanket of pastoral green fields with the snowcapped Rockies in the background. In addition, with over 250 RV and tent sites, there is no shortage of places to camp. This is a great place to unwind and relax for a bit. The hikes are short, the fishing is decent, and the neighbors are typically friendly.

Hiking Ridgway State Park

There are 17 named trails in the park, but the majority of them are under one mile and many are connectors from one campground loop to another. The most popular hikes are listed below.

Mear's Bay Trail

Easy – (1.0 mi / 1.6 km), one-way trip, allow 30 minutes, each way

Paved and wheelchair accessible, this trail allows for an ambling walk along the reservoir's southern shore. The San Juan Mountains frame the horizon with opportunities to view wildlife along the way, especially at dawn and dusk. Mear's Bay Trail is ideal for twilight hour strolls or a morning run. This trail starts from the Dutch Charlie section of the park and connects with the more strenuous Enchanted Mesa Trail. The combined distance of both trails is 3.5 miles.

Marmot Run Trail

Easy – (1.8 mi / 2.9 km), one-way trip, allow 1 hour, each way

This trail is similar to Mear's Bay for accessibility and no fuss hiking, but is about a mile longer. The trail is paved and easy to follow. Lots of picnic sites and restrooms nearby as the trail winds gently along the shoreline. Again, great wildlife viewing, including the trail's namesake, the marmot, which has a moderate population near the southern end of the path. From the southern end, this trail continues another four miles into the town of Ridgway along a nice path that parallels Highway 550 and the Uncompahgre River for the most part. This section is great for biking into town for local fare.

Enchanted Mesa Trail

Moderate to Strenuous – (5.0 mi / 8.0 km), round trip, allow 2 – 3 hours

The nickname for this park is "Switzerland of America" and when it comes to the trail that aligns best with that moniker, look no further than the Enchanted Mesa Trail. What makes this hike a must for anyone staying at the park is the scenery. You get 360-degree views of the countryside with the reservoir down below. There are bridges to cross and ponds to walk past, with wooded areas emerging into wide-open fields. The Cimarron and Sneffel segments of the San Juan Mountains can be seen. Within the Cimarron's, it is possible to see the prominent Chimney Rock next to Courthouse Mountain.

There are some switchbacks along this trail that could arguably be defined as strenuous. However, the journey here is worth every step, as the green landscape, white capped mountains and deep blue waters mix together in a beautiful and serene melody of nature. Access is via either the Pa-Co-Chu-Puk or Dutch http://www.americasstateparks.org/park_maps/Ridgway%20Trail%20Map.pdf Charlie sections.

Cookie Tree Trail

Moderate – (1.8 mi / 2.9 km), round trip, allow 1 hour

Cookie Tree Trail connects the Dutch Charlie and Dallas Creek park areas. The elevation gain is a little more than 100 feet; however, there are some short but steep areas to be found. Along the trail are great views of the reservoir and the surrounding area. The trail's namesake, the Cookie Tree Ranch, lies at the bottom of the reservoir, one of the many sacrifices in the creation of man made lakes.

Black Canyon of the Gunnison National Park

Quick Facts

Official Park Website: http://www.nps.gov/blca

Visitor Center: (970) 641-2337

Park Accessibility:

- Okay for 2WD and RVs

- Day and Overnight Use

Experience Level:

- Family Friendly – Backcountry Hiker

Deeply carved Black Canyon

Camping in Park:

- South Rim: 88 T/RV, 2 accessible sites, hookups at some sites, drinking water, vault toilets, some sites reservable at http://www.recreation.gov/

- North Rim: 13 T/RV, drinking water seasonally, vault toilets, no hookups, no dump station, first come–first served

- East Portal: 15 T only, road to campground not suitable for vehicles longer than 22 feet, drinking water seasonally, vault toilets, first come–first served

Lodging and Dining in Park:

- None

Nearest Town with Amenities:

- Montrose, CO is 13 mi / 21 km from park

Getting There:

- From Denver, CO: Take US-285 South to US-50 West. Total distance is 262 mi / 422 km to park entrance

What Makes Black Canyon of Gunnison Special

- Gazing at the craggy rock spires and following the view over 2,000 feet down sheer cliffs to the mercurial line of the Gunnison River
- Knowing that you are looking at some of the oldest rock in North America
- Being at the bottom and getting that special feeling of the sun on your face during the few hours of direct sunlight that hits the canyon floor

Most people have never even heard of this park, which is one of the many reasons it is so special. Getting just 5% of the traffic as the Grand Canyon, the Black Canyon of the Gunnison National Park is refreshing and stunning at the same instance. The surrounding land is lightly forested, providing a pleasant duff of green at the top of the cliffs and within the draws. This provides an almost artistic contrast to the canyon itself, a gapping maw of stone ruggedness, hardened gneiss, and schist marbled together along a canvas of cliff 2,250 feet high in some spots. As the eye travels down the canyon walls, it is finally resolved with a thin liquid silver line set in motion. This line is the Gunnison River, a fast-paced steeply cutting engine of water, creating the Black Canyon, so named because it only receives a few hours of direct sunlight on any given day.

A visit to the Black Canyon of the Gunnison is one of those places that effects people in unexpected and positive ways. Friends may ask what you did while you were there and it becomes one of those places that are hard to put into words. In fact, you find yourself not really even wanting to as if some of the magic you experienced would be lost in trying to describe it. It is not as big or as epically southwest as the Grand Canyon, but in many ways, it is as special.

Color on the rim

Hiking Trails Not in the Inner Canyon

Hiking the inner parts of Black Canyon require a permit and are amongst the steepest and most strenuous of the designated trails within the entire National Park System. Fortunately, there are quite a few trails that don't require a permit and are very pleasant both in grade, pace and the scenery presented to the hiker. These hikes are presented below by rim. Inner Canyon hikes are described separately.

SOUTH RIM

Rim Rock Nature Trail
Moderate – (1.0 mi / 1.6 km), round trip, elev. Δ: 199 ft / 61 m, trailhead at Black Canyon Visitor Center

A pleasant mostly flat trail that gives great views of the Black Canyon, in some places all the way down to the Gunnison River. The canyon gives different views as one hikes along the pinyon juniper covered rim and while the views are dramatic, the trail stays at a healthy distance from the edge. Look for both animals and plants, including deer and Dusky Grouse.

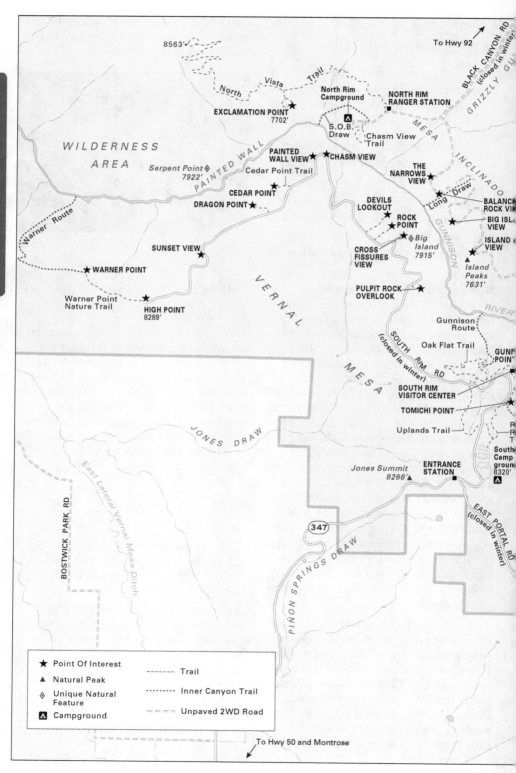

8563'

To Hwy 92

BLACK CANYON RD (closed in winter)

GRIZZLY GU

North Vista Trail

North Rim Campground

NORTH RIM RANGER STATION

EXCLAMATION POINT 7702'

S.O.B. Draw

Chasm View Trail

MESA

INCLINADO

WILDERNESS AREA

Serpent Point 7922'

PAINTED WALL

PAINTED WALL VIEW

CHASM VIEW

Cedar Point Trail

THE NARROWS VIEW

Long Draw

BALANC ROCK VI

CEDAR POINT

DRAGON POINT

DEVILS LOOKOUT

ROCK POINT

BIG ISL. VIEW

GUNNISON

ISLAND VIEW

SUNSET VIEW

CROSS FISSURES VIEW

Big Island 7915'

Island Peaks 7631'

WARNER POINT

Warner Route

Warner Point Nature Trail

HIGH POINT 8289'

VERNAL

PULPIT ROCK OVERLOOK

RIVER

Gunnison Route

Oak Flat Trail

SOUTH RIM RD (closed in winter)

GUN POIN

MESA

SOUTH RIM VISITOR CENTER

TOMICHI POINT

Uplands Trail

R R T

JONES DRAW

East Lateral Vernal Mesa Ditch

Jones Summit 8266'

ENTRANCE STATION

South Camp groun 8320'

BOSTWICK PARK RD

347

EAST PORTAL RD (closed in winter)

PIÑON SPRINGS DRAW

★ Point Of Interest
▲ Natural Peak
◇ Unique Natural Feature
🅰 Campground

------ Trail
·········· Inner Canyon Trail
==== Unpaved 2WD Road

To Hwy 50 and Montrose

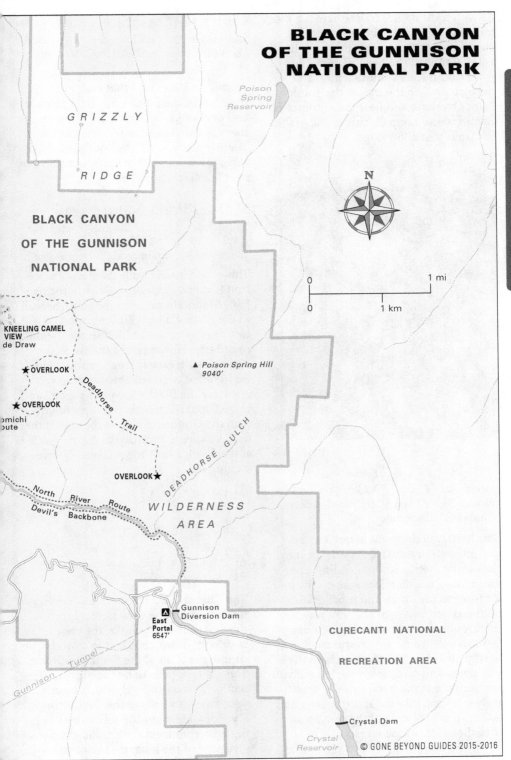

BLACK CANYON OF THE GUNNISON NATIONAL PARK

Poison Spring Reservoir

G R I Z Z L Y

R I D G E

BLACK CANYON

OF THE GUNNISON

NATIONAL PARK

N

0 — 1 mi

0 — 1 km

KNEELING CAMEL VIEW
de Draw

★ OVERLOOK

▲ *Poison Spring Hill*
9040'

★ OVERLOOK

Deadhorse

omichi
ute

Trail

OVERLOOK ★

DEADHORSE GULCH

North River Route
Devil's Backbone

W I L D E R N E S S
A R E A

Gunnison
Diversion Dam

▲ East
Portal
6547'

CURECANTI NATIONAL

Tunnel

RECREATION AREA

Gunnison

Crystal Dam

*Crystal
Reservoir*

© GONE BEYOND GUIDES 2015-2016

As with most nature trails, there is a nice trail guide that describes some of the plants and geology. The guide as well as the trailhead itself can be picked up at the South Rim Visitor Center. You can also pick up the trail at the Tomichi Point Overlook and near the entrance of Campground Loop C. This is one of the few trails that allow dogs.

Painted Wall

Oak Flat Loop Trail

Strenuous – (2.0 mi / 3.2 km), round trip, elev. Δ: 349 ft / 106 m, trailhead at Black Canyon Visitor Center

This loop trail descends about 350 feet and gives an immersive experience into the canyon itself without needing a permit. Hiking counterclockwise on the loop is more steeply down and more gradual on the ascent back up. The trail travels through thickets of Douglas fir and Gambel oak. There are several respites to stop and enjoy the view both on the way down and on the way back up. If you are camping at the park, this is a great early morning hike for spotting deer and taking in the solitude of the canyon along with the scents of the forests.

Cedar Point Nature Trail

Easy – (0.7 mi / 1.1 km), round trip, elev. Δ: 40 ft / 12 m, trailhead at Cedar Point trailhead

A wide and easy trail that ends at an overlook of the Black Canyon. There are two overlooks, both giving a clean uninterrupted view of the Gunnison River. There is also a great view of the Painted Wall, the tallest cliff in Colorado, coming in at 2,250 feet high.

Warner Point Nature Trail

Moderate – (1.5 mi / 2.4 km), round trip, elev. Δ: 158 ft / 48 m, trailhead at end of Highway 347, main road for South Rim

This is very nicely built there and back trail that gives excellent views of the San Juan Mountain range to the south as well as the Black Canyon. There is a bit of elevation gain, about 300 feet for the full round trip. However, the trail is constructed with easy hiking in mind, with well-crafted steps suitable for most hikers. Here the Black Canyon is rugged and jagged, looking treacherous and mighty, with the Gunnison seen at the end of the trail. Be sure to pick up the nature guide at the South Rim Visitor Center before starting out.

NORTH RIM

Chasm View Nature Trail

Easy – (0.3mi / 0.5 km), round trip, elev. Δ: 70 ft / 21 m, trailhead is near North Rim Campground

The Chasm View Nature Trail is definitely high on the wow factor. From the first of two overlooks, the view is straight down 1800 feet to a nicely running section of the Gunnison River. This also happens to be the narrowest section at the rim level, which means your fellow tourists at the South Rim Overlook are just 1100 feet away. Looking upstream from the second overlook gives one of the longest canyon views possible in the park. As well, the Painted Wall is unavoidably incredible from the overlook. Standing at 2250 feet, this epic cliff is the tallest in Colorado. Now if that isn't enough to lure you to take this short hike, it's also dog friendly and easy enough for use by outdoor strollers.

North Vista Trail

Moderate to Exclamation Point– (3.0 mi / 4.8 km), round trip, elev. Δ: 154 ft / 47 m, trailhead at North Rim Ranger Station

Strenuous to Green Mountain– (7.0 mi / 11.3 km), round trip, elev. Δ: 956 ft / 291 m, trailhead at North Rim Ranger Station

This trail can seem more like two trails then one. Most head to Exclamation Point only, but the trip up to Green Mountain, the highest point in the park is very rewarding.

The hike to Exclamation Point is very popular. From the overlook, there is a long continuous view both up and down river. It can be argued this is one of the best views in the park. There is an overlook prior to Exclamation Point but it is lacking a guardrail so use caution.

From Exclamation Point, it's definitely worth the two miles up to the top of Green Mountain. The hike itself climbs at a steady manageable grade, using long switchbacks for much of the trail up. The trail climbs through old growth pinyon juniper and gives an almost aerial view of the Black Canyon as one slowly climbs above it. The top also gives expansive views of the surrounding area, including the San Juan Mountains, the Grand Mesa, and the Uncompahgre Plateau.

Deadhorse Trail

Moderate – (5.0 mi / 8.0 km), round trip, elev. Δ: 447 ft / 136 m, trailhead at Kneeling Camel Overlook

The hike starts out on a gravel service road passing an old ranger station along high country hillside. The service road gives way to an older path, now more trail than the road it once was. One heads past a spring fed stocking pond and the lowest point on the trail at about the one-mile mark.

From here, the trail begins to climb steadily through brush until reaching a fence. From here, the trail follows the fence line until the overlook and end of the trail is reached. From the overlook, there is a good view of the East Portal and a small dam that aids in the diversion of the Gunnison for irrigation use within the Uncomphagre Valley. The trail's namesake, the Deadhorse Gulch, can be seen as the large side canyon located east of the overlook.

The diversion itself was no easy feat to build. True work started in 1904 and it was completed in 1909, the diversion is a tunnel that was cut 5.8 miles through solid rock. At the time of its completion, it was the longest irrigation tunnel in the world. A total of 26 folks died making it. Digging from both ends, when they met in the middle, they were only 18 inches off. The tunnel has a capacity of 1300 cubic feet per second.

Fall at the park

Hiking Trail Within the Inner Canyon

All hikes within the inner canyon are by permit only. Permits are available at the South Rim Visitor Center, North Rim Ranger Station, and East Portal registration board (located west of the campground). The number of permits available daily are limited, and permits are distributed on a first come-first serve basis. Besides obtaining a permit, neither dogs nor campfires are allowed in the inner canyon.

Here are the posted regulations from the National Park Service:

- Wilderness Use permits are required.

- Open fires are prohibited. Use camp stoves only.

- No pets.

- A valid Colorado Fishing license is required, and Gold Medal Water regulations apply.

- No hunting.

- Collecting wood, flowers, plants, animals, and rocks is prohibited.

- Bury all human waste in 6" deep holes at least 100 feet from the river. If pit toilets are available, please use them.

- Pack out all trash, including toilet paper.

Hiking down to the Gunnison River is incredibly steep and difficult. There are no marked trails and while there are routes, they can be extremely difficult to follow in places. It is very possible to cliff out in areas as not all ravines lead all the way down to the river or back up to the rim. Given the steepness of the terrain, the last thing a hiker will want to do is double back again to find the correct route.

With that, get a decent map and study the terrain of the chosen route and the surrounding areas before you go. Look for areas that may present problems. If you aren't well versed in knowing your terrain, both via reading a map and while on the route, including knowing how to memorize the way back up as you head down, this may not be the best place to learn. Most hikers run into difficulty on the ascent in that the terrain is so steep, it is difficult to assess the correct ravine. All hikers must be prepared to self-rescue.

Other things to note. Be prepared to filter all water. Be bear safe. One of the coolest things is seeing a bear along the Gunnison, but hopefully on the other side and not rummaging in your stuff. This is no place for anything but sturdy hiking boots, keep the shoes and sandals back at the top. Oh, and there is an unavoidable amount of poison ivy along these routes. Definitely wear pants and even long sleeves when hiking up and down the routes.

On the descriptions, the term "River Access" denotes the maximum distance available to the hiker once they get to the canyon floor. This distance is approximate and is calculated at low water levels (300-350 cfs). The water of the Gunnison is pretty chilly (about 50 degrees Fahrenheit) plus the rocks are often fall on your butt slick. This river has taken a fair amount of people to their deaths, be careful if you plan to go in.

If you've read all this and you still want to head down, awesome! The inner canyon is a place literally encapsulated by nature. It surrounds and envelopes the hiker. Plus, the hike down is strenuous enough to force one to forget anything else that may be on their minds. To this, the inner canyon sheds whatever you may have thought was important and puts into perspective that which really matters. It is truly one of those raw "you and the elements of nature" type of adventures.

A typical moment at the canyon floor

SOUTH RIM ROUTES

Tomichi Route

Strenuous – (Distance: 1.0 mi / 1.6 km), Vertical Drop: 1,960 feet (597 m), 0.5 miles of River Access with two campsites

Tomichi is arguably the steepest route along the South Rim and the loose rocks combined with head on sun for most of the day make this one of the most difficult. That said, it looks deceptively doable on a map for some. The route is, in essence, a very steep bowling alley or in other words, a rock avalanche chute. Use extreme caution with the loose rocks.

Take the Rim Rock Trail to post #13 and descend on down a minor ravine before connecting to the main draw that will quickly take you down to the river. At the junction to the main draw, be sure to memorize how you came down to make going up a little easier. It takes about 1.5 hours or so to get down and about 4.5 hours to get back up.

Gunnison Route

Strenuous – (Distance: 1.0 mi / 1.6 km), Vertical Drop: 1,800 feet (549 m), 0.75 miles of River Access with three campsites

All of the routes described here are very steep and there are moments where one wonders if the journey back up will ever end. These thoughts are slightly less prevalent along the Gunnison Route, which is the easiest of the routes to the river. Don't be mistaken, this journey is still very much a strenuous one but it is the recommended route for first timers and is thus the most popular. There is even a nice chain that helps you keep you footing for about 80 feet.

The route begins at the South Rim Visitor Center from the Oak Flat Trail. Follow the trail until you see a sign that says "River Access. Permit Required". This is your indication to either a) go back and get a permit or b) begin the scramble down with permit stowed somewhere safely on your person. Unlike the other routes and perhaps a foretelling of its popularity, there is an outhouse located a bit upstream near the campsites at the bottom. It takes about 1 ½ hours to get down and about 2 hours to get back up.

Warner Route

Strenuous – (Distance: 2.75 mi / 4.4 km), Vertical Drop: 2,722 feet (829 m), 1 miles of River Access with five campsites

The Warner Route is the longest of the paths to the inner canyon but is a little more rational of a way down as long as you plan on doing it as an overnight run. Start from the Warner Point Nature Trail and enjoy the scenery until you hit a sign that says "Serviceberry Bush", aka post #13 of the nature trail. This is where the Warner Route begins. Follow the path that leads off to the left and take the second gully down, avoiding the first one. Continue west to the lowest saddle on the ridge you are on and descend from there to the river. Campsites are located up and downstream. It takes about 2 - 2 ½ hours to get down and about 4 hours to get back to the rim.

Red Rock Canyon

Strenuous – (Distance: 3.4 mi / 5.5 km), Vertical Drop: 1,330 feet (405 m), 1 mile of River Access with 8 people total allowed per day in season

Whether day hiking or backpacking, the only way into the Red Rock Canyon in the western section of the park is by permit. The canyon is accessed through an easement that passes through private property so the amount of traffic allowed is limited. Permits are allocated via a lottery and the area is open seasonally. Exact dates the canyon are open varies from year to year, but in general, it is from May to October. To learn how to apply for the lottery and a host of other details, go here: http://www.nps.gov/blca/planyourvisit/redrockinfo.htm

Aside from the limited access, the Red Rock Canyon route is much less steep than any of the other routes. The first mile of the trail is on a double track dirt road and then starts a downward trend of 1,330 feet over the last couple of miles. There is a trail, but it is narrow. Also, be sure to stay near the creek, as it is easy to

Rainbow across the Overlooks

veer off trail, though once in the canyon proper, the trail is easier to stay on. There are several creek crossings along the way. Once you reach the Gunnison, continue upstream and negotiate a final steep hill and short cliff to obtain a wide stretch of river access. There are good fishing spots here along with some good camping spots farther upstream prior to a cliff wall that blocks further access for most.

NORTH RIM ROUTES

S.O.B. Draw

Strenuous – (Distance: 1.75 mi / 2.8 km), Vertical Drop: 1,800 feet (549 m), 2 miles of River Access with six campsites

The NPS material lists the S.O.B. Draw as a suggested route for first timers to the inner canyon. In general, the route is slightly more navigable and takes a wider approach down. That said, this is a very strenuous hike, with plenty of ledges and boulders to navigate as you make your way down a steep incline. There is also an abundance of poison ivy, so wear suitable clothes, such as pants and long sleeve shirts.

Pick up the S.O.B Draw at an access ladder east of the North Rim campground along the fence line. The route follows across the rim to the entry point downward. As with all of these routes, there is no trail and no one best route, so once in, navigate where others have gone before, and keep to a line that leads you down the easiest path while keeping an eye back up to see where you've been.

The descent typically takes 2 hours, with the ascent about 3 hours. Campsites are located a short distance downstream.

Long Draw

Strenuous – (Distance: 1.0 mi / 1.6 km), Vertical Drop: 1,800 feet (549 m), 0.25 miles of River Access with 1 campsite

The Long Draw is suitable for a tiring but doable day hike. The descent down takes about 1.5 hours with the ascent taking double. The canyon and the route start literally at a bend in the road about 1.5 miles south of the North Rim Ranger Station on G74 Road. You are getting close when you get to the Balanced Rock Viewpoint.

The route heads downwards from the onset, passing a small stand of Box Elders and much bouldering, scrambling and steepness from there. Like most of the routes, there is a plethora of poison ivy, especially towards the bottom. Once down, the river access is limited to about a quarter mile of exploring and one campsite.

Slide Draw

Strenuous – (Distance: 1.0 mi / 1.6 km), Vertical Drop: 1,620 feet (494 m), 0.75 miles of River Access with two campsites

The Slide Draw can be found at the last bend in the road past Kneeling Camel Viewpoint, just before the end of the road (4 miles south from North Rim Ranger Station on G74 Rd). Park at Kneeling Camel View. This route is one of the steepest routes into the inner canyon. Unlike Long Draw, which takes one of the longer side gullies down, Slide Draw is a very short and thus very steep gully. To add to the challenge, there is a 30-foot climb at the start of the route. Of the three routes down from the North Rim, this is the least recommended due to the loose rock and steepness.

It takes about 1.5 hours to get down and 4 hours to get back up. If you lose your footing completely, shorten these times considerably for the descent and lengthen them if coming back up. Seriously, this is a sickly steep route to the river, which is truly felt on the way back up. This is also a route that has multiple ravines, be sure to make note of your route down so you can get back up. Once down, there is a nice camping area on the river that can accommodate two campsites.

Curecanti National Recreation Area

Quick Facts

Official Park Website: http://www.nps.gov/cure

Visitor Center: (970) 641-2337

Park Accessibility:

- Okay for 2WD and RVs
- Day and Overnight Use

Experience Level:

- Family Friendly – Experienced Hiker

Camping in Park:

- There are 10 campgrounds and 385 campsites at Curecanti NRA. For full details go here: http://www.nps.gov/cure/planyourvisit/camping.htm

Lodging and Dining in Park:

- Pappy's Restaurant and Pub, open seasonally, located on Blue Mesa Reservoir

Nearest Town with Amenities:

- Gunnison, CO is 17 mi / 27 km from the park

Getting There:

- From Durango, CO: Take US-550 North to US-50 East. Total distance is 156 mi / 251 km to park entrance.

- From Grand Junction, CO: Take US-50 East. Total distance is 110 mi / 177 km to park entrance

What Makes Curecanti NRA Special

- Where the lone serenity of the high desert meets the playful oasis of water

- With three reservoirs, each visit brings something new to see and do

- Being close to Black Canyon of the Gunnison National Park

Curecanti NRA is a multi-use park consisting of three dams and thus three reservoirs spread out over an area of about 43,000 acres. The dams hold back the Gunnison River and are all upstream from the nearby Black Canyon of the Gunnison National Park. Curecanti was built for water storage, hydroelectric energy production, and recreation.

Within the park is just about everything one can think of, from dramatic vistas, secluded waterways, hiking, camping, fishing, personal boating and boat tours, scenic waterfalls, overlooks and even a restaurant. There are 3 visitor centers, 10 campgrounds, and 385 campsites, more if you include the primitive and boating campsites.

The largest reservoir and the furthest upstream is Blue Mesa Reservoir. At 20 miles long and with 96 miles of shoreline, it is Colorado's largest body of water. It is also the largest lake trout and Kokanee salmon fishery in the United States. Blue Mesa Reservoir has the most robust set of amenities of the three bodies of water. One standout is Dillon Pinnacles, an iconic beacon that can be seen from many parts of the reservoir and is a favorite trek for hikers.

Next downstream is the Morrow Point Dam, which creates the 12-mile-long Morrow Point Reservoir. Morrow Point Dam was designed primarily to produce hydroelectricity over water storage and is a fairly narrow body of water. As a result, boating here is more intimate, with canyon walls towering above the visitor on each side. Highlights here are the Curecanti Needle and the thinly flowing Chipeta Falls.

In between Morrow Point Dam and Black Canyon of the Gunnison NP is Crystal Dam. Crystal Reservoir is only six miles long and is even narrower than Morrow Point Reservoir. The main focus of this section is hydroelectric power generation, though there is some hiking and camping as well.

Hiking in Curecanti National Recreation Area

Since many readers may find Curecanti NRA to be a nice side trip to nearby Black Canyon of the Gunnison NP, the hikes listed here go in order of distance from the national park, from shortest to longest distance.

Crystal Creek Trail

Moderate to Strenuous – (5.0 mi / 8.0 km), round trip, allow 2 - 3 hours

Crystal Creek is a wonderful there and back trail that starts at 8,900 feet elevation and gradually climbs a ridge, ending at an overlook into Black Canyon 1,800 feet below. Apart from the elevation, which pushes this trail into the strenuous category, the hike itself is straightforward. Often the trail can be seen in front of you as you walk through low-lying vegetation, providing sweeping view all along the way. This is a great hike in the spring or fall, with abundant wildflowers along the trail to greet you.

The Cimarron Valley as well as the West Elk and San Juan Mountains can be seen. The San Juan's are the highest overall of Colorado's mountain range as an average elevation. Uncompahgre Peak (14,321 feet) is prominent as the large horn shaped peak to the left of the range. The other stand out horn to the right is Wetterhorn Peak (14,015 feet).

Mesa Creek Trail

Strenuous down/up, easy along shore – (1.5 mi / 2.4 km), round trip, allow 30 – 60 minutes

Mesa Creek Trail travels a short distance down to the end of Crystal Reservoir and subsequently the head of Morrow Point Dam. The trail follows down along the rushing Mesa Creek to the shoreline. From here, the trail crosses a footbridge and ambles downstream along the shore for a stretch before ending. Return by retracing your steps.

While there is an abundance of water all along this trail, the surrounding landscape is sparsely forested. This is a great hike to see a dam up close as well as an easy access into the towering walls of Black Canyon. There is also a picnic area on the north shore.

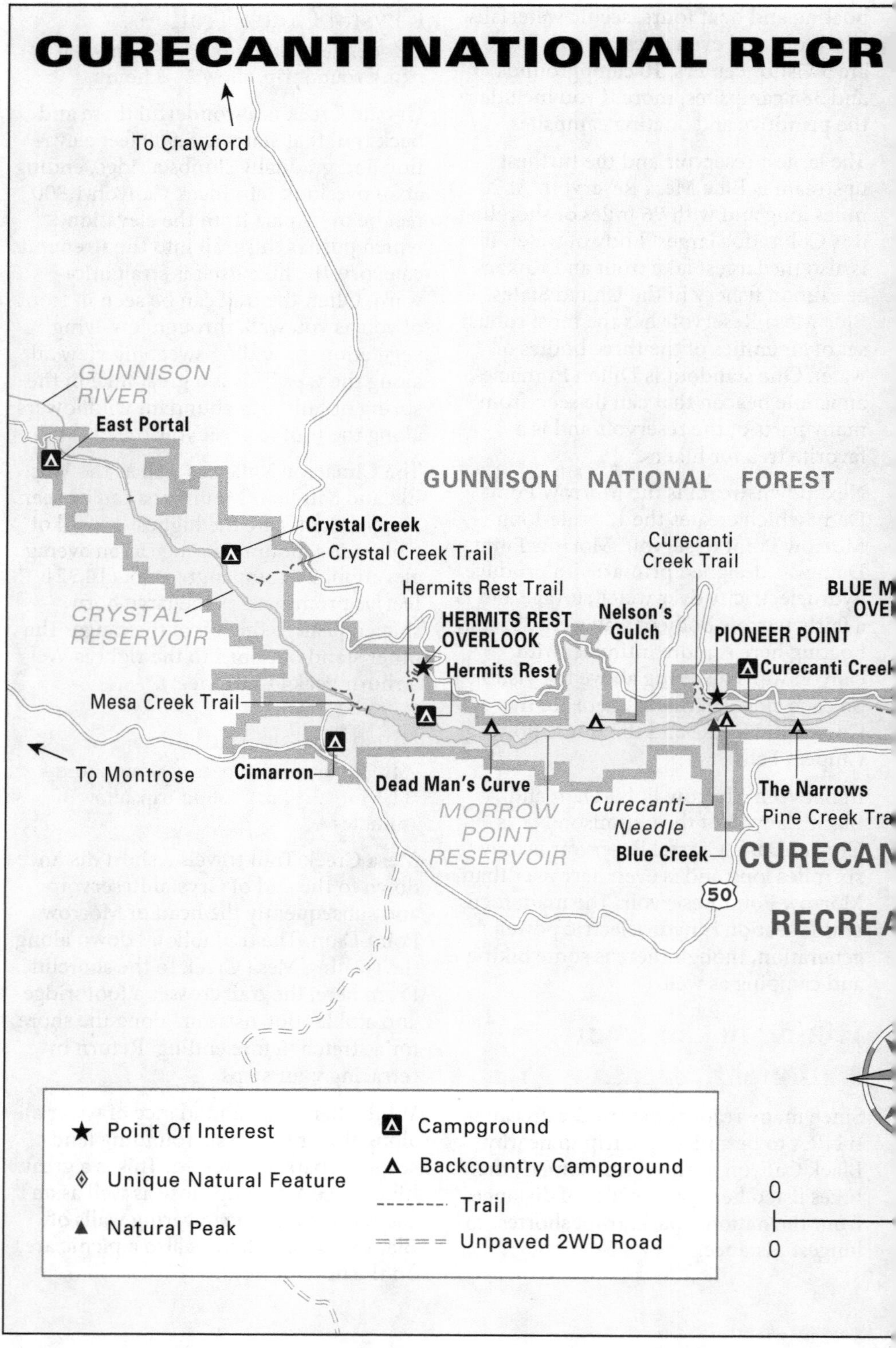

CURECANTI NATIONAL RECR

To Crawford

GUNNISON
RIVER
East Portal
⛺

GUNNISON   NATIONAL   FOREST

Crystal Creek
⛺ Crystal Creek Trail

Curecanti
Creek Trail

Hermits Rest Trail

CRYSTAL
RESERVOIR

**HERMITS REST
OVERLOOK**
★ **Hermits Rest**

Nelson's
Gulch

BLUE M
OVE

PIONEER POINT
★ ⛺ Curecanti Creek

Mesa Creek Trail

To Montrose ←   ⛺ **Cimarron**

△   △   △△   △

Dead Man's Curve

MORROW
POINT
RESERVOIR

Curecanti
Needle

Blue Creek

The Narrows
Pine Creek Tra

CURECAN

(50)

RECREA

Legend

★	Point Of Interest	⛺	Campground
◊	Unique Natural Feature	△	Backcountry Campground
▲	Natural Peak	-------	Trail
		====	Unpaved 2WD Road

0

0

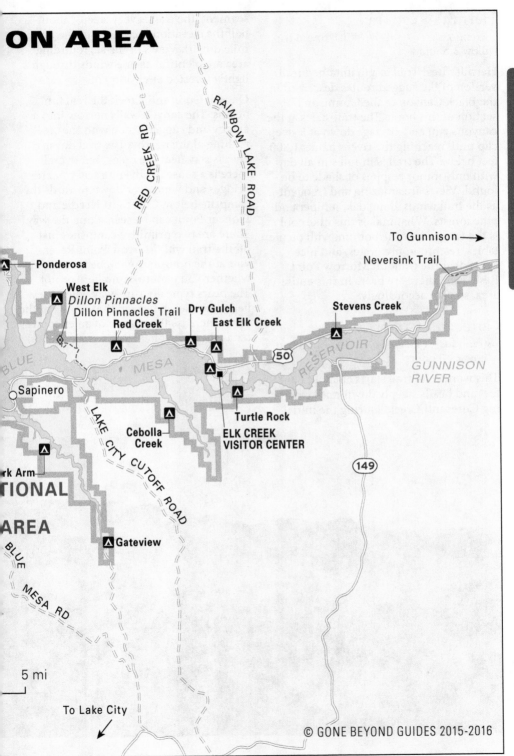

ON AREA

RED CREEK RD

RAINBOW LAKE ROAD

Ponderosa

West Elk

Dillon Pinnacles
Dillon Pinnacles Trail
Red Creek

Dry Gulch

East Elk Creek

To Gunnison →

Neversink Trail

Stevens Creek

50

RESERVOIR

MESA

*GUNNISON
RIVER*

BLUE

Sapinero

Turtle Rock

ELK CREEK
VISITOR CENTER

Cebolla
Creek

LAKE CITY CUTOFF ROAD

149

rk Arm

TIONAL

AREA

Gateview

BLUE

MESA RD

5 mi

To Lake City

© GONE BEYOND GUIDES 2015-2016

55

Hermit's Rest Trail

Strenuous – (6.0 mi / 9.7 km), round trip, allow 3 hours

Hermit's Rest Trail is a maintained trail version of the rugged routes described in the Black Canyon of the Gunnison NP section of this book. The trail starts at the canyon's rim and zig zags down at a steep clip until reaching the river's banks 1,800 feet below. The trail is in full sun all day with only minor respites of shade to be found. Views are amazing and frequent as the trail winds along oak, juniper and pine forests. What makes this hike cool is the campsite at the bottom, with picnic tables, restroom, fire grates, and nice spots near the tranquil Morrow Point Reservoir. There are bears in this entire area, so plan accordingly.

Curecanti Creek Trail

Strenuous – (4.0 mi / 6.4 km), round trip, allow 2 - 3 hours

This wonderful trail starts at about 8,000 feet and heads steeply down until reaching Curecanti Creek. During the initial segment, the trail is very steep, (about half the elevation is covered in the first mile down). Views of the surrounding area are plentiful as one winds through a lightly forested environment.

Once at Curecanti Creek the real fun begins. The canyon walls narrow into a craggy and rugged scene with the creek rushing along nearby. The trail doesn't always stay near the creek, but overall, there is a sense of adventure as you cross bridges and wind ever down towards the campsite below. Curecanti Needle and Pioneer Point can be seen along the way. There are two primitive campsites just off the trail with Morrow Point Reservoir at the bottom. Again, be bear aware whether you plan to camp here or not. The bears typically run away when they hear a human, however, the sounds of the water increase the chance of an encounter as they won't hear you (or vice versa).

Pine Creek Trail

Moderate – (2.0 mi / 3.2 km), round trip, allow 1 hour

This is an interpretive trail that describes the history of the narrow gauge railroad that once went through Black Canyon. The trail heads quickly to the shore through lush woodlands along Pine Creek before heading along the banks of Morrow Point Reservoir. This section is quite peaceful and easy for strolling along and taking it all in.

The trail is also used as the starting point for a boat tour. Be sure to get tickets beforehand, as there are no ticket sales at the dock itself. The boat tour is very much a worthwhile activity and a great side trip for families. Tours are given twice daily in season. Please call (970) 641-2337, ext. 205 or stop by the Elk Creek Visitor Center (15 miles west of Gunnison off of Highway 50) to make reservations.

Dillon Pinnacles Trail

Moderate – (4.0 mi / 6.4 km), round trip, allow 2 - 3 hours

One of the best hikes in Curecanti. The trail starts along the shores of Blue Mesa Reservoir through high desert landscapes. Views of the Dillon Pinnacles are nearly omnipresent along the hike along with the reservoir and San Juan Mountains in the distance. The hike heads away from the shore after about a mile and towards the pinnacles, which are volcanic in origin and as such erode in a unique fashion relative to the rest of the area. The trail takes the hiker to the base of the pinnacles and then makes a small loop at the end for the return. The scenery here is wide open and dramatic, with the tall fins and curtains of the pinnacles on one side, the reservoir, and the San Juan Mountains on the other.

NeversinkTrail

Easy – (1.5 mi / 2.4 km), round trip, allow 30 – 60 minutes

A nice strolling hike along the north bank of the Gunnison River. The hike is lush with riparian flora and fauna and is next to a rookery for the great blue heron. This is a great hike for birdwatching and simply getting a peaceful walk in. This trail is wheelchair accessible.

Dillon Pinnacles

Colorado National Monument

Quick Facts

Official Park Website: http://www.nps.gov/colm

Visitor Center: (970) 858-3617 ext. 360

Park Accessibility:

- Okay for 2WD and RVs
- Day and Overnight Use

Experience Level:

- Family Friendly – Casual Hiker

Camping in Park:

- Saddlehorn Campground: 80 T/RV, pull through sites, drinking water, flush toilets, no hookups, reservations at http://www.recreation.gov/ for some sites, other sites first come-first served, open year round

Lodging and Dining in Park:

- None

Nearest Town with Amenities:

- Grand Junction, CO is 6 mi / 10 km from park

Getting There:

- From Moab, UT: Take US-191 North to I-70 East. Total distance is 103 mi / 166 km to park entrance

Colorado National Monument

What Makes "The Monument" Special

- Tall red rock monoliths within the high desert of Colorado
- Some 40 miles of maintained trails to suit every hiker
- The beautiful and bold views of Monument Canyon

Colorado National Monument is for many one of their favorite parks within the Grand Circle. Within its boundaries are the red rock sandstone formations found in Utah, but with big differences. The park is less crowded then some of the more well known counterparts for one. Colorado NM receives 10% of the visitors to Grand Canyon and about 25% of Zion National Park.

The other big difference is its location. It is of the lands of the red rock, but is also part of the lands that make up the beginning of a journey into the Rocky Mountains. The park in a way sits in both worlds. For instance, Colorado National Monument overlooks the Grand Mesa, which is the largest flattop mountain in the world. However, unlike the majority of mesas in Utah, Grand Mesa's top is thickly forested. The park itself is known for its red rock sculptures, but it sits on a layer of harder gneiss and schist. There is a juxtaposition of these layers. Seemingly, the spires and mesas of the various sandstone formations float on top of the harder rock they sit on.

The monument is a big park, over 20,000 acres, with plenty of hiking opportunities. The trails range from easy to more strenuous and long. With 40 miles of hiking potential, there is something for everyone here.

Hiking Colorado National Monument

Devils Kitchen Trail

Easy, moderate at very end– (1.5 mi / 2.4 km), round trip, allow 1-2 hours

This is a great short trail that ends at a playground of sandstone hoodoos, alcoves and a rock grotto collectively known as Devils Kitchen. While the trail itself can be quickly hiked, allow time to explore once you get there.

The trailhead is shared with No Thoroughfare Canyon, Echo Canyon, and Old Gordon Trails. There are good signs to point out the way, but in general, at the first fork go right and at the second, keep to the left trail and follow it across a wash. The trail becomes actual steps carved into the sandstone at certain points. There are a couple of "unofficial trails" along this part of the journey, simply keep to the most established trail. Once you see the rock formation, going around it from the left will reveal "the kitchen".

Echo Canyon

Easy – (3.0 mi / 4.8 km), round trip, allow 2 hours

This is a nice there and back trail leading to a box canyon. At the end is a rocky alcove, which seasonally contains a pool of water as well as a rather shallow mineshaft. The terrain along this hike is varied, starting out with crossing a seasonal stream before climbing up a hill into a thicket of growth produced from a nearby seep at the mouth of Echo Canyon. From here, follow the streambed up the canyon, walking past some cool and unusual rock structures before hitting the alcove at the end. The hike gets accolades for having variety in the scenery and for being a trail less traveled, potentially giving the hiker an entire canyon all to themselves.

Note: return the same way you came, don't take the spur trail at the end, which will take you out of your way back towards the entrance of the park.

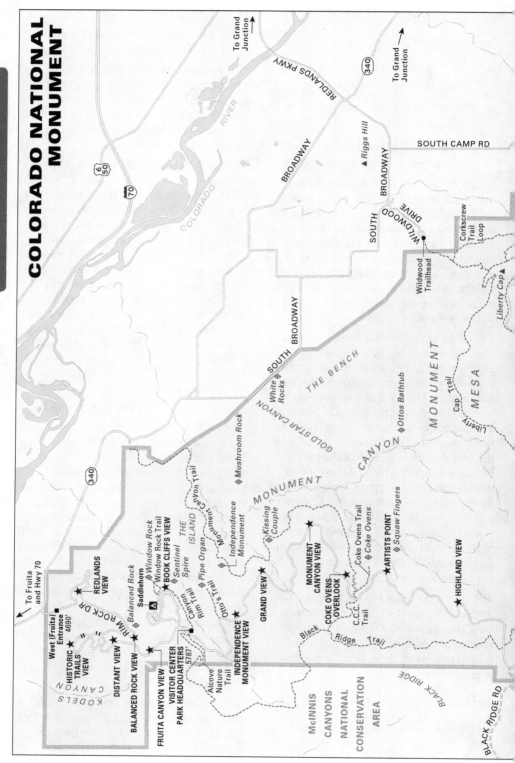

COLORADO NATIONAL MONUMENT

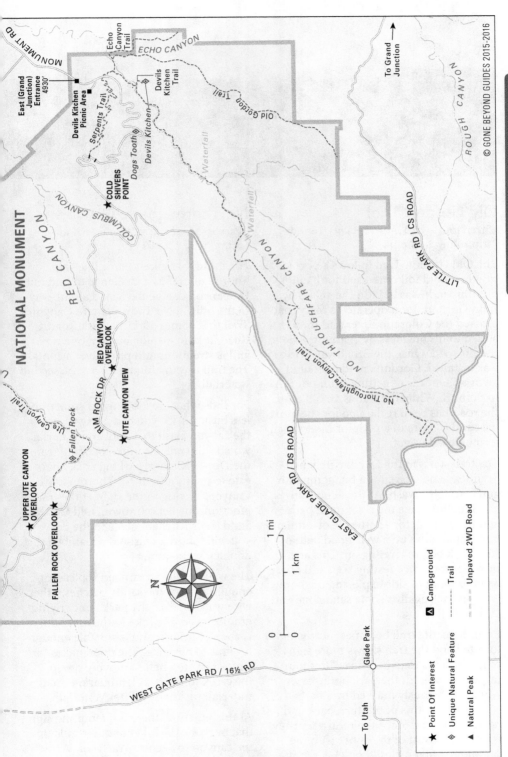

COLORADO NM

COLORADO NM — NATIONAL MONUMENT

MONUMENT RD

East (Grand Junction) Entrance 4930'

Echo Canyon Trail
ECHO CANYON

Devils Kitchen Picnic Area

Devils Kitchen Trail

Serpents Trail

Devils Kitchen

Dogs Tooth

Waterfall

Old Gordon Trail

COLD SHIVERS POINT

COLUMBUS CANYON

RED CANYON

Waterfall

NO THOROUGHFARE CANYON

To Grand Junction

ROUGH CANYON

LITTLE PARK RD / CS ROAD

RED CANYON OVERLOOK

RIM ROCK DR

UTE CANYON VIEW

Ute Canyon Trail

Fallen Rock

UPPER UTE CANYON OVERLOOK

FALLEN ROCK OVERLOOK

No Thoroughfare Canyon Trail

EAST GLADE PARK RD / DS ROAD

1 mi

1 km

N

WEST GATE PARK RD / 16½ RD

Glade Park

To Utah

★ Point Of Interest
◇ Unique Natural Feature
▲ Natural Peak
△ Campground
------- Trail
==== Unpaved 2WD Road

© GONE BEYOND GUIDES 2015-2016

Colorado NM   SOUTHWEST COLORADO

61

Old Gordon Trail

Strenuous – (8.0 mi / 12.9 km), round trip, allow 5-6 hours

The Old Gordon Trail follows a portion of an old toll road used for hauling out timber. It was built in the 1880's by John Gordon. John operated a ferry that crossed the Colorado River and then added to his business by charging a fee to use his road. Once the Broadway Bridge was installed, Gordon's road fell out of favor as a means of getting from point A to point B. While the trail is an old road, the road has been reclaimed for the most part and is more of a path for hikers than for horse led wagons

The trail starts at the Devils Kitchen Trailhead and descends a bit, going into and through a wash. At the Echo Canyon junction, take the right most path and head uphill for another ¾ of a mile. The trail follows up a well-lined path of slick rock before leveling off. This area provides for a nice resting spot and offers a fair amount of side exploring or simply leaning back against some sandstone and taking it all in.

From here, the trail becomes increasingly forested and the trail shows more signs of its previous road heritage. After four miles, you will hit the park boundary, which is obviously marked by a barbed wire fence. At this point, turn back and head for the car. Since the return journey is downhill most of the entire way, the car and the hiker should quickly reunite.

No Thoroughfare Canyon

Easy to Moderate – (4.0 mi / 6.4 km), round trip, 2 hours

For those that take a name like "No Thoroughfare" as a challenge to find one, the canyon can be navigated all the way to the official No Thoroughfare Canyon Trail that comes off Little Park Road/CS Road. It is an 8-mile journey, one way, and is strenuous and primitive in spots. The trail is unmaintained past the second waterfall.

For those that are looking for something less bush wacky, you can navigate up the canyon wash to a pool and waterfall, which this trail describes. Starting from the Devil's Kitchen parking area, navigate to the mouth of No Thoroughfare Canyon, staying to the right at the trail junctions for Echo Canyon, Old Gordon, and Devils Kitchen. Once in the canyon you will follow a seasonal streambed that doubles as the trail.

The walk up the streambed is pleasant enough, with some sandy patches, otherwise walking over the park's underlying granite layer. The hike to the first pool is about 1 mile in and is suitable enough for kids to navigate. The pool makes for a nice rest stop before moving on up the creek to the next landmark, a small waterfall nicknamed First Waterfall.

At this juncture, there is a tempting sign that beckons the hiker another mile up the canyon to Second Waterfall. While

Panorama of Monument Canyon

it's possible to get to this waterfall and beyond, the trail becomes increasingly primitive after the second falls until you reach Little Park Road/CS Road. It's a five-mile journey that is not for the inexperienced hiker. The route can be tricky to find at times, starting with a 500-foot cliff that one hits shortly after the Second Waterfall. (There is a way around it, look for a route down canyon on your right). Note that the canyon branches in the last mile. Staying to the right will put you eventually on the small but maintained portion of the trail that starts from this road. There are signs of prehistoric lifeways in the upper reach of the canyon, so if you do take this journey, allow extra time to explore the area.

Serpents Trail

Strenuous – (3.9 mi / 6.3 km), round trip, allow 2 hours

Before 1950, this trail was once a road nicknamed "the crookedest road in the world and even when it first became a trail, the trail sign warned hikers not to run on the trail for their safety. The trail offers great views as it winds its way through Wingate Sandstone. At times, the views of Grand Junction, the surrounding rural areas and the Rim Rock Drive can be seen.

The trail has two trailheads. The one near the east entrance of the park has more parking spaces both across from the trailhead and in the Devils Kitchen

Picnic Area. The parking lots are used for multiple trails. Alternatively, there are spaces for no more than five vehicles at the other trailhead, which is about 2.3 miles from the east entrance. If you are looking to take the trail one way, starting at this trailhead will allow for a nice downhill hike.

Ute Canyon Trail

Moderate overall, two steep ascents– (10.3 mi / 16.6 km), round trip, 4-5 hours

Ute Canyon Trail vies for best hike overall within the monument, encompassing many of the traits of a perfect hike. First the scenery is, from the very beginning, massive and grand. Ute Canyon is wide and deep. Once in the canyon, the elevation gain is gradual, allowing one to take in the views of the large sandstone cliff walls, arches, towers and buttes that surround you.

Starting from Wildwood Trailhead, one begins outside of the park's boundaries. Wildwood Trail branches into Liberty Cap and Corkscrew Trails as well as Ute Canyon. All the trails are well marked at their junctions.

The trail begins easily enough in a broad grassland, but the goal of ascending up and into Ute Canyon begins soon after. Here, the trail climbs about 700 feet until it reaches a bench of granite from the Precambrian Era. The geology and scenery along this portion do help to alleviate the pitch up to the first trail junction, one mile into the hike.

A quick two tenths of a mile further and the next junction is reached. Following the signs and keeping to the Ute Canyon trail, the hike now enters fully into Ute Canyon. Here, the sojourn is at a more gradual pace as the trail continues to climb up the canyon's streambed. There are spots that can be a bit overgrown, especially in the spring and monsoon seasons.

You may have the entire canyon to yourself and as you are surrounded by its walls, the canyon brings an intimate experience, wide enough for expansive views, yet enclosed and contained. There are finger arches, large cliff towers, and a little different view with each step as you make your way up the canyon. At 4.5 miles in, the trail climbs steeply again, about 550 feet over one half mile. This portion will bring views back down into Ute Canyon, ending at Rimrock Drive. On this portion is Fallen Rock, a huge section of sandstone that has cleaved from its main counterpart and is now tilted at an angle, yet unmistakably evident that it was once connected.

Returning from Rimrock Drive is straightforward with the added plus that it is mostly downhill all the back to the car.

From the Grand View

Liberty Cap Trail
Moderate – (14.0 mi / 22.5 km), round trip, 6 – 7 hours

The Liberty Cap Trail is named for a large mushroom shaped dome. From the Wildwood trailhead, getting to this popular attraction is 4 miles round trip. Much of the trail follows an old road to Rimrock Drive, giving nice views of the surrounding red rocks as you travel through pinyon juniper forests.

Starting at Wildwood trailhead, quickly climbs up the trail, (about 500 feet in elevation) to place yourself on the top of the mesa. At the first and second junctions, stay to the right trail. After two miles into the hike, you will come upon Liberty Cap, which is referred to as a "remnant sand dune" from the sign near the rock. The formation looks like a liberty cap mushroom, with a fat dome base meeting to a pointy top.

Many turn around here, making this a four-mile hike roundtrip. Continuing on, there is another short steep pitch up to Monument Mesa where the hiker continues to Rimrock Drive via an old jeep trail. This section can be great for wildlife viewing. Once at Rimrock Drive and the end of the trail, wave at a car and then return the way you came.

Corkscrew Trail Loop
Moderate – (3.3 mi / 5.3 km), round trip, 60 – 90 minutes

Corkscrew Trail is typically used as connector or alternative trail for Ute Canyon and Liberty Cap Trails, but is a short fun hike in its own right. The trail starts at the Wildwood Trailhead and is a true loop. The description here is for the counterclockwise direction, but either way is great.

Follow the Wildwood Trail for one-quarter mile until being presented with two trails, which are both Corkscrew Trail. Taking the right one and follow as the

Coke Ovens are in background

trail goes behind a large rock slab and climbs steeply. Take heart that once you see the next sign and trail junction, the ascent portion is behind you. Take the junction on the left that leads to Ute Canyon.

The trail sits high for another quarter mile, giving some spectacular views before again presenting another junction. Take the trail to the left back to where you started; taking the right trail will take you into Ute Canyon. From here, the loop begins its descent with some occasional narrow rocky passages and a steep set of serious switchbacks and the main reason to take this hike in a counterclockwise direction.

Monument Canyon
Moderate – (13.0 mi / 21.0 km), round trip, allow 4 -5 hours

Monument Canyon is one of the most popular hikes in the park. The main attraction is Independence Rock, which is the largest freestanding rock in Colorado National Monument. There is also the Kissing Couple, another freestanding pillar of whimsical rock art, looking like an ancient stone couple locked in an eternal smooch.

This is a there and back trail with trailheads at both ends, giving an option to use a shuttle car to halve the distance. Starting from Red Rock Drive, the trail steeply descends about 600 vertical feet over almost a mile down to the canyon floor.

Once at the bottom, the trail levels out and follows the contours of the canyon. Look for the Kissing Couple after 2.6 miles. Once past this sandstone tomfoolery, Independence Monument is in sight. Continue on the trail to its base. For a nice view of Window Rock, climb up the western slope of Independence Monument. The trail continues another 2.5 miles from here to Highway 340, where you turn around and head back or get in the car you parked at this end of the trail.

Coke Ovens Trail
Easy – (1.0 mi / 1.6 km), round trip, allow 30 – 45 minutes

If you've seen one of the historic beehive shaped charcoal ovens, then spotting these beehive shaped sandstone formations will be easy. This type of erosion is common to Wingate Sandstone after it has lost its harder top cap layer of Kayenta sandstone.

The caress of light on rock

The trailhead begins off Rim Rock Drive as the Monument Canyon Trailhead. For this reason, this hike allows for fantastic views of Monument Canyon. The trail descends into the canyon before leveling off at the fork. Stay right at the fork and continue to the end of the trail. The trail not only will give good views into Monument Canyon, it is fairly well sheltered and level, making it suitable for young kids.

C.C.C. Trail

Moderate – (0.75 mi / 1.2 km), one way, allow 30 – 60 minutes

The C.C.C. Trail gets its name from the Civilian Conservation Corps; a federal program during the depression era of the 1930's to help create jobs. The trail is fairly practical; it connects a hiker from Monument Canyon Trail to the Black Ridge Trail, providing a red rock experience with a finish at the high point in the park. The trail climbs 400 feet to Black Ridge over a three quarter mile distance.

Black Ridge Trail

Moderate – (11.2 mi / 18.0 km), round trip, allow 4-5 hours

Black Ridge Trail is a great trail for getting expansive views of the San Juan Mountains, Utah and the Grand Valley of Colorado. This is the highest trail in the park and was once a pioneer road called the Old Fruita Dugway. It was built in the 1880's to drive cattle from Fruita to Glade Park. The trail begins at the visitor center and follows the Black Ridge, ending at the Liberty Cap Trailhead on Rim Rock Drive.

Starting from the visitor center, look for the trailhead as a wide gravel fire road across the street. Ascend briefly until coming to the BLM/NPS boundary about one half mile into the hike. Now on BLM land, continue to climb until leveling out into a pygmy Juniper Pinyon forest. The poor soils here are just enough to sustain this ecosystem, but the flora is stunted. Along the way, take in the views of the Grand Mesa, the world's largest flattop mountain and the Book Cliffs.

By about 1.5 miles in you are now hiking on an open grassy plain with dotted swaths of juniper. This area is known for being a favorite of big horn sheep in spring and summer. Go early in the morning or late afternoon for the best viewing opportunities. At about two miles, the trail narrows to just 10 feet wide with canyons on either side. There are great views in all directions here. This is a decent place for a turnaround spot if you want to shorten the hike to 4 miles round trip.

You will reach a gate at 2.9-miles that marks the boundary back into the monument. Note that rather than undoing the chain on the gate, there are slotted steps in poles near the gate that make for an easier and cooler way to climb over the fence. Your next stop is at the C.C.C. Trail, which is also the third access point to the trail from Monument Canyon.

The C.C.C. Trail is 3.5 miles into the hike and another half mile puts you at the high point of the trail at 6,740 feet. From here, the final two miles are downhill for the most part, ending at Rim Rock Drive. It is possible to pick up Liberty Cap Trail from this point and continue.

Otto's Trail
Easy – (1.0 mi / 1.6 km), round trip, allow 30 – 45 minutes

John Otto was a pretty special guy. He lived in the area in the early 1900's and after exploring the area that is now Colorado National Monument, he started building roads to it. This effort put a spotlight of preservation on what had been previously considered inaccessible land. The roads allowed President Taft himself to pay a visit, which played a part in the president declaring the area a national monument in 1911. John Otto then became the park's first ranger, getting paid $1 a month initially and

working as a ranger for 16 years. Hats off to the tenacity of folks like John Otto!

The trail itself is very special, allowing in a short distance some of the best views of Monument Canyon. One can see the spires of Independence Monument and Sentinel Spire, as well as the rock formations known as Pipe Organ and Praying Hands. The trail is picked up about a mile from the Saddlehorn Visitor Center.

Alcove Nature Trail
Easy – (1.0 mi / 1.6 km), round trip, allow 30 minutes

This easy hike is suitable for families with small children. The hike is level for the most part and heads into a box canyon with an alcove at the end. There is a nice trail guide that is available at the visitor center and at the trailhead that helps explain the scenery as you walk.

Window Rock Trail
Easy – (0.5 mi / 0.8 km), round trip, allow 15 minutes

Window Rock Trail is a short and level loop through pinyon juniper forests to an overlook into the Monument and Wedding Canyons. This trail provides sweeping views into the heart of this park. The trail's namesake, Window Rock, can be seen here as well. This trail is often combined with the Canyon Rim Trail, described below.

Canyon Rim Trail
Easy – (1.0 mi / 1.6 km), round trip, allow 30 minutes

The Canyon Rim Trail extends the expansive and incredible views of Window Rock Trail with a focus on Wedding Canyon. The views along this hike are absolutely stunning. This is a great compliment hike to Window Rock Trail. If taking both trails, the total distance is 2 miles and takes about 90 minutes.

Rifle Falls State Park

Quick Facts

Official Park Website: http://cpw.state.co.us/placestogo/parks/RifleFalls

Visitor Center: (970) 625-1607

Park Accessibility:

- Okay for 2WD and RVs
- Day and Overnight Use

Experience Level:

- Family Friendly to Casual Hiker

Camping in Park:

- Rifle Falls Campground: 13 T/RV plus 7 walking tent sites, drinking water, restrooms, showers, hookups, reservable at www.reserveamerica.com

Lodging and Dining in Park:

- None

Nearest Town with Amenities:

- Rifle, CO is 13 mi / 21 km from the park

Getting There:

- From Grand Junction, CO: Take I-70 East to US-6 East to CO-325 North. Total distance is 73 mi / 117 km to park

Rifle Falls State Park

What Makes Rifle Falls State Park Special

- Amazing set of waterfalls good enough to be the back drop for weddings
- Limestone caves open for exploration
- The views leading to the falls and within the park

Rifle Falls State Park surrounds a portion of East Rifle Creek. The area is secluded and lush, with two highlights, a picturesque set of three waterfalls, and a set of limestone caves that one can explore. This is not a "grand" park, it is less than 50 acres soaking wet. This is however, a fun and delightful little place, with swimming holes and fish to catch and summer light falling effortlessly onto a riparian watershed. There are several walk in tent sites along the creek. Most of the other campground sites are along the creek as well.

Hiking Rifle Falls State Park

Coyote Trail
Moderate – (3.0 mi / 4.8 km), round trip, allow 90 minutes

This trail leads to both of the main attractions of the park, the falls, and the caves. The trail is ADA compliant to the base of the falls, where a truly picturesque view of three separate cascades falling at approximately equal lengths can be seen. The lighting is soft and the mists keep the surrounding vegetation fresh and green,

making this spot a favorite for weddings and photographers. It is possible to see the falls from their backside by walking to the alcoves behind them. If you decide to explore the caves, make sure to bring a flashlight.

Bobcat Trail
Moderate – (2.0 mi / 3.2 km), round trip, allow 1 hour

The Bobcat Trail is new to the park and connects to the nearby Rifle Falls State Fish Hatchery. The hike is pleasant, following along the creek with many fishing spots to be found before heading towards the hatchery through a grassy meadow.

The Rifle Falls State Fish Hatchery is definitely worth checking out. This is the largest state owned fish hatchery in Colorado, producing most of the rainbow and cutthroat trout for the western portion of the state. It is open year round from 8 AM to 4 PM. There is a visitor center and self-guided tours as well as food dispensers and a fishing pond for the kids.

Squirrel Trail
Moderate – (3.0 mi / 4.8 km), round trip, allow 90 minutes

The first 0.25 miles is ADA compliant and passes by the walk in tent site area along East Rifle Creek. The trail then crosses the creek and climbs to an overlook of the valley. From here, the trail heads north for a mile along the Grass Valley Canal before crossing the creek again back to the campground area. You can return the way you came via either the trail or walk back through the campground.

Dinosaur National Monument

Quick Facts

Official Park Website: http://www.nps.gov/dino

Visitor Center:

- Quarry Visitor Center in Utah (staffed year round): (435) 781-7700

- Canyon Visitor Center in Colorado (staffed only in summer): (970) 374-3000

Park Accessibility:

- Okay for 2WD and RVs

- Day and Overnight Use

Experience Level:

- Family Friendly – Casual Hiker

Camping in Park:

- Green River Campground: 79 T/RV, drinking water, flush toilets, no hookups, some sites reservable through www.recreation.gov

- Split Mountain Campground: Four group sites, drinking water, flush toilets, no hookups, some sites reservable through www.recreation.gov

- Rainbow Park Campground: 4 walk in tent sites, no water, vault toilets, picnic table, (plus bonus fire grate with half burned log left by last guy at some sites), first come-first served

- Echo Park Campground: 17 T/RV + 4 walk in sites, water available seasonally, vault toilets, first come-first served

- Deerlodge Park Campground: 7 walk in tent sites. Prone to flooding when Yampa River exceeds 18,000 cfs. Drinking water available seasonally, vault toilets, first come-first served

- Gates of Lodore Campground: 19 T/RV, 1 is ADA compliant, water available seasonally, vault toilets, first come-first served

Nearest Town with Amenities:
Jensen, UT is 7 mi / 11 km from the park

Getting There:

- From Grand Junction, CO: Take I-80 East to US-40 East to UT-149. Total distance is 190 mi / 306 km to park

Rare fossil of a sauropod

What Makes Dinosaur National Monument Special

- Seeing the Wall of Bones, a two story section of exposed dinosaur quarry, showcasing thousands of dinosaur bones excavated in place
- Relaxing and rafting the Green River
- Exploring the unique and expansive set of trails within the park

In 1909, paleontologist Earl Douglass discovered what would become one of the most prolific dinosaur fossil quarries in the world. His work received worldwide fame and recognition, with National Geographic covers and postage stamps celebrating the find. His initial find was also a home run. He uncovered the most complete Apatosaurus skeleton ever found at the time. This monster of an animal was over 70 feet long (the length of a modest house) and could weigh up to 80 tons. Some folks know this dinosaur as the brontosaurus, which was the name popularized by Douglass' find and continues to be the more known term for this species despite scientific reclassification.

Whatever the name is, the animal was tremendous and is among the 1,500 dinosaur bones that folks can see in the Dinosaur Quarry, a sheltered and comfortable museum built around Douglass' original quarry. The exhibit is very well done with the highlights being the "Wall of Bones", full skeletal reconstructions and even some 149-million-year-old bones laying around that one can touch.

While the dinosaur fossils alone are enough to warrant a visit, the park offers much more. The surroundings offer some of the best scenery and hiking in the Grand Circle and at cooler temperatures. The geology of the land is a mixture of jutting sandstone buttes, the sedimentary Morrison Formation and conglomerates.

The park sits in both Colorado and Utah, protecting a decent portion of the Green and Yampa Rivers, which flows through the entire park. If relaxing by a river isn't enough, the park also hosts a number of vibrant and unique Fremont rock art sites. To round out the activities, auto tours, river rafting, guided tours, and stargazing are also offered. In many ways, this park is a hidden gem, packing a lot of variety into a park named just for its dinosaurs.

Hiking in Dinosaur National Monument

Fossil Discovery Trail

Moderate – (2.4 mi / 3.9 km), round trip, allow 1 – 2 hours

See fossils in their natural habitat along this trail. There is a trail brochure that one can pick up at the Quarry Visitor Center to help provide interpretation along the way. Great place to see and touch naturally exposed fossil fragments.

River Trail

Moderate – (4.0 mi / 6.4 km), round trip, allow 2 – 3 hours

River trail is a nice hike connecting the Green River and Split Mountain Campgrounds. Great for a pleasant evening or early morning hike, abundant wildlife and views of Green River along the way.

Box Canyon Trail

Easy – (0.5 mi / 0.8 km), round trip, allow 30 minutes

One of two hikes that can be done in a day from the Cub Creek Road. Box Canyon Trail lives up to its name. This is a pleasant and often cool hike to the end of a box canyon with little elevation gain. Great family hike. Petroglyphs can be seen on the way just off Cub Creek Road. See Hog Canyon Trail for details on the other hike in this area.

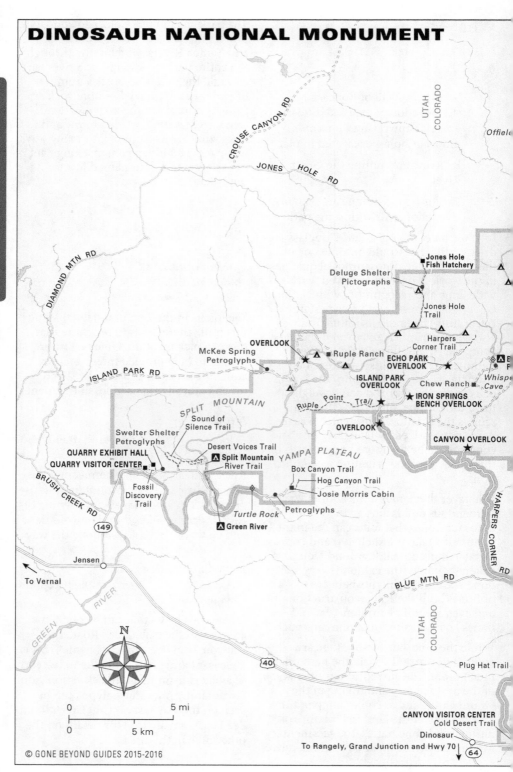

DINOSAUR NATIONAL MONUMENT

CROUSE CANYON RD

JONES   HOLE   RD

UTAH
COLORADO

Offiele

DIAMOND MTN RD

Jones Hole
Fish Hatchery

Deluge Shelter
Pictographs

Jones Hole
Trail

Harpers
Corner Trail

OVERLOOK

McKee Spring
Petroglyphs

Ruple Ranch

ECHO PARK
OVERLOOK

ISLAND PARK RD

ISLAND PARK
OVERLOOK

Chew Ranch

Whispe
Cave

B
P

SPLIT   MOUNTAIN

Ruple Point   Trail

IRON SPRINGS
BENCH OVERLOOK

Sound of
Silence Trail

Swelter Shelter
Petroglyphs

OVERLOOK

CANYON OVERLOOK

Desert Voices Trail

YAMPA PLATEAU

QUARRY EXHIBIT HALL
QUARRY VISITOR CENTER

Split Mountain
River Trail

Box Canyon Trail

Hog Canyon Trail

Josie Morris Cabin

BRUSH CREEK RD

Fossil
Discovery
Trail

Petroglyphs

HARPERS   CORNER   RD

Turtle Rock

(149)

Green River

Jensen

To Vernal

GREEN   RIVER

BLUE MTN RD

UTAH
COLORADO

N

Plug Hat Trail

0 _____ 5 mi

0 _____ 5 km

(40)

CANYON VISITOR CENTER
Cold Desert Trail

Dinosaur
To Rangely, Grand Junction and Hwy 70

(64)

© GONE BEYOND GUIDES 2015-2016

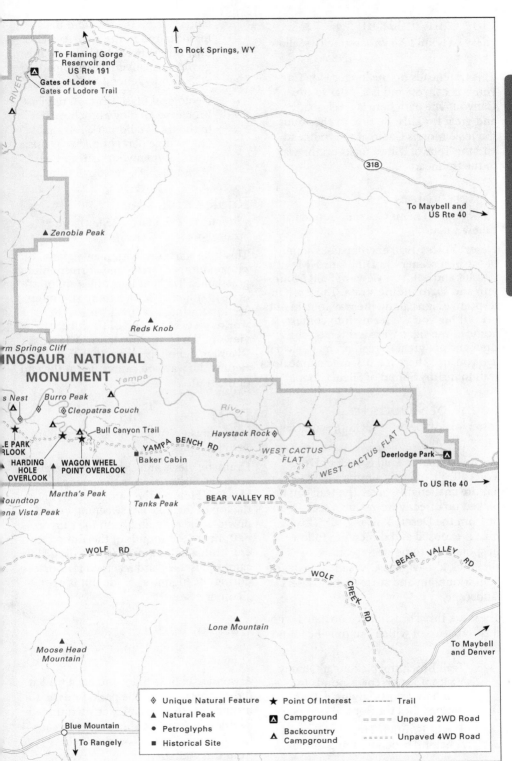

To Flaming Gorge
Reservoir and
US Rte 191

To Rock Springs, WY

Gates of Lodore
Gates of Lodore Trail

RIVER

318

To Maybell and
US Rte 40

▲ Zenobia Peak

▲ Reds Knob

rm Springs Cliff

NOSAUR NATIONAL
MONUMENT

Yampa

s Nest   Burro Peak
◇ Cleopatras Couch

Bull Canyon Trail

River

Haystack Rock ◇

E PARK
RLOOK
HARDING   WAGON WHEEL
HOLE   POINT OVERLOOK
OVERLOOK

YAMPA BENCH RD

Baker Cabin

WEST CACTUS
FLAT

WEST CACTUS FLAT

Deerlodge Park ▲

To US Rte 40 →

oundtop
ena Vista Peak

Martha's Peak

Tanks Peak ▲

BEAR VALLEY RD

WOLF RD

BEAR VALLEY RD

WOLF CREEK RD

To Maybell
and Denver

Lone Mountain ▲

▲
Moose Head
Mountain

Blue Mountain ○
↓ To Rangely

◇ Unique Natural Feature   ★ Point Of Interest   ------- Trail

▲ Natural Peak   🄰 Campground   ==== Unpaved 2WD Road

● Petroglyphs   △ Backcountry   ===== Unpaved 4WD Road
                              Campground

■ Historical Site

73

Hog Canyon Trail

Easy – (1.5mi / 2.4 km), round trip, allow 1 hour

This trail heads up the longer Hog Canyon box canyon and is similar to Box Canyon. The path here is level, shady, and great for kids. Be sure to check out the Josie Morris Cabin at the trailhead and the Tour of Tilted rocks on the way to the trailhead.

Desert Voices Trail

Moderate – (1.5mi / 2.4 km), round trip, allow 1 hour

Desert Voices Trail encompasses some of the best scenery in Dinosaur NM with vibrant and colorful views of Split Mountain and surrounding strata. There are interpretive signs along the way to help put everything you are seeing into context. Some of the signs were written by children and are great to read no matter what age you are. There is a 0.3-mile connector trail to nearby Sound of Silence loop.

Sound of Silence Trail

Strenuous – (3.0 mi / 4.8 km), round trip, allow 1 hour

Sound of Silence Trail is west of Desert Voices Trail, offering similar views within a more challenging hike. The trail can be picked up directly from Cub Creek Road or from the Desert Voices Trail. This hike is exposed and difficult to follow in spots with some steep sections of slickrock to navigate. Gives great views of Split Mountain and surrounding desert landscape.

There are three brochures associated with this trail, two of which can only be found online.

- Trail Brochure: pick up at Quarry Visitor Center, corresponds to numbered posts, giving details on geology and the flora.

- Travel Through Time Brochure: A helpful brochure tying in the landscape on the trail and the fossils found in the area. Available only online here: http://www.nps.gov/dino/planyourvisit/upload/SOS-Guide-general-online.pdf

- Geological Blast Through the Past Brochure: Geology brochure tied to the trail's landmarks. Available only online here: http://www.nps.gov/dino/planyourvisit/upload/SOS-and-FDT-geology-online.pdf

Ruple Point Trail

Strenuous – (9.5 mi / 15.3 km), round trip, allow 4 – 5 hours

This hike starts out within an expanse of pinyon juniper forests and corresponding grasslands. The first four miles are moderate in difficulty with a more strenuous section leading to a great "top of the world" view at the end of the hike. The views of the Split Mountains and Green River are definitely worth the effort. Return the way you came once at the end of the trail.

Bull Canyon Trail

Strenuous – (3.0 mi / 4.8 km), round trip, allow 2 hours

Dramatic views and sheer canyon walls greet the visitor on this steep hike to Harding Hole on the Yampa River. From the top of the hike are sweeping views down to the river and from the canyon bottom are the sounds of the Yampa River within a narrow canyon. Harding Hole campsite is used and reserved for boaters during the high use season but is open to all otherwise.

Gates of Lodore Trail

Easy – (1.5 mi / 2.4 km), round trip, allow 1 hour

A wonderful little there and back trail at the northern end of the park. Ends at a meander of the Green River surrounded by dramatic canyon views from a peaceful overlook. There is no river access from this trail.

Island Park Trail

Strenuous – (16.0 mi / 25.7 km), round trip, long day trip or multi-day backpacking trip

This and Jones Hole are considered by many to be the prettiest trails in the park. Dynamic and grand views are found along with shaded areas within Ely Creek. The trail offers a number of different routes. For either Island Park or Jones Hole Trails, it is best to purchase the appropriate topo maps and consult with the park rangers prior to heading out.

Jones Hole Trail

Strenuous – (8.5 mi / 13.7 km), round trip, allow 4 hours or multi-day backpacking trip

Jones Hole is a great hike, long enough to allow for an immersive experience, but easy enough as it is along a level canyon floor near a small creek. The hike offers spur trails to Ely Falls via the Island Park Trail about two miles from the trailhead. Other features include Fremont rock art sites and large canyon wall views.

Cold Desert Trail

Easy – (0.5 mi / 0.8 km), round trip, allow 30 minutes

Located in the southern Canyon Visitor Center, Cold Desert Trail is a short interpretative walk describing the flora of the desert in this region.

Plug Hat Trail

Easy – (0.3 mi / 0.4 km), round trip, allow 15 minutes

A paved and wheelchair accessible walk to a broad view of the northern Uintah Basin. The view is well worth the short walk.

Harpers Corner Trail

Moderate – (3.0 mi / 4.8 km), round trip, allow 2 hours

This is a continuation of Harpers Corner Road at roads end. The trail follows the ridgeline to a sweeping view of the Green River and surrounding desert panorama. The overlook sits 2,500 feet above the Green River, giving a commanding view of the park.

Confluence of the Green and Yampa Rivers

Northwest New Mexico

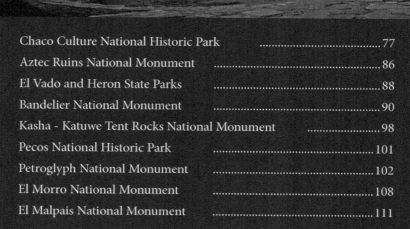

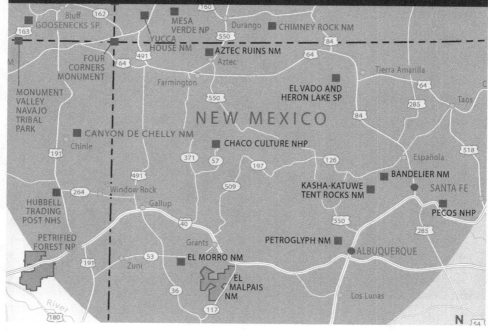

Chaco Culture National Historic Park

Quick Facts

Official Park Website: http://www.nps.gov/chcu

Visitor Center:

(505) 786-7014 ext. 221

Park Accessibility:
- Okay for 2WD and RVs
- Day and Overnight Use

Experience Level:
- Family Friendly to Casual Hiker

Camping in Park:
- 34 RV/T sites plus 15 tent only, 2 group sites, non-potable water at site, drinking water at visitor center, restrooms no hookups, dump station

Lodging and Dining in Park:
- None

Nearest Town with Amenities:
- Bloomfield, NM is 61 mi / 98 km from park

Getting There:
- Chaco Canyon can only be accessed by driving on dirt roads. For those in RV's not camping in the park, it is recommended to leave the RV at the paved section and take a car in. There are many spur roads that are not recommended and it is not recommended to rely on GPS directions from one's phone. Best directions are found on the NPS website: http://www.nps.gov/chcu/planyourvisit/directions.htm

Pueblo del Arroyo windows

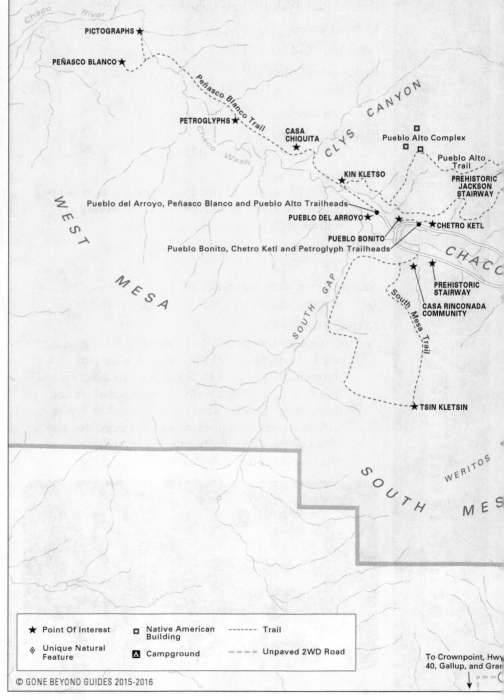

CHACO CULTURE NATIONAL HISTORICAL PARK

Chaco River

PICTOGRAPHS ★

PEÑASCO BLANCO ★

Peñasco Blanco Trail

PETROGLYPHS ★

Chaco Wash

CASA CHIQUITA ★

CLYS CANYON

Pueblo Alto Complex

Pueblo Alto Trail

KIN KLETSO ★

PREHISTORIC JACKSON STAIRWAY

Pueblo del Arroyo, Peñasco Blanco and Pueblo Alto Trailheads

PUEBLO DEL ARROYO ★

★ CHETRO KETL

PUEBLO BONITO

Pueblo Bonito, Chetro Ketl and Petroglyph Trailheads

CHACO

WEST MESA

SOUTH GAP

South Mesa Trail

PREHISTORIC STAIRWAY

CASA RINCONADA COMMUNITY

★ TSIN KLETSIN

SOUTH MESA

WERITOS

SOUTH MES

Legend

★	Point Of Interest	◻	Native American Building	--------	Trail
◈	Unique Natural Feature	▲	Campground	═══	Unpaved 2WD Road

To Crownpoint, Hwy 40, Gallup, and Gran

© GONE BEYOND GUIDES 2015-2016

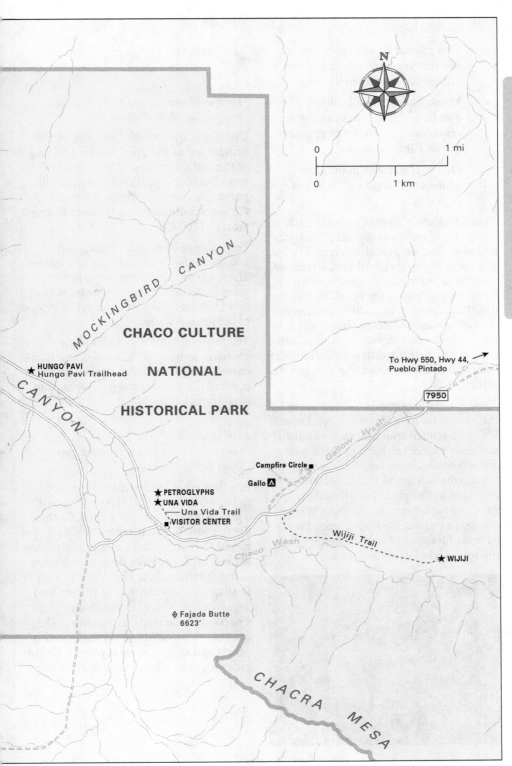

MOCKINGBIRD CANYON

CHACO CULTURE

NATIONAL

HISTORICAL PARK

CANYON

★ HUNGO PAVI
Hungo Pavi Trailhead

To Hwy 550, Hwy 44,
Pueblo Pintado

7950

Gallow Wash

Campfire Circle ■

Gallo ▲

★ PETROGLYPHS
★ UNA VIDA
— Una Vida Trail
■ VISITOR CENTER

Chaco Wash

Wijiji Trail

★ WIJIJI

◇ Fajada Butte
6623'

CHACRA MESA

0 — 1 mi
0 — 1 km

What Makes Chaco Special

- Exceptional Ancestral Puebloan site that contains not just of one village but an entire city

- Kivas, multistoried buildings, plazas, and doorways exhibiting remarkable examples of engineering and architecture

- One of the largest population centers of this period in North America

Chaco Culture National Historic Park is likely one of the most special places you will ever visit, on par with seeing Machu Picchu or the ruins of Athens. The sheer number of buildings is awe inspiring in its own right, but as the eye dials into the details, you see an incredible intelligence in architecture and design here. It is a place where one can wonder and continually see something different, continually remain transfixed in awe that this place is actually real.

There are six major sites located along the nine-mile-long Canyon Loop Drive with self-guided trail brochures available at the visitor center. Each of these is described below; however, there is a wealth of information in the trail brochures provided by the park. For all of these sites, the park requests traveling in small groups to protect the fragile sites. Please be mindful here of trash, of stepping off the trail, and of dropping food.

Penasco Blanco

Hiking Chaco Culture National Historic Park

Una Vida

Easy to Moderate – (1.0 mi / 1.6 km), round trip, allow 45 minutes

Una Vida, Spanish for "one life," is the fifth largest of the great houses and one of the earliest created. Tree rings dating from the oldest portions of the building put initial construction in the mid 800 CE with continued construction through around 1100 CE.

The ruins of Una Vida contain some 160 rooms, with some being two stories. There are four kivas, plus one to two great kiva sites. The complex is laid out in a D-shaped floor plan, which is typical of the great houses.

The round trip trail includes some excellent petroglyph examples and is the closest site to the visitor center. Some parts of the trail are steep in places and slippery when wet.

Hungo Pavi

Easy – (0.25 mi / 0.4 km), round trip, allow 30 minutes

Another great house, Hungo Pavi, contains 140 to more than 150 rooms and a great kiva and is unexcavated. In the north room block, there are three rows of rooms that stand three stories high along the rear wall and then drop to one story along the plaza. Like Una Vida, the site is D-shaped. Construction of Hungo Pavi began in late 900s with multistory construction in the mid-11th century. The fact that this site was never excavated is telling and shows an example of a Chaco great house in a more undisturbed state.

A visit to Chaco is akin to stepping back through time

Pueblo Bonito

Easy – (0.5 mi / 0.8 km), round trip, allow 45 - 60 minutes

Pueblo Bonito is the largest and best-known great house in the park, with 600 rooms, 40 kivas, and three great kivas. It is a place to wander in wonder, both in its scale and its artistry of design and architecture. At its peak, this great house rose four stories along the arc of northern rooms with the majority of the plaza-facing rooms being one story tall. In between were rows of rooms that were two or three stories tall.

Pueblo Bonito has undergone five excavations, the two most prominent being the Hyde Exploring Expedition of 1896, sponsored by the American Museum of Natural History, and the expedition conducted by the National Geographic Society from 1921–1927. For the Chaco culture, this was their main township, the center of their known world. Within its urban heart, innovations were born out of necessity as the populations grew and became denser. Researching even the ground plan reveals how they managed growth, in many ways coping with it in a manner that retained an enduring spirit that can be seen even today.

Ranger-led walks of Pueblo Bonito are offered year-round. Check in at the visitor center for more information.

Chetro Ketl

Easy, occasional steep steps – (0.5 mi / 0.8 km), round trip, allow 45 - 60 minutes

Chetro Ketl, located a little more than a quarter mile from Pueblo Bonito, is the second largest great house. The provenance of the name Chetro Ketl goes back to a report in 1849 by Lieutenant Simpson; however, the meaning of the term is less clear.

While there is evidence of earlier rooms, an analysis in 1983 revealed that the principal construction of Chetro Ketl began around 1040 A.D. and continued into the early 12th century. As a result, evidence of some of the advancements made in architectural design can be seen in this great house. It is thought that the north side rose to four stories, and stretching along the north pueblo wall is evidence of a balcony, which is distinctive. Another unique architectural highlight is a colonnade (row of columns) built along a portion of the plaza wall in the northern room block. The colonnade was later filled in for unknown reasons and is no longer visible today.

Overall, there is a subtle play in the design, and the circular shapes of the kivas blend nicely with the straighter edges of the walls and surfaces. One needs to use his imagination, but there is an eye for flow in the design of Chetro Ketl.

Pueblo del Arroyo
Easy – (0.25 mi / 0.4 km), round trip, allow 30 - 45 minutes

The fourth largest of the great houses, holding around 300 rooms and 17 kivas, is located about 900 feet west of Pueblo Bonito. There are two unique aspects of Pueblo del Arroyo. The first is its location, which is away from the northern cliff face and oriented to the east rather than to the south. As a result of this, the site has had more erosional battles with flash floods from the nearby wash.

The other distinction of Pueblo del Arroyo is the tri wall construction. Some research suggests this was the first tri wall design built. While there are examples of tri wall construction elsewhere in the Chacoan culture, this is the only one found at the Chaco Culture park. Interestingly, the tri wall was prehistorically razed (the people built it, then tore it down, likely for stone reuse), leaving the foundation intact. Pueblo del Arroyo is Spanish for "town by the wash."

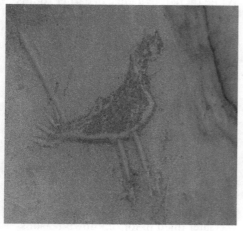

Pictograph

Casa Rinconada
Easy – (0.5 mi / 0.8 km), round trip, allow 30 - 45 minutes

Isolated from the great houses, Casa Rinconada is a great kiva, located on the southern edge of the canyon atop a ridge directly across from Pueblo Bonito. There are a number of masonry rooms adjoining the kiva, including a one-room antechamber to the south and the north. The interior diameter of this great kiva is 63 feet (19.2 m). As with many of the great kivas, there is an inner bench, seating pits, a firebox, and 34 niches encircling the structure. The kiva also has a 39-foot-long (12m) underground passage that is three feet deep by three feet wide. The underground chamber may have allowed either spirits or the Chacoan shaman to enter, potentially in a dramatic fashion.

Petroglyph Trail
Easy – (0.25 mi / 0.4 km), round trip, elev. Δ: negligible, trailhead between Chetro Ketl and Pueblo Bonito

This trail travels between the Pueblo Bonito and Chetro Ketl great houses along the cliff face. The trail shows many examples of petroglyphs of the Chacoan people. Some are high up the cliff face (How did they do that?), so bring binoculars. If you plan to visit both great houses, make sure to include time for this worthwhile hike. There are interpretive trail guides at either end of the trail.

Penasco Blanco Trail
Moderate, Strenuous when hot – (7.2 mi / 11.6 km), round trip, allow 4 - 6 hours, elev. Δ: 160 ft / 49 m, trailhead at west end of park road, near Pueblo del Arroyo

This trail is the longest in the park that showcases a number of archaeological sites, pictographs, and petroglyphs. The highlight for most visitors is the "supernova" pictograph. This ancient painting shows a bright star near a sickle-shaped moon with a hand above. While the

The Supernova petroglyph

NORTHWEST NEW MEXICO

Chaco

meaning is up to interpretation, the Crab Nebula is in fact the remains of a supernova that exploded in 1054. Could this be a depiction of that event?

The trail starts out flat and wide enough for a vehicle. For all points described here, they are well labeled on the trail. The first stop is a small ruin site named Kin Kletso.

With the trail still wide enough for a bus full of tourists, the next stop is the great house Casa Chiquita. There have not been any formal excavations of this site, which contains around 34 ground floor rooms and a central kiva that is elevated relative to the rooms. The entire structure is believed to have been built in one period of construction around the early 12th century, given certain elements of its design. One interesting side note is the large masonry dam that lies northeast of Casa Chiquita. This may have held water for agricultural use.

One mile in, the trail narrows to single track with a half mile to the next destination, the Petroglyph Trail. The trail does indeed contain many petroglyphs,

though in some areas, modern intrusions can be seen. This trail can be done in either direction and is flat.

The next stop, the supernova pictograph, is 1.2 miles farther on. There is something rather artistic and auspicious about this particular ancient painting. The supernova of A.D. 1054 has been recorded in Chinese and Japanese literature and would have been visible to the Chacoans as well. The explosion of a star would certainly give reason to record it. There are some amateur astronomers who have returned during one of the 18.5-year cycles when the sky would look much like it did in 1054 and found the Crab Nebula was indeed to the left of a crescent moon.

There is one other point that was made by the Chacoans who created this pictograph, if indeed this is a depiction of the supernova of A.D. 1054. The moon is shown lit by the sun from the top. If you look at the crescent moon at night, the moon is always lit from the side or the bottom. It is only during the day, when the sun is "above us" that you would see a crescent moon lit from the top, as is shown in the pictograph. The point here is that the Chacoans are telling us that the supernova was bright enough to be visible during the day. If this point is to be believed, then the size of the supernova relative to the size of the moon could also be meant to depict the actual size of the explosion in the sky relative to the moon, very large indeed.

The final 0.8 miles to Penasco Blanco wind past some odd rock structures, an arch, and some petroglyphs before climbing a bit for the last half mile to the ruins themselves. The ruins of Penasco Blanco are extensive and very much worth the hike. It is the westernmost and third largest of the Chaco great houses. The oval ground plan is quite different from the classic D shape of the other great houses. The site contains evidence of multiple stories and four great kivas, which is the largest number of any of the great houses. The return trip is completed by turning around and walking back.

Pueblo Alto Trail

Moderate to Strenuous – (5.1 mi / 8.2 km), round trip, allow 3-4 hours, elev. Δ: 270 ft / 82 m, trailhead at west end of park road, near Pueblo del Arroyo

This trail gives impressive and expansive views of Pueblo Bonito, Pueblo Arroyo, and Chetro Ketl. The hike up is steep and narrow in places, with a 270-foot elevation gain over one mile. From the top, it is possible to see the breadth of the Chaco culture and the land within which they lived.

If you do carry on to Pueblo Alto and New Alto, it will be exposed and hot in the summer, so come prepared. The remainder of the hike has a little more climbing before summiting at a grassy mesa to the ruins. Both ruins are the only great houses atop the mesa north of the canyon and are definitely worth visiting. Along the way are clearly marked Chacoan stairs that seem to be carved right out of the cliff wall. Look for the trail sign marked "Jackson Stairway".

Once the ruins have been completed, the trail loops back to the Bonita Overlook and back down to the main area.

South Mesa Trail

Moderate to Strenuous – (3.6 mi / 5.8 km), round trip, allow 3-4 hours, elev. Δ: 450 ft / 137 m, trailhead near Casa Rinconada

Looking down from Pueblo Alto Trail

Detail of Chetro Ketl Great Kiva

The South Mesa is a great hike. It's not terribly long, isn't the most popular hike in the park and gives the hiker plenty of both solitude and archaeological sites in a lonely and yet inviting land. Going clockwise, the hike starts as single track and begins to climb almost immediately. There are many areas where rock cairns point the way and the trail takes the hiker past some cool looking sandstone mini arches and other oddities that can be best described as sandstone Swiss cheese. The trail climbs 450 feet and does so rather quickly. Soon the valley floor expands out, giving great views of the ruins and distant mesas.

After summiting to the top of the mesa, continue on a dusty single track through desert grasslands until you reach Tsin Kletzin. This portion of the hike is wonderfully remote, with the big sky above and expansive grasslands in every direction. Tsin Kletzin is 1.3 miles from the trailhead and is a great house consisting of 80 room and 3 kivas, two of which are elevated. The site is unexcavated and was constructed later than some of the other great houses, dating to early 12th century. Look for a rectangular enclosure to the north. In the southern portion of the ruins is an arced plaza. There are pottery shard remnants that have been found by

hikers and then left for others to view. Please do not remove anything that you find. The complex provides line of site to six other great houses.

The trail continues through the mesa top before winding downwards via the help of rock cairns in some areas. Look for rock art either inscribed or otherwise along the way (and in fact along the entire trail). Ultimately, the trail ends at Case Rinconada and the parking lot.

Wijiji Trail

Moderate – (3.0 mi / 4.8 km), round trip, allow 2 hours, elev. Δ: 20 ft / 6 m, trailhead at Gallo Campground parking area

This is an up and back trail, heading 1.5 miles to a later period C shaped great house. The trail itself is fairly flat and great for mountain biking. It is a two-lane road until the final approach to the ruins themselves.

The Wijiji ruins contain a smaller sized great house built in period around A.D. 1110. It contains 100 rooms, but no great kivas or enclosing wall for the plaza area. The room blocks stood as high as three stories and overall, there is a symmetry to the east and west wings, inferring designed thought of the entire complex prior to its construction.

Aztec Ruins National Monument

Quick Facts

Official Park Website: http://www.nps.gov/azru

Visitor Center: (505) 334-6174 ext. 230

Park Accessibility:

- Okay for 2WD and RV's
- Day Use Only

Experience Level:

- Family Friendly

Camping in Park:

- None

Lodging and Dining in Park:

- None

Nearest Town with Amenities:

- Aztec, NM is 1.5 mi / 2.4 km from the park

Getting There:

- From Aztec, NM: take NE Aztec Road to Road 2900 for 1.5 mi / 2.4 km to the park

What Makes Aztec Ruins Special

- Isolated setting allows for a more intimate look at the Ancestral Puebloan people

- Contains the largest and oldest reconstructed kiva in North America

- Some of the best preserved ruins in the Grand Circle

Not to be confused with the Aztec people that lived much further south in Mexico, this ruin is an example of the Ancestral Puebloans. Built approximately 900 years ago, the ruins are heavily influenced by the Chaco architecture styles. Like Chaco, the development was planned out and cleared before the building began. The ruins of over 400 rooms can be seen in the excavated portion of the site.

The best part of this site is that it was over engineered, which has allowed much of the ruins to remain intact. One can see many examples of original timbers and along the northwest room block, it is possible to walk inside intact rooms, with original ceilings and walls. There is also the Green Wall, which is a wall with a line of green limestone incorporated along with custom hewn timbers for decoration and style.

For some, the highlight of the park is the Great Kiva, which was completely reconstructed. One can walk inside and see what it is like to stand under the roof of a painted and fully detailed kiva. The Great Kiva is the largest and oldest reconstructed kiva in North America and is definitely worth seeing.

The site is located just outside the small town of Aztec, New Mexico and doesn't get as much attention as Chaco Culture National Historic Park further south. This is the park's biggest advantage as it provides a more up close and intimate window into the world of these original inhabitants. The site is one of the most well preserved examples of the Chacoan lifeway, rivaling Chaco Culture National Historic Park in some aspects.

Hiking Aztec Ruins National Monument

A self-guided trail takes the visitor along and inside the ruins. The trail is accessed from the visitor center and is about half a mile in distance. Visitors can step inside intact rooms, with original ceiling timbers and stone work. In some places, the fingerprints of the workers can be seen in the masonry.

Aztec Ruins

El Vado and Heron State Parks

Quick Facts

Official Park Website:

- El Vado Lake State Park: http://www.emnrd.state.nm.us/SPD/elvadolakestate-park.html

- Heron Lake State Park: http://www.emnrd.state.nm.us/SPD/heronlakestatepark.html

Visitor Center:

- El Vado Lake State Park: (575) 588-7247

- Heron Lake State Park: (575) 588-7470

Park Accessibility:

- Okay for 2WD and RVs

- Day and Overnight Use

Experience Level:

- Family Friendly to Casual Hiker

Camping in Park:
Sites reservable online or by calling (877) 664-7787

- El Vado Lake State Park: 8 Campgrounds, 80 total T/RV sites plus 4 group camp-grounds, drinking water, showers, vault toilets, some hookups and pull thru sites, dump station.

- Heron Lake State Park: 250 total T/RV sites plus group camp-grounds, drinking water, showers, vault toilets, some hookups and pull thru sites, dump station.

Lodging and Dining in Park:

- None

Nearest Town with Amenities:

- Rutheron, NM is 11 mi / 18 km from park (nearest town is relative to where you are within these two lakes)

Getting There:

- From Santa Fe, NM: Take US-285 North to US-84 West/North to NM-95 South. Total distance is 109 mi / 175 km to park

- From Durango, CO: US-160 East and US-84 East to NM-95 South. Total distance is 132 mi / 212 km to park

What Makes Both Parks Special

- Nice peaceful high desert lakes with big skies and deep blue waters
- Seeing the dramatic views of the Brasos Cliffs
- Hiking along the Rio Chama, a major tributary of the Rio Grande

The El Vado and Heron Lakes are both man made recreational reservoirs created for multiple purposes including camping, fishing, boating, cross-country skiing and hiking. They are within a 5.5-mile hike of each other. Heron Lake, at 5,900 acres (24 km2), is the larger of the two lakes and has three times the campsites. El Vado is 3,200 acres (13 km2) in size and is split into two major finger lakes, which is in contrast to Heron, which is one large body of water.

Both sit in the lower elevation of the Southern Rockies in a transitional ecosystem known as the Foothill Woodlands and Shrublands. These areas are dominantly populated by ponderosa pine, oak and sagebrush set in a semiarid region. Both lakes sit at an elevation of around 7,200 feet (2,190 m).

Hiking in El Vado Lake State Park

Rio Chama Trail
Moderate to Strenuous – (5.5 mi / 8.9 km), one way, allow 4 hours

The Rio Chama Trail is a scenic hike that connects from El Vado Lake to Heron Lake. The trail was built by the Youth Conservation Corp in the early 1980's. Pick up the trail north of the Elk Run Campground near Shale Point in El Vado Lake State Park. The trail stays to the east and above the Rio Chama for most of the hike in conifer woodlands, giving spectacular views of Heron Lake and the Southern Rockies. Near the comple-

tion of the hike at Heron Lake, the trail descends and crosses the Rio Chama via a suspension bridge. Rio Chama (or the Chama River) is a major tributary of the Rio Grande. The river is 130 mi (209 km) long and has an average discharge of 571 cu ft/s (16.17 m3/s).

Heron Lake

Hiking in Heron Lake State Park

East Meadow Trail
Moderate – (2.4 mi / 3.9 km), one way, allow 2 hours

The trail begins easily enough at the Heron Lake visitor center and ambles up through conifer woodlands and pleasant meadows. The trail ends at an overlook of the narrow Willow Creek finger of Heron Lake as well as the Brazos Cliffs to the east. This is a great place to watch the late afternoon sun against the Brazos Cliffs, but allow enough time to return before dark.

Salmon Run Trail
Easy to Moderate – (5.0 mi / 8.0 km), one way, allow 4 hours

Like the East Meadow Trail, this trail starts at the Heron Lake visitor center. The trail heads south above and along the lakeshore through coniferous forests and sagebrush. This hike is a great way to see different views of Heron Lake. Keep an eye out for mule deer, elk, and osprey. Bald eagles are regularly spotted in winter.

Bandelier National Monument

Quick Facts

Official Park Website: http://www.nps.gov/band

Visitor Center: (505) 672-3861 ext. 517

Park Accessibility:

- Okay for 2WD and RVs
- Day and Night Use
- Day Use Only for trails

Experience Level:

- Family Friendly – Backcountry Hiker

Camping in Park:

- Juniper Campground: 66 T/RV sites, some tent only, pull through sites, no hookups, drinking water, and restrooms

- Ponderosa Group Campground: reservations required, 2 group sites

Lodging and Dining in Park:

- Bandelier Trading Company, gift shop and snacks

Nearest Town with Amenities:

- Los Alamos, NM is 15 mi / 24 km from park

Getting There:

- From Los Alamos, NM, take NM-501 West to NM-4 East to park entrance

Bandelier ruins

What Makes Bandelier Special

- Knowing that while the park protects some very special Ancestral Puebloan cliff dwellings, over 70% of the 33,000-acre park is wilderness

- The extensive hiking opportunities in the canyon and mesa country of New Mexico

- The elevation change of the park, which starts at the Rio Grande River nearly a mile high to the top of Cerro Grande at 10,199 feet

Bandelier National Monument holds some unique Ancestral Puebloan ruins in a tranquil forested setting. The uniqueness of the ruins is twofold. First, the setting of many of the ruins is complete enough to allow the visitor to imagine the entire village as it was over a thousand years ago. It is easy to transport oneself back in time and connect with the experiences the original inhabitants played out in their daily lives.

The other unique aspect is the cavates, which are small cave like alcoves built into the soft rock walls of the area. The land was covered in ash from the Jemez Volcano, which left over 1,000 feet of ash in its wake at the time of its eruption. This ash has transformed into a tuft, a soft rock that makes up the area's pinkish cliff rocks. The Ancestral Puebloans carved living quarters into this material, which are themselves, fascinating to see.

The main attractions aside, the park is 70 percent wilderness and this means many opportunities to hike on a trail and have the land to yourself for a while, just as the Puebloans did. It is a heartwarming territory, with green forested carpets covering a once, more rugged volcanic terrain.

Hiking in Bandelier National Monument

Main Loop Trail

Easy – (1.2 mi / 1.9 km), round trip, allow 1 hour

The Main Ruins Loop Trail is a spectacular trail for seeing Ancestral Puebloan ruins. It is an easy loop from the visitor center and is the only trail that is maintained during the winter. The trail contains 21 interpretive trail markers along the way (be sure to get the guide at the visitor center for a small fee, it's worth it). Look for the trailhead marker just behind the visitor center.

The trail goes past a circular kiva used for ceremonies and Tyuonyi; a meeting area thought to have been three stories in height and held 400 rooms. The trail heads next to a canyon wall where there are some cavates, the cave dwellings carved out by the original inhabitants. These dwellings are well preserved and there are three ladders to allow entrance to some of them. The perspective once inside the dwellings is definitely amazing; don't pass up climbing up each one.

The next portion of the trail heads to the Long House within the Cliff Dwellings. Here are ruins of multi-story buildings. Petroglyphs and pictographs can be found in this area. After marker 21, the trail makes a beeline to Frijoles Creek where you pass over a log bridge and head south back to the visitor center.

Tyuonyi Overlook Trail

Easy – (2.2 mi / 3.5 km), round trip, allow 1-2 hours

This trail is a pleasant easy walk with much to offer. The destination is an eagle's view of the Tyuonyi Ruins, a circular Ancestral Pueblo site that contained 400 rooms and housed about 100 people. Access to this village was through a single opening within the circular design and the inner plaza contained three kivas.

BANDELIER NATIONAL MONUMENT

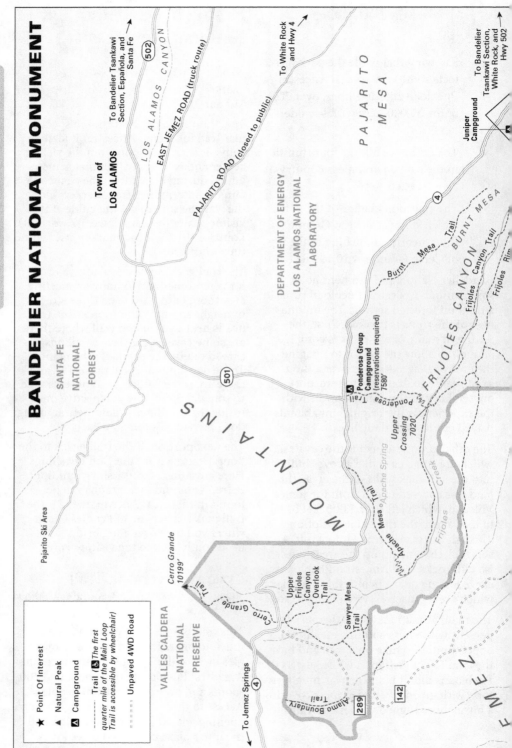

Legend:
- ★ Point Of Interest
- ▲ Natural Peak
- 🅰 Campground
- ---- Trail (🅰 The first quarter mile of the Main Loop Trail is accessible by wheelchair)
- ===== Unpaved 4WD Road

SANTA FE NATIONAL FOREST

Pajarito Ski Area

Town of LOS ALAMOS

To Bandelier Tsankawi Section, Española, and Santa Fe

502

LOS ALAMOS CANYON

EAST JEMEZ ROAD (truck route)

PAJARITO ROAD (closed to public)

To White Rock and Hwy 4

PAJARITO MESA

DEPARTMENT OF ENERGY LOS ALAMOS NATIONAL LABORATORY

Juniper Campground

To Bandelier Tsankawi Section, White Rock, and Hwy 502

4

BURNT MESA

Burnt Mesa Trail

Frijoles Canyon Trail

Frijoles Rim

FRIJOLES CANYON

501

Ponderosa Group Campground (reservations required) 7580'

Ponderosa Trail

Upper Crossing 7020'

Apache Spring

Frijoles Creek

Apache Mesa Trail

VALLES CALDERA NATIONAL PRESERVE

Cerro Grande 10199'

Cerro Grande Trail

Upper Frijoles Canyon Overlook Trail

Sawyer Mesa Trail

MOUNTAINS

JEMEZ

To Jemez Springs

4

Alamo Boundary Trail

289

142

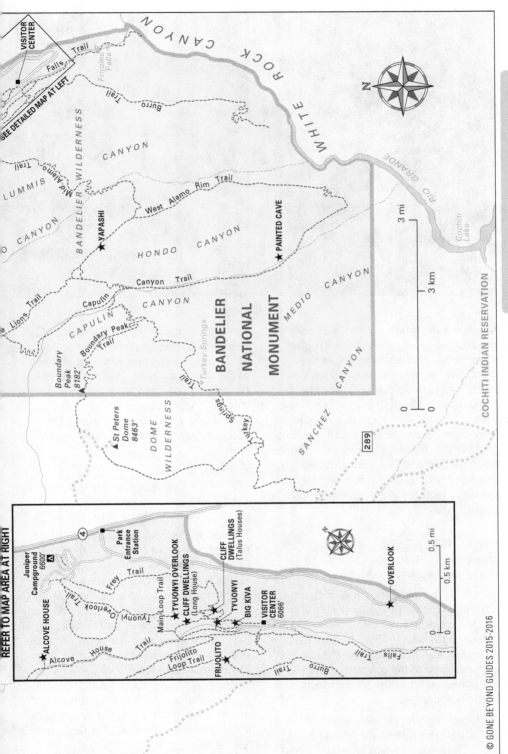

Bandelier

BANDELIER NATIONAL MONUMENT

COCHITI INDIAN RESERVATION

WHITE ROCK CANYON

RIO GRANDE

Cochiti Lake

N

3 mi

3 km

0

0

VISITOR CENTER

Falls Trail

Frijoles Falls

SEE DETAILED MAP AT LEFT

BANDELIER WILDERNESS

Mid Alamo Trail

Burro Trail

CANYON

LUMMIS

★ YAPASHI

West Alamo Rim Trail

HONDO CANYON

★ PAINTED CAVE

O CANYON

Canyon Trail

Lions Trail

Capulin

CAPULIN CANYON

MEDIO CANYON

Boundary Peak 8182'

Boundary Peak Trail

Turkey Springs

Turkey Springs Trail

SANCHEZ CANYON

▲ St Peters Dome 8463'

DOME WILDERNESS

289

REFER TO MAP AREA AT RIGHT

Juniper Campground 6600'

4

Park Entrance Station

Frey Trail

Main Loop Trail

Tyuonyi Overlook Trail

★ TYUONYI OVERLOOK

★ CLIFF DWELLINGS (Long House)

CLIFF DWELLINGS (Talus Houses)

★ TYUONYI

BIG KIVA

VISITOR CENTER 6066'

★ ALCOVE HOUSE

Alcove House Trail

Frijolito Loop Trail

★ FRIJOLITO

Burro Trail

Falls Trail

★ OVERLOOK

N

0.5 mi

0.5 km

0

0

The unique cavates of Banelier

While the destination of both Tyuonyi and the great views of the Frijoles Canyon are enough to motivate the hiker, the journey to the overlook end point is equally fulfilling. There are agricultural ruins that are passed along the way, including one that is thought to have been ceremonially used to promote good crops. This trail can be picked up from the Juniper Campground and is a dead end trail to the Overlook. Near the overlook look for a spur trail that leads to a small ruin.

Frey Trail

Moderate to Strenuous – (1.5 mi / 2.4 km), one way, allow 1-2 hours

Frey Trail connects the Juniper Campground to the main visitor center and was the original road into Frijoles Canyon until the late 1930's. The trail itself is wide, flat, and inviting from the Juniper Campground along a serene mesa and with great views of the Jemez Mountains to the north.

At the edge of the canyon, stay to the left and follow the sign to the Main Loop Trail. Here the trail descends about 550 feet to the canyon floor via a series of switchback. From here look for a view of the large central meeting area known as the Tyuonyi Ruins. The trail ends at the Main Loop Trail, veer left for a direct route to the visitor center. This trail has little shade and can be hot in the summer. As always, bring plenty of water.

Alcove House

Easy to Moderate, some exposed elevation – (1.0 mi / 1.6 km), round trip from Main Loop Trail, allow 0.5 -1 hour

Alcove House is a branch trail half way through the Main Loop Trail near the Frijole Creek. This trail was damaged by floods and while it has since reopened and is marked, expect some navigating through the debris field. Most of the trail follows along the creek before heading to the ruins themselves. The ruins are accessible via four wooden ladders and some stone steps that ascend 140 feet to a deep alcove containing many ruins. There is a reconstructed kiva; however, it is closed due to an unstable roof. The access is exposed and this trail is not for those with a fear of heights.

Falls Trail

Moderate to Strenuous – (1.5 mi / 2.4 km), one way from Main Loop Trail, allow 1-2 hours

Besides ending at the beautiful Upper Falls, this hike follows Frijole Creek for much of the way and is pleasant in its own right. The waterfall is definitely worth the walk, though the trail does descend 400 feet. The Upper Falls are the only falls accessible. The trail did descend further to the lower falls and on to the Rio Grande, but the flash floods in the summer of 2011 not only took out portions of the trail, it scoured the vegetation that once framed the Upper Falls.

Tsankawi

Moderate to Strenuous – (1.5 mi / 2.4 km), round trip, allow 1-2 hours

This village site is an extension of Bandelier National Monument on Highway 4, near State Route 502 and about 12 miles from the main park section. It is easy to miss if coming from Santa Fe, as there are no signs from that direction.

The hike has a number of things going for it, including cavates, ruins, agricultural fields, and petroglyphs. Ladders are used in parts of the hike and some of the trail was used by the villagers themselves. There is a great view as well from the top of the mesa. If you are going past the main visitor center, pick up the trail guide to help bring a deeper experience to the hike. The trail guide is also available online here: http://www.nps.gov/band/learn/photosmultimedia/tt-vt-intro.htm.

Frijolito Loop Trail

Strenuous – (2.5 mi / 4.0 km), round trip, allow 2-3 hours

This trail starts at the Cottonwood Picnic area near the main visitor center. The trailhead is deceptively marked "Bandelier Backcountry", though this is backcountry in the Bandelier NM, so technically, it's not wrong. The trail ascends from the start. At the three-way split take the center trail marked "Frijolito Ruins". The trail climbs out of the Frijoles Canyon via a strenuous set of steep switchbacks, which reward the hiker with views of the canyon, cave dwellings, and the Jemez Mountains.

Continue to cross the mesa until coming to an unexcavated set of ruins, which are unassuming and can be easily missed. Look for small dirt mounds covered with grass and the occasional rock wall stub. Unassuming or not, the ruin is extensive and gives a good visual of what an unexcavated site looks like.

Continue until about 1.5 miles where you will want to turn right at the split to Long Trail to head back to the canyon floor. There is another obvious split at about 2.2 miles, stay to the right to head back to the trailhead or left to take a side trip to the Alcove House. The trail can be very icy in the winter and is hot and strenuous in the summer.

Burnt Mesa Trail

Easy – (5.0 mi / 8.0 km), round trip, allow 2-4 hours

This is a pleasant and relatively flat trail passing through pinyon juniper woodlands giving expansive views. The trail is a great spot to simply "walk amongst nature" with many opportunities for flora and fauna viewing. This is an in and out trail with no connector trails, ending after 2.5 miles at a side canyon of Frijoles Canyon. The trail is not well marked from the road but as there is not much else out this way, it is easy to find. Head west on Highway 4. Los Alamos Labs will be on your right, the park on your left. Look for a Los Alamos Labs sign labeled "Tech Area 49". Drive past this sign for less than 0.5 miles to reach the trailhead.

Cerro Grande Route

Easy to Moderate – (4.6 mi / 7.4 km), round trip, allow 2-4 hours

Cerro Grande Route offers up a route to the highest point in Bandelier National Monument, Cerro Grande Peak. With an elevation of 10,199 feet, (3109 meters), this hike travels through alpine meadows, mixed conifer forests and with ample wildflowers in the summer. In addition, the views from the top are remarkable.

The trail is considered easy to moderate due to the altitude and the infrequent steep patches. Once on the trail, follow the yellow diamonds up about 1200 feet to reach the summit. As this is at elevation, be mindful of thunderstorms in the summer and presence of snow later in the season.

Also, be sure to bring plenty of water, easy to digest foods and sunscreen. At higher altitudes, there is less oxygen, which makes digesting proteins more difficult and can contribute to cramping for some. Simpler carbs such as granola bars or a nice chunk of chocolate are easier to digest. In addition, dehydration is increased at altitude, hence the increased importance of water for these types of hikes. Finally, sunscreen is a no brainer at any time, but at altitude, the thinner atmosphere increases the amount of UV rays that get through.

Alamo Boundary Trail

Easy – (2.6 mi / 4.2 km), round trip, allow 2-3 hours

The Alamo Boundary Trail is tucked away in the northeastern corner of Bandelier NM, which is its highest quality as there aren't many who venture on this hike. While it is a little more of a drive to get to the trailhead, the chances are good that solitude awaits. The trail gently climbs 400 feet total for the 1.3 miles one way and gives opportunities for wild flower viewing in the summer. The trail does connect with the Coyote

Call Trail within the neighboring Valles Caldera National Preserve where the trail descends more steeply. To get here, take Highway 4 west and turn left onto Forest Service Road 289. After about 1.7 miles, look for a parking area on your right.

Frijoles Canyon and Rim Trail

Strenuous – (up to 13 mi / 21 km), depending on route taken

The Frijoles Canyon and Rim Trails step into the heart of Bandelier National Monument. That said, the Las Conchas fire swept through this area in 2011 and burned hot in some areas, destroying much of the vegetation. Then, in 2013 and again in 2014, the area flooded, leaving much chaos, including logjams and even some trail closures. One favorite part of this hike, the Narrows, is still accessible and is a wonder filled section as you hike along the creek with vertical walls on either side.

Given this part of the park is undergoing continual change, check first with the park ranger on conditions and best approaches to take. Also, plan on being out of the canyon before the afternoon thunderstorms since the canyon is more susceptible to flash floods. This long but rewarding loop has changed dramatically due to the power of fire and water, showing only another side to the cycles of nature. From destruction comes life and even within destruction not all is destroyed. The uniqueness of seeing this first hand makes this a worthwhile hike.

Painted Cave

Strenuous – (up to 22 mi / 35 km), depending on route taken, recommend two days, can be done as a long day hike, allow 8 - 10 hours

The Las Conchas Fire and the subsequent flooding are part of this entire backcountry. This means that at times, the trail is nonexistent including the trail signs. Still, the trail is highly rewarding, offering expansive views and a few untouched areas. The Painted Cave is an alcove about fifty feet above the trail within Capulin Canyon. The alcove contains many pictographs of various animals in primarily red, black and white pigments. The Painted Cave is off limits to the visitor and is considered an active sacred place by the folks at the Cochiti Pueblo. Be sure to bring binoculars and a good telescopic lens if you want to photograph these colorful markings.

Many folks take on this route as a backpacking trip but it is possible to do as a long day hike. There are two access points. If you don't have a high clearance vehicle, start at the visitor center to access the Mid Alamo Trail. This portion crosses multiple canyons with some steep and strenuous sections, especially Alamo Canyon. Follow the trail along to the West Alamo Rim Trail, staying to the left or south at the fork. This trail keeps to the rim for the most part before turning north and descending down into Capulin Canyon and becoming the Capulin Canyon Trail. Painted Cave is about 1.2 miles from the northward bend. The Capulin Canyon Trail continues along the canyon floor and ends at the Stone Lions Trail, however for this route, veer right at the split up a side canyon towards Yapashi and back to the West Alamo Trail. This route also passes the Shrine of the Stone Lions as you head back to the visitor center.

If you have a high clearance vehicle, it's possible to cut the distance down to 14.5 miles round trip by starting from the Dome Trailhead off Forest Service Road 142. This route does cut off some of miles but is quite strenuous with some decent elevation change. Whichever route taken, it's best to consult with the visitor center rangers before heading out to get the most up to date information. Given the flooding, this area is continually changing.

Exploring the cavates

Yapashi Pueblo and Stone Lions Trail

Strenuous – (13.0 mi / 20.9 km), round trip, allow full day

The Yapashi Pueblo is an unexcavated ruin 6 miles from the Bandelier visitor center. The hike is, as one hiker put it, "a grunt", as you pass first down and then up the other side of the Mid Alamo Canyon. This portion changes 500 feet in less than a quarter mile. Take the Mid Alamo Canyon Trail to the Stone Lions Trail, staying to the right at the obvious fork. The Stone Lions Trail is named after twin rock carvings of a pair of lions in a protective posture. These carvings are unique and are definitely worth seeing. Pre historic bas-relief carvings are extremely rare; please treat this area with great respect by not touching or walking within the shrine. This is considered a sacred area.

Kasha - Katuwe Tent Rocks

Kasha - Katuwe Tent Rocks National Monument

Quick Facts

Official Park Website: http://www.blm.gov/pgdata/content/nm/en/prog/NLCS/KKTR_NM.html

Visitor Center:
- Monument: (505) 331-6259
- Park Ranger: (505) 761-8955

Park Accessibility:
- Okay for 2WD and RVs
- Day Use Only

Experience Level:
- Family Friendly – Casual Hiker

Camping in Park:
- None

Lodging and Dining in Park:
- None

Nearest Town with Amenities:
- Bernalillo, NM is 38 mi / 61 km from the park

Getting There:
- From Albuquerque, NM: Take I-25 North to NM-22 North to Indian Service Route 92 for 54 mi / 87 km to park entrance
- From Santa Fe, NM: Take I-25 South to NM-16 North to Indian Service Route 92 for 40 mi / 64 km to park entrance

Eroded volcanic ash that create the tent rocks of Kasha-Katuwe

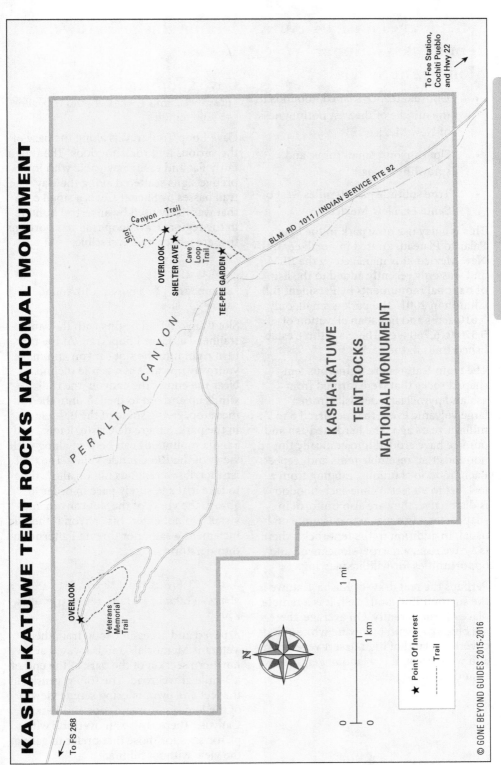

KASHA-KATUWE TENT ROCKS NATIONAL MONUMENT

OVERLOOK

Veterans Memorial Trail

To FS 268

PERALTA CANYON

Slot Canyon Trail

OVERLOOK

SHELTER CAVE

Cave Loop Trail

TEE-PEE GARDEN

BLM RD 1011 / INDIAN SERVICE RTE 92

To Fee Station, Cochiti Pueblo and Hwy 22

KASHA-KATUWE TENT ROCKS NATIONAL MONUMENT

N

★ Point Of Interest
------ Trail

0   1 mi
0   1 km

© GONE BEYOND GUIDES 2015-2016

Kasha - Katuwe Tent Rocks

What Makes Kasha-Katuwe Tent Rocks National Monument Special

- Unusual teepee shaped hoodoos in the middle of the vast nothingness of New Mexico

- Slot canyons, small ruins, and sprawling vistas

- True solitude just 40 miles west of Santa Fe, New Mexico

This is a day use only park in the lonely Pajarito Plateau, located in north central New Mexico. It is managed by the BLM and was only recently added to the list of national monuments by President Bill Clinton in 2001. The park is small, only 5,610 acres and lies at an elevation of 5,570 to 6,760 feet. There are three established trails in the park.

The main features are numerous tent shaped rocks that were formed from ash and pyroclastic deposits from a large volcanic event that occurred 6 to 7 million years ago. The hardened ash and pumice have eroded into conically tipped hoodoos that resemble tents and teepees. Each hoodoo is unique, ranging from a few feet to 90 feet. While each hoodoo is distinctive, they are also uniform in shape, creating a visual that is quite unusual. In addition to the tent rocks, there is a cave ruin, a narrow slot canyon and opportunities for wildlife viewing.

Perhaps the real draw of Kasha-Katuwe is the surrounding land itself. It is a remote place of true serenity. On average, there are blue skies with billowing white clouds covering a land of high desert vegetation and white rock. It is a land of gentle power and humbling silence.

Hiking Kasha-Katuwe Tent Rocks

Cave Loop Trail

Easy – (1.2 mi / 1.9 km), round trip, allow 45 – 60 minutes

Cave Loop Trail travels along the base of the various tent rock hoodoos. The trail is fairly flat and easily navigable with interpretive signs scattered along the way. The trail passes by Shelter Cave, a small cave that was likely used by ancestral hunters in the region. Cave loop trail has portions that are wheelchair accessible.

Slot Canyon Trail

Strenuous – (2.8 mi / 4.5 km), round trip, allow 2 hours

Slot Canyon Trail begins with the same trailhead as Cave Loop Trail. At the fork, turn right into the slot canyon and make your way upwards at a gentle incline. Near the end of the canyon, the trail winds up and out to the left onto the mesa top, giving some of the best views in the park. Sangre de Cristo, Jemez, and Sandia mountains can be seen along with views of the Rio Grande Valley. The trail isn't terribly strenuous but do allow time to take it at a leisurely pace in order to absorb the views of the slot canyon and vistas. Do not enter this canyon if there is inclement weather or threat of afternoon thunderstorms.

Veterans Memorial Trail

Easy – (1.0 mi / 1.6 km), round trip, allow 30

A paved and accessible loop trail, the Veterans Memorial Trail is located at the northern section of the park at the end of a 3-mile gravel road. The trail is gentle on the feet and eyes, offering serene views of the Jemez mountain tops and Peralta Canyon. There is also an overlook with picnic sites for those that prefer to gaze at the view without hiking.

Pecos National Historic Park

Official Park Website: http://www.nps.gov/peco

Visitor Center:

- None in park, contact (775) 289-1693 (message only)

Park Accessibility:

- Okay for 2WD and RVs
- Day Use Only

Experience Level:

- Experienced Hiker – Casual Hiker

Camping in Park:

- None

Lodging and Dining in Park:

- None

Nearest Town with Amenities:

- Pecos, NM is 2 mi / 3 km from park

Getting There:

- From Santa Fe, NM: Take I-25 North to NM-50 to Peach Drive. Total distance is 28 mi / 45 km to park

Within the many protected ruins sites in the Southwest, Pecos National Historic Park is unique in a few aspects. At its height, the village held buildings that were five stories tall and sustained a population of 2,000 Ancestral Puebloans. The people here lived in the area for over 400 years. Close by and within the park are the ruins of Mission Nuestra Señora de los Ángeles de Porciúncula de los Pecos, a Spanish mission built in 1619. A visit to Pecos is to understand the struggle of imposing one culture onto another, of trying by coercion or by force to change one's fundamental beliefs. A symbolic response of this effort was a kiva built in front of the mission in 1680 as an outright rejection of the Spanish's belief system.

The park sits just outside of the designated Grand Circle on the edge of the Plains southeast of Santa Fe, NM. There is a small 1.25-mile self-guided tour on a paved trail that allows for interpretation of both the Pecos ruins and the mission. Guided tours are also available.

Pecos NHPS also protects two very different sites preserving some of the westernmost areas of the Civil War. These are located in separate units close to the Pecos Ruins. The most accessible is the Gaviota Pass Battlefield. Dubbed the "Gettysburg of the West", this set of two parcels was the location of a pivotal Civil War battle that saw a retreat of the Confederate Army. The Confederates attempted to break the Union Army's possession of the West along the base of the Rockies. They were able to push the Union Army back through Gaviota Pass at first. However, in the skirmish they lost a critical supply train and many of their pack animals and horses, forcing a retreat and victory to the Union soldiers.

One can explore this area via the 2.3-mile Civil War Battlefield Trail. This area is closed to the public by default, but can be accessed by asking the ranger for the gate code at the visitor center. The ranger will hand out an interpretative trail guide as well. The ruins make for some good photo opportunities and the walk is pleasant.

Petroglyph National Monument

Quick Facts

Official Park Website: http://www.nps.gov/petr

Visitor Center: (505) 899-0205

Park Accessibility:

- Okay for 2WD and RVs
- Day Use Only, 8 AM to 5 PM MST

Experience Level:

- Family Friendly – Casual Hiker

Camping in Park:

- None

Lodging and Dining in Park:

- None

Nearest Town with Amenities:

- Albuquerque, NM is 10 mi / 16 km from park to center of town

Getting There:

- From Albuquerque, NM: take I-40 to Exit 154/Unser Blvd. and head north 3 miles to Western Trail. Turn left on Western Trail to park visitor center.

- Alternately, from I-25, take Exit 232/Paseo del Norte and head west to Coors Road. Take Coors Road south to Western Trail. Turn right on Western Trail to park visitor center.

The volcanic landscape of Petroglyph National Monument

Stepping off at Petroglyph National Monument

What Makes Petroglyph National Monument Special

- A chain of dormant volcanic fissures near the city of Albuquerque that hold one of the largest concentrations of petroglyphs in the Grand Circle

- Hiking amongst hundreds of archeological sites and nearly 24,000 petroglyphs of animals, humans, symbols, and brands from Ancestral Puebloans to Spanish settlers

- Trying to make sense of the macaw petroglyph, given there are no macaws in New Mexico

With the backdrop of Albuquerque in the distance and the Rio Grande just two miles to the east, Petroglyph NM is a definite, dry, and rugged landscape filled with tens of thousands of petroglyphs.

The hikes are more akin to walking through an ancient art museum. Some images invoke a clear meaning while others invoke more questions than answers mixed with a sense of wonder. While they are more artful to modern visitors, the reasoning behind their creation is not entirely known. One theory is that these images are meant to help the spirit of the deceased Ancestral Puebloan leave this world and head to the next. Nearly all of the petroglyphs are carved into the dark desert varnish of volcanic rock, exposing the lighter rock underneath.

The park also contains five small volcanic cones near the western boundary, which can be explored. Part of the monument is co-managed between the NPS and the City of Albuquerque. The ecoregion the park sits in is known as the Albuquerque Basin, known for being drier and warmer than the surrounding areas with primarily desert grasslands for vegetation. The Albuquerque Basin sits at about 6,000 feet (8,851 km).

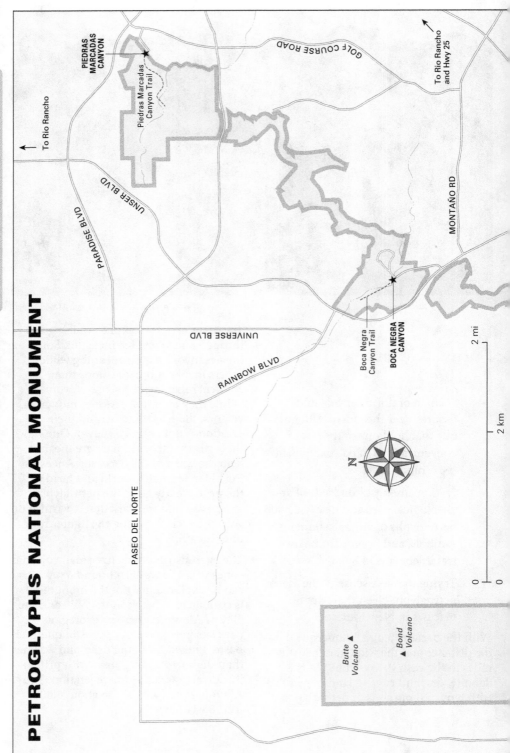

PETROGLYPHS NATIONAL MONUMENT

PIEDRAS MARCADAS CANYON

Piedras Marcadas Canyon Trail

GOLF COURSE ROAD

To Rio Rancho

UNSER BLVD

PARADISE BLVD

To Rio Rancho and Hwy 25

MONTAÑO RD

UNIVERSE BLVD

Boca Negra Canyon Trail

BOCA NEGRA CANYON

RAINBOW BLVD

PASEO DEL NORTE

N

2 mi

2 km

0

0

Butte Volcano ▲

▲ Bond Volcano

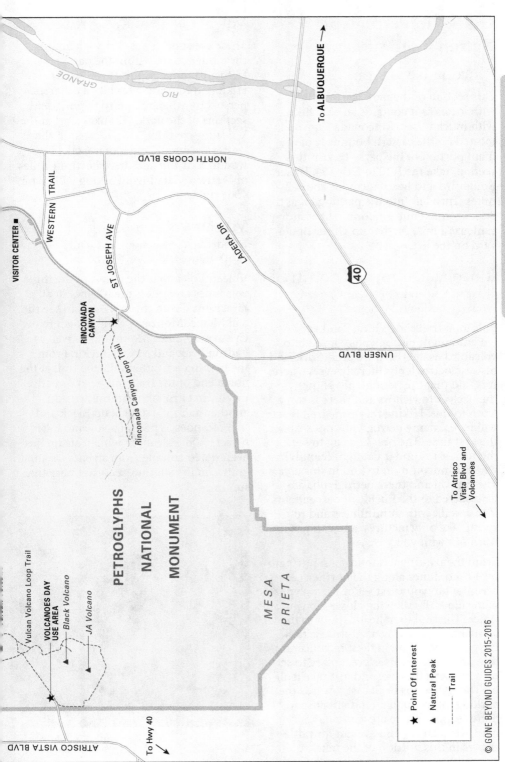

Petroglyph

VISITOR CENTER ■

WESTERN TRAIL

ST JOSEPH AVE

NORTH COORS BLVD

LADERA DR

40

UNSER BLVD

RINCONADA CANYON ★

Rinconada Canyon Loop Trail

PETROGLYPHS

NATIONAL

MONUMENT

MESA PRIETA

RIO GRANDE

To ALBUQUERQUE →

To Atrisco Vista Blvd and Volcanoes ↓

Vulcan Volcano Loop Trail

VOLCANOES DAY USE AREA

Black Volcano ▲

JA Volcano ▲

ATRISCO VISTA BLVD

To Hwy 40 ↓

★ Point Of Interest
▲ Natural Peak
- - - - Trail

© GONE BEYOND GUIDES 2015-2016

105

Hiking in Petroglyphs National Monument

Rinconada Canyon

This section of the park is a favorite with locals as it contains an easy hike with much to see. Rinconada Canyon is located off the eastern boundary of the main portion of the park. To visit this section, take the I-40 to Exit 154, Unser Boulevard and head north for about 2 miles. Turn left into the parking lot at the St. Joseph Avenue junction. The visitor center is a mile further up Unser Boulevard on the left.

Rinconada Canyon Loop Trail
Easy to Moderate – (2.5 mi / 4.0 km), round trip, allow 2-3 hours

This loop trail shows a vast and varied amount of petroglyphs carved into volcanic basalt. There are prehistoric and historic petroglyphs literally everywhere. It is said that the petroglyphs show themselves to visitors and there is some truth to this. Hiking this same trail twice will reveal many petroglyphs not seen the first time. The best lighting to see the rock art is under flat light (cloudy), which is uncommon to find in this area. The canyon and these petroglyphs are held sacred to the Puebloan descendants. Please walk with mindfulness and respect, take only pictures, and carry your trash out with you.

From the parking lot, follow a sandy path over sand dunes along the northern escarpment to your first set of petroglyphs with side trails allowing closer viewing at times. The trail then heads south to the west end of the canyon. At this section, the petroglyphs are highest in concentration and variety, this is great place to set up a break in the hike and just take it all in. The trail loops back east towards the parking lot through an indistinct sand dune section. There are trail markers here. Keep an ear and eye out for rattlesnakes in this portion of the hike.

Volcanoes Day Use Area

These are short hikes that walk among the cinder cones within the park, collectively known as the Three Sisters. Hiking in this area provides a different perspective than the petroglyph-laden sections of the park. All hikes start at the Volcanoes parking area, located in the western section. To get there, take I-40 west to Exit 149 and drive north 11 miles on Atrisco Vista Blvd. Parking will be on your right.

Vulcan Volcano Loop
Moderate to Strenuous – (2.0 mi / 3.2 km), round trip, allow 2-3 hours

Vulcan Volcano is the tallest of the three volcanoes and offers great views in all directions. From the top, one can see the San Mateo, Monzano, Sandia, Sangre de Cristo and Jemez Mountains as well as Ladron Peak and Mount Taylor. From the parking lot, either take the trail at the north end of the trail and head directly to Vulcan (1 mile to summit) or add another half mile to pick up Black and JA Volcanoes as part of a volcano hike trifecta. On Vulcan, in winter, steam has been noted coming from a vent in a small grotto on the southwest corner near the summit

Spiraling onwards

Boca Negra Canyon

The Boca Negra Canyon is a 70-acre section that contains approximately 200 petroglyphs. One of the most eye raising glyphs is of a macaw, a parrot like bird of South America. There are two theories here, that the Puebloan culture either had contact with or migrated from the Central and South American cultures.

To get to Boca Negra Canyon, take the I-40 to Exit 154, Unser Boulevard and head north 4.5 miles, passing the visitor center. Turn right onto Atrisco Drive to the well-designated Boca Negra Canyon parking lot.

There are three short trails here, all with a difficulty of "Easy", ranging from 0.1 miles to 0.4 miles. Macaw Trail includes its namesake, the macaw petroglyph. Cliff Base Trail holds an exceptional array of glyphs and Mesa Point, which also includes petroglyphs but also gives a commanding 360-degree view of the Boca Negra escarpment

Piedras Marcadas Canyon

The most northern section of park, Piedras Marcadas Canyon contains hundreds of petroglyphs; however, this area is bordered on many sides by suburban Albuquerque. This section of the park is maintained by the City of Albuquerque.

Take Usner Road from Black Negra Canyon north until it ends, then turn right onto Paradise Boulevard. After a short distance, make a right onto Golf Course Road then a quick right onto Jill Patricia Street. The parking for this area is well marked, though you will wonder if you didn't drive into someone's neighborhood during the last section.

"Oh the stories I could tell"

Piedras Marcadas Canyon Trail

Easy to Moderate – (1.5 mi / 2.4 km), round trip, allow 1-2 hours

The trailhead starts after a short well-marked distance from the parking lot. Bear left at the gate to begin the loop and continue on a sandy fire road. The trail narrows as it enters into Piedras Marcadas Canyon proper. Look for interpretive signs along the way. Bear right and walk along the canyon wall, looking for additional markers identifying petroglyphs. At the end of the trail, you can either turn around or walk through the center of the canyon to cut off about 0.4 miles of distance.

El Morro National Monument

Quick Facts

Official Park Website: http://www.nps.gov/elmo

Visitor Center: (505) 783-4226 ext. 801

Park Accessibility:

- Okay for 2WD and RVs
- Day Use Only, seasonal hours

Experience Level:

- Family Friendly – Casual Hiker

Camping in Park:

- None

Lodging and Dining in Park:

- None

Nearest Town with Amenities:

- Gallup, NM is 56 mi / 90 km from the park, limited lodging and food within 1 mile of park

Getting There:

- From Gallup, NM, take I-40 to NM-602 South and NM-53 East to park entrance

Iconic 1873 photo of El Morro by Timothy Sullivan

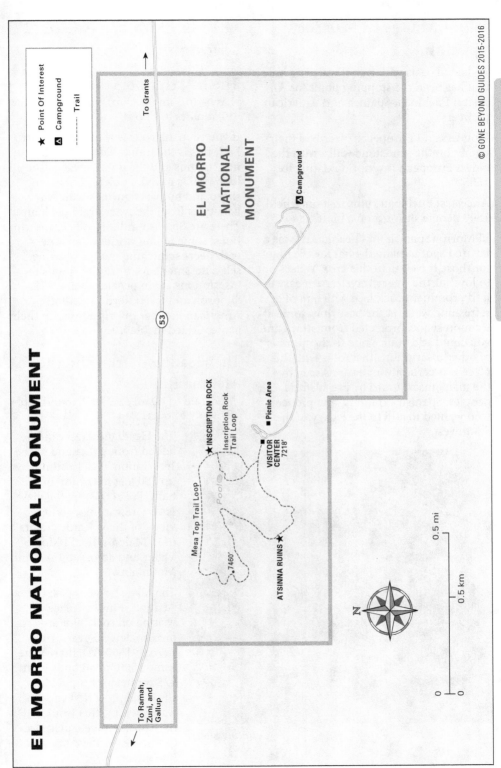

EL MORRO NATIONAL MONUMENT

Point Of Interest
★ Point Of Interest
△ Campground
------- Trail

To Grants

EL MORRO
NATIONAL
MONUMENT

53

To Ramah,
Zuni, and
Gallup

Mesa Top Trail Loop

Pool

7460'

★ INSCRIPTION ROCK

Inscription Rock
Trail Loop

★ ATSINNA RUINS

■ Picnic Area

VISITOR
CENTER
7218'

△ Campground

N

0   0.5 km
0   0.5 mi

What Makes El Morro Special

A shaded oasis with a cool watering hole that has been the stopping point for Ancestral Puebloan, Spanish and American pioneers

Pioneers and Europeans inscribed their names on the sandstone walls, with the oldest European inscription dating to 1605

Ancestral Puebloan ruins that once held 1500 people sitting atop a bluff

El Morro (Spanish for "headland") was a favored spot to hang the hat for the night for those traveling in this area. What's not to love for the weary traveler? An easy to find prominent rock face with a pool of refreshing water at the base of it, some afternoon shade, protected from attack and you could add your name to the number of other inscriptions that folks left. This place was certainly an oasis as seen by the many inscriptions by pre-historic peoples, Spanish explorers, and pioneers who wanted to add to the legacy of the Southwest.

Counting Sheep

Hiking El Morro National Monument

The Inscription Trail

Easy – (0.5 mi / 0.8 km), round trip, allow 30 minutes to 1 hour

If you've made your way out to El Morro NM, this is the trail to take to see the inscriptions and the pool of water. The loop trail is paved. Look for big horn sheep and human figurines with crazy hairstyles from the Ancestral Puebloans. There are Spanish military officer inscriptions, some telling stories of greatness with peers scratching out the glowing self-assessment. Many of the Spanish inscriptions are in ornate cursive. J.H. Simpson and R. H. Kern kicked off American Pioneer inscriptions with their names added in 1849.

The Headland Trail and the Atsinna Ruins

Moderate – (2.0 mi / 3.2 km), round trip, allow 1 - 2 hours

The Headland Trail can be added from either end of the Inscription Trail to climb up 250 feet to the top of the bluff. From the top, the view is very rewarding, giving views of the volcanic craters of El Malpais, the El Morro Valley and across to the Zuni Mountains.

The hike also goes past the Atsinna ruins or "place of writing on rock". For approximately 50 years, from 1275 to 1350 AD, there were some 1500 inhabitants with 875 rooms in this pueblo site. Well protected and with water nearby, this would have been an ideal place to call home for the Ancestral Puebloans.

El Malpais National Monument

Quick Facts

Official Park Website: http://www.nps.gov/elma

Visitor Center: (505) 876-2783

Park Accessibility:

- Okay for 2WD and RVs
- Day Use Only

Experience Level:

- Family Friendly – Experienced Hiker

Camping in Park:

- None

Lodging and Dining in Park:

- None

Nearest Town with Amenities:

- Grants, NM, 27 mi / 43 km from park

Getting There:

- From Grants, NM, take I-40 to NM-117 East for 28 miles / 45 km

An assortment of pottery shards at El Malpais National Monument

El Malpais

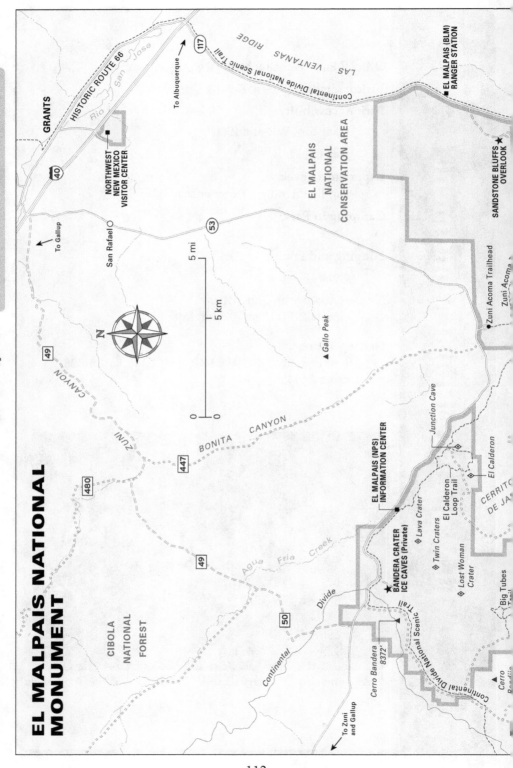

EL MALPAIS NATIONAL MONUMENT

GRANTS

HISTORIC ROUTE 66

Rio San Jose

To Albuquerque

117

Continental Divide National Scenic Trail

LAS VENTANAS RIDGE

NORTHWEST NEW MEXICO VISITOR CENTER

To Gallup

San Rafael

53

EL MALPAIS NATIONAL CONSERVATION AREA

EL MALPAIS (BLM) RANGER STATION

SANDSTONE BLUFFS OVERLOOK

N

5 mi

5 km

▲ Gallo Peak

Zuni Acoma Trailhead

Zuni Acoma

49

ZUNI CANYON

480

CIBOLA NATIONAL FOREST

447

BONITA CANYON

EL MALPAIS (NPS) INFORMATION CENTER

Junction Cave

El Calderon

49

Agua Fria Creek

BANDERA CRATER ICE CAVES (Private)

★ Lava Crater

El Calderon Loop Trail

CERRITO DE JA

Twin Craters

50

Divide

Lost Woman Crater

Continental Divide National Scenic Trail

Cerro Bandera 8372'

Big Tubes

Continental Divide

To Zuni and Gallup

Cerro

112

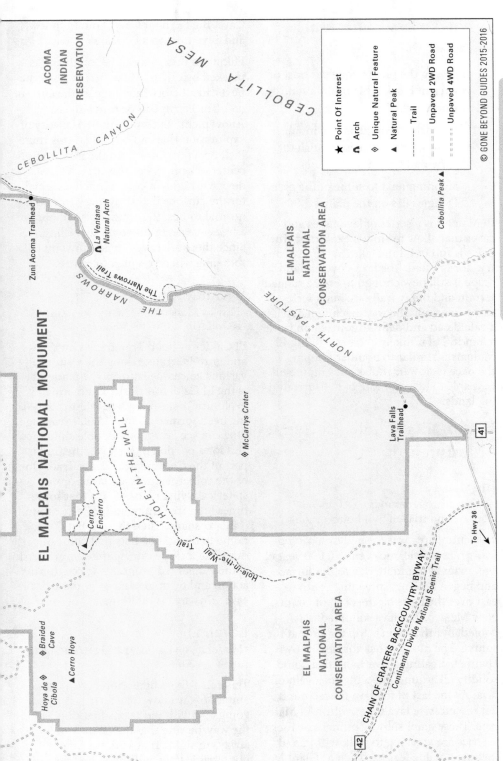

EL MALPAIS NATIONAL MONUMENT

EL MALPAIS NATIONAL CONSERVATION AREA

EL MALPAIS NATIONAL CONSERVATION AREA

ACOMA INDIAN RESERVATION

CEBOLLITA MESA

CEBOLLITA CANYON

THE NARROWS

NORTH PASTURE

HOLE-IN-THE-WALL

Zuni Acoma Trailhead

La Ventana Natural Arch

The Narrows Trail

McCartys Crater

Cerro Encierro

Hole-in-the-Wall Trail

Braided Cave

Hoya de Cibola

Cerro Hoya

Lava Falls Trailhead

CHAIN OF CRATERS BACKCOUNTRY BYWAY

Continental Divide National Scenic Trail

To Hwy 36

41

42

Cebollita Peak ▲

Point Of Interest ★
Arch ∩
Unique Natural Feature ◈
Natural Peak ▲
Trail ----
Unpaved 2WD Road ====
Unpaved 4WD Road =====

© GONE BEYOND GUIDES 2015-2016

What Makes El Malpais Special

- Seeing the picturesque contrast of ancient black lava within a sandstone basin

- Exploring lava tubes in a monument whose name is Spanish for "The Bad Country"

- Standing next to some of the oldest Douglas firs on the planet

El Malpais is a series of lava tubes and caves that allow for much exploring. The place is fun but don't take this "bad country" for granted. The lava-covered landscape is still new enough to create rugged terrain and many trails are but a series of cairns marking the way. Each footstep is a calculated and definite conclusion from a handful of unlikely choices. Hiking El Malpais is similar to boulder hopping, the pace is slower, and as a result, the hiker is able to take in more of the surrounding lands.

Hiking El Malpais National Monument

Big Tubes
Moderate to Strenuous – (2.0 mi / 3.2 km), round trip, allow 4 hours or longer

This entire area was created by a geologically recent volcanic event. 10,000 years ago, magma found its way to the surface and began flowing, spreading south to east over the large basin south of Grants, New Mexico. The lava solidified as it cooled, but that didn't stop the flow at the source. The molten rock formed its own channel, creating a riverbank that could solidify all around like a big rock vein of lava. As the last of the lava flowed out it left the massive lava tubes within El Malpais. These giant subway tunnel size rock arteries are amazing to walk within and include notable features such as Giant Ice

Cave, Big Skylight Cave, Four Windows, and Seven Bridges Overlook.

Hiking in this area can be tough and is marked by cairns. Make sure you see the next cairn before moving past the current one. The cairns can be tough to see. Allow plenty of time as there is plenty of exploration that can be had on this route. Pick up a brochure from the information center or online. For this hike, a GPS device is highly recommended, especially for the curious that stray away from the normal routes. Remember also to obtain a free cave permit before proceeding. Since these are caves, make sure you tell someone when you plan to return.

El Calderon Loop Trail
Easy to Moderate – (3.8 mi / 6.1 km), round trip, allow 4 – 5 hours

El Calderon Loop Trail travels on dirt and gravel terrain, taking the visitor to various volcanic features. The namesake is the El Calderon cinder cone, which is geologically speaking a newcomer, having been formed about 115,000 years ago. One can see lava tubes, double sinkholes, and for a portion of the hike, the trail is part of the Continental Divide Trail. One of the cooler features are lava bombs, spherical flying blobs of lava that sometimes hit a tree trunk and solidify around it in a U shape. Then there is Bat Cave, a home to over 5,000 bats that come out at dusk like a cloud during the summer. Ask about ranger led programs to see this in action and by no means go into the bat cave. This area is off limits.

Lava Falls
Moderate – (1.1 mi / 1.8 km), round trip, allow 2 - 3 hours

This cairn-filled hike shows great examples of lava flow. The terrain is tough going and with the cairns marking the way, be sure that the next cairn is always in sight. That said, the hike is not terribly long and shows a variety of lava formations. These include lava toes, ropy pahoehoe (Pahoehoe is a Hawaiian term for smooth textured lava) and glass like lava known as tachylite. The namesake of the trail is a lava fall, an area where lava flowed over itself as it cascaded down a steep incline. Be sure to pick up the interpretive trail guide from the information center to help make sense of what you are seeing.

Zuni Acoma Trail

Strenuous due to rugged terrain at times – (7.5 mi / 12.1 km), one way, allow 5 - 7 hours

The Zuni Acoma trailheads start at one highway and ends at another (Highways 117 and 53), making this trail a good candidate for the two car shuttle method of hiking. Allow about 40 minutes for the 38-mile drive from one highway to other. Neither trailhead is that well marked, however, with some good navigational skills and the fact there is nothing else out this way, nor are they hard to find. The more obvious route is from Highway 53. If coming from the other direction, keep an eye out for the split off the Continental Divide Trail near the end of the hike.

The Zuni Acoma Trail follows the Continental Divide National Scenic Trail, which runs 3,100 miles starting in Canada and ending in Mexico. Hiking even a small portion of this natural divide is cool enough in its own right. This portion has double significance as portions of the trail also commemorate the 1776 Dominguez Escalante expedition, which was the first attempt to find an overland route from Santa Fe to Monterey, California. Hiking the Zuni Acoma Trail is more than just seeing some great scenery over an open expanse; it is retracing both history and the trail that divides the continent.

The trail is marked with cairns on the open lava fields of El Malpais and here the area lives up to its name. The terrain is challenging and slow going. That said, the hike is one of the hidden gems of this park. It is easy to visualize what it would be like to be one of the first people to trek across this land. Besides the cairns marking the Zuni Acoma Trail, look for Continental Divide Trail Blazes and Concrete posts, the latter of which marks the Dominguez –Escalante expedition.

El Malpais

Great scenery at "El Malpais"

Northeast Arizona

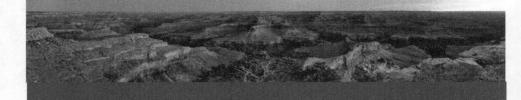

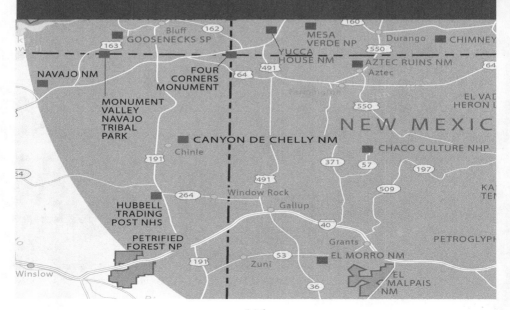

Canyon de Chelly National Monument

Quick Facts

Official Park Website: http://www.nps.gov/cach

Visitor Center:

- (928) 674-5500

Park Accessibility:

- Okay for 2WD and RVs
- Day and Overnight Use

Experience Level:

- Family Friendly – Casual Hiker

Camping in Park:

- Cottonwood Campground: 93 T/RV, flush toilets, drinking water, dump station, no hookups, some pull thru sites, first come-first served

Lodging and Dining in Park:

- None

Nearest Town with Amenities:

- Chinle, AZ is 1 mi / 1.6 km from park

Getting There:

- From Flagstaff, AZ, take I-40 East to AZ-87 North to Indian Route 15. Turn left on AZ-77 to Indian Route 15 to AZ-191 North to Indian Route 7 for 183 mi / 294 km to park

Looking down into Canyon de Chelly

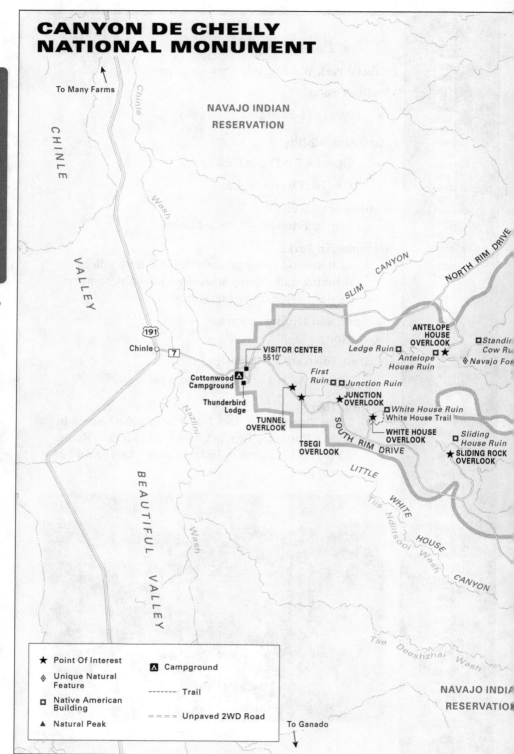

CANYON DE CHELLY NATIONAL MONUMENT

To Many Farms

Chinle

NAVAJO INDIAN
RESERVATION

CHINLE

Wash

VALLEY

SLIM
CANYON

NORTH RIM DRIVE

US 191

Chinle 7

ANTELOPE
HOUSE
OVERLOOK

Ledge Ruin □

□ Standin
Cow Ru

VISITOR CENTER
5510'

*Antelope
House Ruin*

◈ Navajo For

Cottonwood
Campground

*First
Ruin* □ *Junction Ruin*

Thunderbird
Lodge

JUNCTION
OVERLOOK

□ *White House Ruin*
White House Trail

TUNNEL
OVERLOOK

SOUTH RIM DRIVE

WHITE HOUSE
OVERLOOK

*Sliding
House Ruin*

TSEGI
OVERLOOK

SLIDING ROCK
OVERLOOK

Nazlini

BEAUTIFUL

LITTLE

WHITE

Tiis Ndíitsooi Wash

VALLEY

Wash

HOUSE

CANYON

Tse Deeshzhai Wash

NAVAJO INDIA
RESERVATIO

Legend	
★ Point Of Interest	▲ Campground
◈ Unique Natural Feature	------- Trail
□ Native American Building	==== Unpaved 2WD Road
▲ Natural Peak	

To Ganado

NORTHEAST ARIZONA

Canyon de Chelly

To Tsaile
and Hwy 191

Tsaile
Lake

12

Black
Pinnacle

To Window Rock →

CANYON   DEL   MUERTO

MASSACRE CAVE
OVERLOOK
□ Massacre Cave
□ Yucca Cave Ruin
□ Mummy Cave Ruin
MUMMY CAVE
OVERLOOK
6838'

LITTLE   MIDDLE   MESA

▲ Black
Wood Hill

▲ White Butte

NAVAJO INDIAN
RESERVATION

DEFIANCE

CK   ROCK   CANYON

▲ Black Rock Butte
7622'

CANYON   DE   CHELLY

Face
Rock
◇ Spider Rock
SPIDER ROCK
OVERLOOK
6871'
FACE ROCK
OVERLOOK

CANYON DE CHELLY

NATIONAL MONUMENT

PLATEAU

N

BAT CANYON

MONUMENT CANYON

7

0   1 mi

0   1 km

© GONE BEYOND GUIDES 2015-2016

What Makes Canyon de Chelly National Monument Special

- Arguably the oldest continuously inhabited location in the United States

In writing about nearly 80 parks, all of them remarkable, there are a few that are truly unique. Canyon de Chelly is one of these places. The land was established by the National Park Service in 1931, but is not federally owned. Chelly is a Spanish interpretation of the Navajo word Tséyi' which means "inside the rock". This series of finger canyons have been home to a history of people for over 5,000 years. Today, 40 Navajo families live and farm the land. In many respects, the ways of the past are the way of the present here. To peer over the edge is to catch a glimpse of the ancient past. To take a guided tour is to bring this past into the present.

Canyon de Chelly is entirely operated by the Navajo Nation and is the only park to be operated in this manner. As it is also home to 40 families and as such, there are restrictions in visiting the park. In visiting, the most common approach is to take one of the two scenic drives and gaze over one of the ten overlooks. That said, private tours offer a more immersive experience. There are many tour operators and many options, including overnight camping, horseback riding, and backcountry backpacking with guide and jeep tours. To ensure you are able to get the tour you want, it is highly advisable to make reservations. There is no entrance fee to the park.

White House Trail is the only established hike in the park. All backcountry travel must have a backcountry permit and be accompanied by an authorized guide. Off road vehicles are prohibited in the park. All this is to protect the privacy of the residents.

On the subject of privacy, don't be frustrated if you are asked not to photograph the residents and their homes, etc. This is living cultural preserve. To allow a window into the lives of these people is rare enough, enjoy the tour for what it is. If that doesn't work, imagine what your life would be like if you had a parade of people coming to your house in jeeps and horses to watch your activities every single day. It makes sense when you turn this experience around. This is a very unique experience from that context. If you are a photographer, it is very frustrating as there are some amazing shots. That said, be respectful of their wishes.

The 800 foot spire named Spider Rock

Hiking Canyon de Chelly National Monument

As stated above, except for the trail listed below, all backcountry hiking requires an authorized guide and a backcountry permit.

White House Trail

Strenuous – (2.5 mi / 4.0 km), round trip, allow 2 hours

This there and back trail follows a series of switchbacks 600 feet down to the canyon floor. There is one tunnel and a bridge at the bottom to cross, with the end of the trail being the magnificent White House Ruins. What makes this set of ruins so stunning is the sheer water stained cliff wall that towers above the cliff dwelling and floor ruins. The ruins themselves are well preserved and some of the exterior walls still have the original plaster. There is a fence at the perimeter of the ruins to help protect them.

The fresh green colors of mature Cottonwood trees and cacti create an uplifting and peaceful setting against the reds and dark stains of the sandstone that frame them. Bottom line, though there is but one hike in Canyon de Chelly, this one does not disappoint.

Canyon de Chelly

Come for the ruins, stay for the water stained cliff murals

Four Corners Monument

Come on, you know you want to stand here!

Official Park Website: http://www.navajonationparks.org/htm/fourcorners.htm

Visitor Center:

None in park, contact: Four Corners Monument Park Office, P.O. Box 861, Teec Nos Pos, AZ 86514, Phone: (928) 206-2540

Park Accessibility:

- Okay for 2WD and RVs
- Day Use Only

Experience Level:

- Family Friendly

Camping in Park:

- None

Lodging and Dining in Park:

- Seasonally open snack stand

Nearest Town with Amenities:

- Cortez, CO is 41 mi / 66 km from park

Getting There:

- From Moab, UT: Take US-191 South to UT-262 East to US-160 West to NM-597. Total distance is 145 mi / 233 km to park

- From Cortez, CO: Take US-160 West/US-491 South to NM-597. Total distance is 41 mi / 66 km to park

- From Gallup, NM: Take US-491 North to US-64 West to US-160 East to NM-597. Total distance is 124 mi / 200 km to park

- From Flagstaff, AZ: Take US-89 North to US-160 East to NM-597. Total distance is 227 mi / 365 km to park

What Makes Four Corners Special

- The only place you can play a game of four state Twister!

- Being in the center of the Grand Circle! (Well, not really, in fact, not at all, but go with it)

- Trying to find that unique Four Corner keepsake from stall after stall of folks selling the same thing

If there is an anchor to the Grand Circle, it is the Four Corners. It isn't the center of the circle, which is a shame from a perfect symmetry standpoint, but it is the symbolic center. In this one spot are captured four of the five states that make up the Grand Circle, namely Utah, Colorado, New Mexico and Arizona. Part of the overall allure of the Grand Circle is "Where does that highway lead to?" The answer to this question here is it leads to a magical place where one can stand in four states at the same time.

The park is run by the Navajo Nation and consists of a large marker indicating the location of the four corners, suitable for family photos and what not. Surrounding this marker on all four sides is a row of vendor stalls. Each stall is run by a local merchant selling the usual collection of jewelry, carved stones, arrows, feathered earrings, dream catchers, and spirit animals. While it would seem that the initial intent was to have New Mexico crafts on one side and Colorado goods on the other, at this point all of the merchants are for the most part selling Navajo crafts. Sometimes there is some Zuni and Hopi representation as well.

The flea market vibe aside, the merchants are all great folk and perhaps the best part of the monument. They come each day; they all know each other and are worth getting to know a little. Most are willing to share a little of their life with you if you invite them into a conversation. There is Navajo bread and other goodies for sale and basic bathroom facilities, however true to being the center of nowhere, there is no electricity, phone service, or running water here.

Time isn't used, it's experienced ~ Hopi proverb

123

Monument Valley Navajo Tribal Park

Quick Facts

Official Park Website:

- http://www.navajonationparks.org/htm/monumentvalley.htm

Visitor Center:

- Contact Monument Valley Navajo Tribal Park at: PO Box 360289, Monument Valley, Utah 84536, Phone: (435) 727-5874, (435) 727-5879, (435) 727-5870

Park Accessibility:

- Okay for 2WD and RVs
- Day and Overnight Use

Experience Level:

- Family Friendly – Casual Hiker

Camping in Park:

- The View Campground: 90 T/RV, no water, no hook-ups, restrooms, shower, reservations: (435) 727-5802

Lodging in Park:

- The View Lodge, reservations: (435) 727-5555

Dining in Park:

- The View Restaurant

Nearest Town with Amenities:

- Oljato-Monument Valley, UT – adjacent to park

Getting There:

- From Flagstaff, AZ: take US-89 North, US-160 East and US-163 North to Monument Valley Rd in Olja-to-Monument Valley
- From Moab, UT: take US-191 South to Oljato-Monument Valley
- From Cortez, CO: take UT-162 West and US-163 South to Oljato-Monument Valley

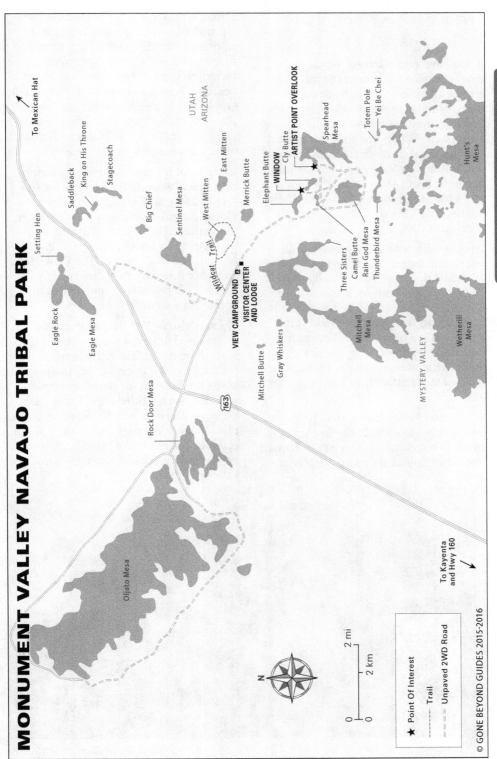

MONUMENT VALLEY NAVAJO TRIBAL PARK

To Mexican Hat

Setting Hen

Saddleback

King on His Throne

Stagecoach

Big Chief

Sentinel Mesa

West Mitten

East Mitten

Merrick Butte

Elephant Butte

Cly Butte

WINDOW

ARTIST POINT OVERLOOK

Spearhead Mesa

Totem Pole

Yei Be Chei

Hunt's Mesa

UTAH
ARIZONA

Eagle Rock

Eagle Mesa

Rock Door Mesa

Wildcat Trail

VIEW CAMPGROUND

VISITOR CENTER AND LODGE

Gray Whiskers

Mitchell Butte

163

Three Sisters

Camel Butte

Rain God Mesa

Thunderbird Mesa

Mitchell Mesa

Wetherill Mesa

MYSTERY VALLEY

Oljato Mesa

To Kayenta and Hwy 160

N

★ Point Of Interest

- - - - - Trail

= = = = = Unpaved 2WD Road

0
0

2 mi

2 km

© GONE BEYOND GUIDES 2015-2016

Monument Valley

What Makes Monument Valley Special

If you have ever watched the classic movie Stagecoach, one of the top westerns of all time, you will notice one thing. No matter where that stagecoach is heading, they are always passing through Monument Valley. The movie was John Wayne's breakthrough role and arguably put Monument Valley on the map for America. From 1939, when the movie was made, to present, Monument Valley has become THE definitive icon of the Southwest.

The problem with any icon is it tends to become larger than reality itself and we are let down when we finally meet it. The good news with Monument Valley is it will not disappoint in this way. It is as sweeping and epic in real life as it is on film. It is a place where time seems to slow down and watching the late afternoon sun slowly slip off the monuments is a memory that will stick with you for life.

Monument Valley is easy to drive through, but to capture the impact of this area it is recommended to stay overnight. The campground set up by the Navajo Tribal Park offers some of the best viewing real estate in the park. The campsites sit on a sandy hill overlooking many of the most recognized monuments, including the Mittens. The View Hotel nearby is also recommended. The famed Goulding's Lodge is another favorite place to stay and was home for the cast and crew of the movie Stagecoach and other westerns.

In terms of hiking, the land is privately owned and actively used by the Navajo. The Wildcat Trail is the only hike that a visitor can take without a Navajo escort in the park. The trail is a 3.2-mile loop that goes completely around the West Mitten. The trail starts at The View Hotel and once down in the valley is fairly flat. Allow 2 – 3 hours to complete this hike and bring water.

There is also a 17-mile scenic drive on a maintained unpaved road, which is highly recommended. The drive is suitable for most cars and is open for day use only. If you are looking for more immersion, you can take a guided tour. These tours are really the only way to see some of the places within the park. All of the official tour operators are listed here: www.navajonationparks.org/htm/monument-valleytours.htm

West Mitten Butte, Monument Valley

Navajo National Monument

Quick Facts

Official Park Website:

- http://www.nps.gov/nava

Visitor Center:

- (928) 672-2700, park is open seasonally

Park Accessibility:

- Okay for 2WD and RVs
- Day and Overnight Use

Experience Level:

- Family Friendly – Experienced Hiker

Camping in Park:

- Sunset View Campground: 33 T/RV, drinking water, restrooms, no hookups, some pull thru sites, no fee site, first come-first served
- Canyon View Campground: 14T, compost toilets, no water, first come-first served

Lodging and Dining in Park:

- None

Nearest Town with Amenities:

- Tsegi, AZ is 18 mi / 11 km from the park

Getting There:

- From Flagstaff, AZ: take US-89 North to US-160 East to AZ-564 North to Indian Route 221 for 140 mi / 225 km to the park

Large alcove protecting Betatakin ruins

NAVAJO NATIONAL MONUMENT

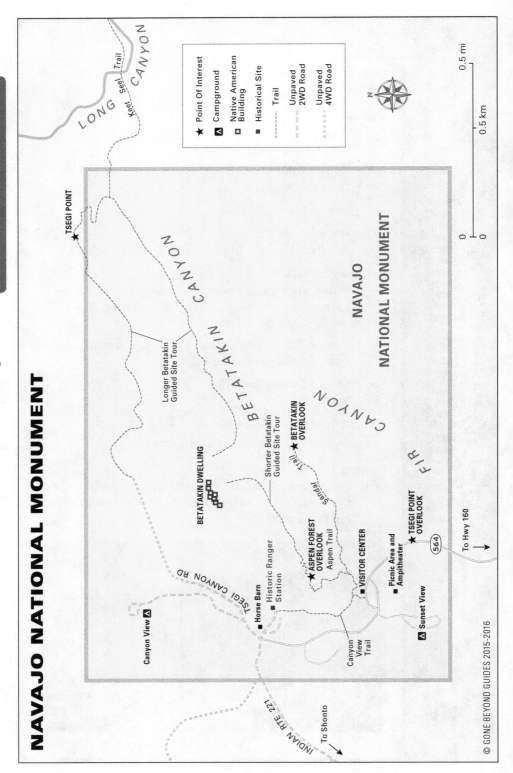

Legend:
- ★ Point Of Interest
- △ Campground
- □ Native American Building
- ■ Historical Site
- ·········· Trail
- — — — Unpaved 2WD Road
- = = = Unpaved 4WD Road

LONG CANYON

Keet Seel Trail

★ TSEGI POINT

BETATAKIN CANYON

Longer Betatakin Guided Site Tour

Shorter Betatakin Guided Site Tour

BETATAKIN DWELLING

★ BETATAKIN OVERLOOK

Sandal Trail

FIR CANYON

NAVAJO NATIONAL MONUMENT

★ ASPEN FOREST OVERLOOK

Aspen Trail

■ VISITOR CENTER

★ TSEGI POINT OVERLOOK

564

To Hwy 160

Picnic Area and Ampitheater

△ Sunset View

Canyon View Trail

■ Historic Ranger Station

■ Horse Barn

TSEGI CANYON RD

Canyon View △

INDIAN RTE 221

To Shonto

0.5 mi
0.5 km
N

© GONE BEYOND GUIDES 2015-2016

128

What Makes Navajo National Monument Special

- Knowing that you are arguably at the best preserved cliff dwelling ruins of the Ancestral Pueblo people
- That first view of the massive rock rainbow-like alcoves that protect the ruins
- Taking the guided tours and not having to pay a dime

Navajo National Monument is comprised of three well-preserved cliff dwellings of the Ancestral Puebloans. While there had been a fair amount of plunder at Mesa Verde prior to its protection, this set of ruins was put under protection in a better state. Keet Seel is considered by some archaeologists to be the best-preserved cliff dwelling in the Southwest and Betatakin wasn't even found until after the park was created.

Besides the cliff dwellings, the redrock canyon setting and even the alcoves themselves are worth the visit. These alcoves are giant grand arcs of rock, with the centerpiece within being the ruins themselves. The first glimpse of these alcoves is breathtaking in their own right.

There are free ranger led tours of the Keet Seel and Betatakin sites. The third site, Inscription House, is currently closed to the public. There is also a short 1-mile walk to an overlook of Betatakin ruins. Amenities include two small campgrounds, picnic area, visitor center, and museum.

Hiking Navajo National Monument

Shorter Betatakin Guided Site Tour

Strenuous – (3.0 mi / 4.8 km), round trip, allow 3 – 4 hours

This is a free ranger led hiking tour to the Betatakin Ruins. The tour follows Sandal and Aspen Trails down to the bottom of the canyon. With an elevation loss of 700 feet, the hike is rather strenuous. The tour is offered seasonally, so check with the visitor center first on exact time. In 2015, the tour was at 10 AM. Folks meet for a briefing with the ranger behind the visitor center and then follow the ranger as he/she describes the people and their culture, as well as flora, fauna and geography. Visitors are welcome to walk back at their own pace. The ranger will be last person out.

Longer Betatakin Guided Site Tour

Strenuous – (5.0 mi / 8.0 km), round trip, allow 3 – 5hours

This free tour takes a different path, using the old Tsegi Point Road to the Betatakin Ruins. As with the other tour, it is ranger led and quite informative. The tour is offered seasonally. To take this tour, start in front of the visitor center at 8:15 AM for a preliminary briefing. Then, the group will need to take their vehicle to end of the navigable portion of Tsegi Point Road. From here, the road becomes trail, following along a wide peninsular portion of the canyon's rim, with alcoves and canyon floor on both sides. This portion of the hike is quite spectacular in its own right. The road ends at Tsegi Point and then climbs steeply down to the canyon floor and the ruins.

Keet Seel

Strenuous – (17.0 mi / 27.4 km), round trip, full day or overnight backpacking trip

It is possible to visit the ruins of Keet Seel. This is considered by some to be the best-preserved cliff dwelling in the Southwest. The ruins are laden with artifacts, both in volume and variety. These include pieces of jewelry, arrowheads, and corncobs. Many of the rooms have the original ceiling beams and exterior plaster still intact. There is a ranger on site who will lead you around once you arrive. For visitors that feel 17 miles is too long for a day hike, there is a primitive campground nearby.

The park limits the number of visitors to Keet Seel to 20 per day. Advanced reservation and a backcountry permit are required. Before receiving a permit, one must listen to orientation, which is held daily at 8:15 AM and 3:00 PM. Keep the permit with you at all times as you hike. Fortunately, it is not difficult to obtain a permit due to the monument's location and the trail's distance.

The route starts in a similar manner as the "Longer Betatakin Guided Site Tour". A permitted visitor takes Tsegi Road to Tsegi Trail down to the canyon floor. From there, look for signs indicating the side canyon for Keet Seel. This primitive trail heads up canyon, crossing the stream multiple times and passes a 100-foot, awe-inspiring waterfall.

Keet Seel is not open in the winter and early spring. In addition, during the summer monsoon season, the park may cancel reservations due to potential flash flooding in the park.

Sandal Trail

Easy – (1.0 mi / 1.6 km), round trip, allow 30 minutes

A paved and accessible trail that leads to an overlook of Betatakin cliff dwelling and surrounding canyon.

Aspen Trail

Moderate – (0.8 mi / 1.3 km), round trip, allow 30 minutes

A spur trail off Sandal Trail that heads lower into the canyon and an old growth grove of Aspen trees.

Canyon View Trail

Easy – (0.4 mi / 0.6 km), round trip, allow 30 minutes

This is an easy walk along the rim, leading from the visitor center and campground to the historic ranger station

Betatakin ruins

Hubbell Trading Post National Historic Park

Official Park Website:

- http://www.nps.gov/hutr

Visitor Center:

- (928) 755-3475

Park Accessibility:

- Okay for 2WD and RVs
- Day Use Only

Experience Level:

- Family Friendly

Camping in Park:

- None

Lodging and Dining in Park:

- None

Nearest Town with Amenities:

- Ganado, AZ is 1 mi / 1.6 km from park

Getting There:

- From Flagstaff, AZ: take I-40 East to AZ-87 North to Indian Route 15 to US-191 South for 156 mi / 251 km to park entrance

Step into the living history of Hubbell Trading Post

What Makes Hubbell Trading Post National Historic Site Special

- Oldest continuously operated trading post within the Navajo Nation

- An amazing step back in time coupled with being a present day active trading post

- Very cool place to browse and see the artistry designs of handcrafted rugs, kachinas, baskets and jewelry

Talk about a unique place, Hubbell Trading Post was created as a center for the Navajo to trade their wares into the non-Navajo world. At the center of it all was John Lorenzo Hubbell, who in 1878, purchased the trading post and became a focal point of trade. Ten years earlier in 1868, the Navajo were decimated as a people and in a depression economically. After the Long Walk of the Navajo, a torturous journey where the Navajo were forced to walk 13 miles a day under poor conditions, they returned to their lands to find their fields and cattle stripped. They rebuilt from what they had left and to obtain goods they didn't have, they traded. The Hubbell Trading Post became a major aspect in this part of their history.

Today, the 160-acre Hubbell homestead is protected as a National Historic Park. It includes the trading post, Hubbell's family home and some out buildings. Tours of Hubbell's home are given for $2. What is especially amazing is that the park is a living cultural preserve. The ranch and the trading post are still active. One can see not only Navajo Churro Sheep, horses and chickens, but also the trading post itself. The look and feel of this place is as if it is a museum where the items are available for purchase. All of the items are authentic. Auctions of items are also held twice a year. Hubbell's is truly a gem within the Grand Circle.

Original basket art

Rug making

Petrified Forest National Park

Quick Facts

Official Park Website:

- http://www.nps.gov/pefo

Visitor Center:

- (928) 524-6228

Park Accessibility:

- Okay for 2WD and RVs
- Primarily day use, overnight use in backcountry allowed with permit

Experience Level:

- Family Friendly – Backcountry Hiker

Camping in Park:

- None

Lodging and Dining in Park:

- Painted Desert Diner

Nearest Town with Amenities:

- Holbrook, AZ is 26 mi / 42 km from park

Getting There:

- From Flagstaff, AZ: take I-40 East 116 mi / 187 km to park entrance

Petrified wood is a mashup of timelessness and beauty

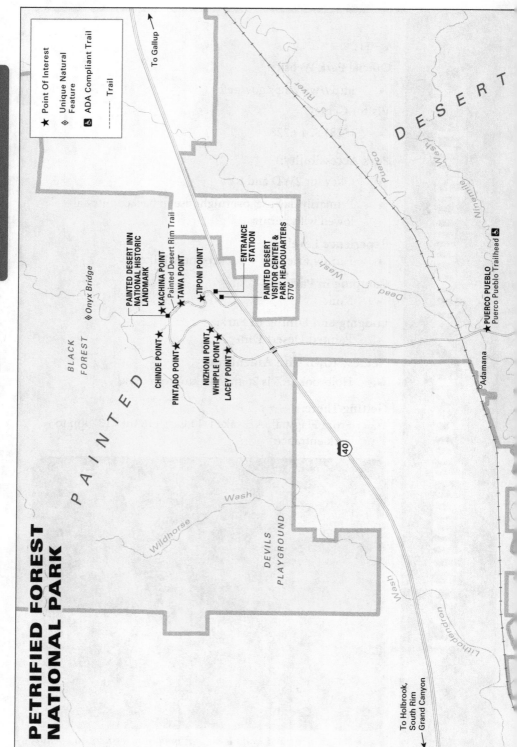

PETRIFIED FOREST
NATIONAL PARK

To Gallup →

Point Of Interest ★
Unique Natural Feature ◈
ADA Compliant Trail ♿
Trail --------

BLACK FOREST

◈ Onyx Bridge

PAINTED DESERT INN NATIONAL HISTORIC LANDMARK
KACHINA POINT ★
Painted Desert Rim Trail
TAWA POINT ★
TIPONI POINT ★

ENTRANCE STATION ■

PAINTED DESERT VISITOR CENTER & PARK HEADQUARTERS 5770' ■

CHINDE POINT ★
PINTADO POINT ★
NIZHONI POINT ★
WHIPPLE POINT ★
LACEY POINT ★

PAINTED

Wildhorse Wash

Wash

DEVILS PLAYGROUND

40

To Holbrook,
South Rim
Grand Canyon ←

DESERT

River

Puerco River

Ninemile Wash

Dead Wash

Adamana

PUERCO PUEBLO ★
Puerco Pueblo Trailhead ♿

Lithodendron Wash

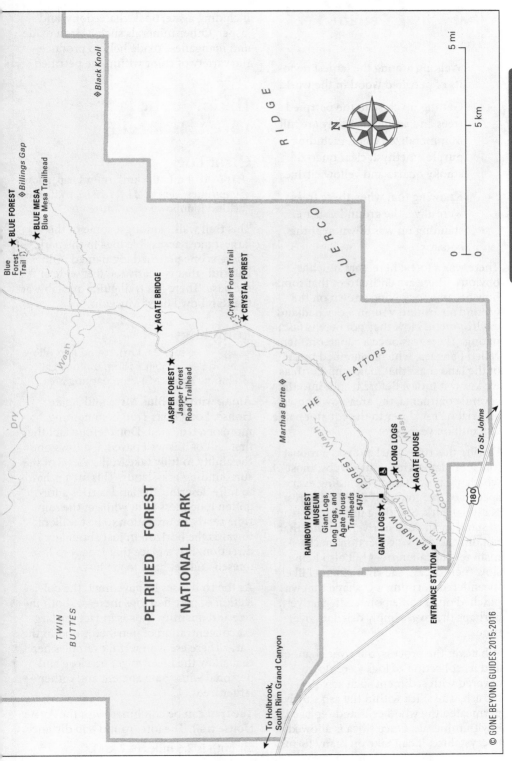

TWIN
BUTTES

PETRIFIED FOREST

NATIONAL PARK

To Holbrook,
South Rim Grand Canyon

Dry

Wash

Blue
Forest
Trail

★ BLUE FOREST

◇ Billings Gap

BLUE MESA
Blue Mesa Trailhead

◇ Black Knoll

R I D G E

P U E R C O

★ AGATE BRIDGE

JASPER FOREST ★
Jasper Forest
Road Trailhead

Crystal Forest Trail
★ CRYSTAL FOREST

Marthas Butte ◇

T H E   F L A T T O P S

F O R E S T

Wash

RAINBOW FOREST
MUSEUM
Giant Logs,
Long Logs, and
Agate House
Trailheads
5476'

★ LONG LOGS
★ AGATE HOUSE

GIANT LOGS ★

RAINBOW   CANYON

Jim   Cottonwood   Wash

ENTRANCE STATION ■

To St. Johns

180

N

0
0

5 km

5 mi

What Makes Petrified Forest Special

- Walking among the largest deposits of petrified wood in the world.

- Getting up close to the petrified trees and seeing that they are full of mineralized color, including purple amethyst, clear quartz, smoky quartz and yellow citrine.

- Knowing that when these trees were alive, the ground you are standing on was down near the equator.

There was a forest here, that much is obvious. There are entire trees that somehow became rock lying strewn on the ground all around you, in a dry badland environment. How they got here is fascinating. There was once a supercontinent called Pangaea, which contained most of the land mass that makes up Earth as we know it today. Before it split into the several continents, the area now known as Arizona sat closer to the equator some 225 million years ago.

During this time, the land was a robust forest of plants, trees and shrubs, most of which are now extinct, including every species of tree found in Petrified Forest National Park. Standing in the park is to stand in an ancient river channel that not only acted as a collection mechanism for the fallen trees but also helped slow their decay. The river channel likely meandered, forming a U shape that was pinched off at some point. Alternatively, perhaps the river simply dried up over time.

Whatever the process, the river channel and its collection of logs were slowly covered with sediment such as volcanic ash. The silica within the ash slowly permeated the wood cells and replaced it with minerals. Once silica is allowed to crystallize, it can take on many forms, including agate, opal, chalcedony, and jasper. Other minerals such as iron oxide and manganese oxide help to produce the variety of color within the petrified wood.

Hiking in the Petrified Forest National Park

Giant Logs

Easy – (0.4 mi / 0.6 km), round trip, allow 30 minutes, elev. Δ: 41 ft / 12 m, trailhead behind Rainbow Forest Museum

This trail walks amongst some of the largest most accessible logs in the park. There is one petrified log named "Old Faithful" that is nearly ten feet wide at the base. There is a trail guide available at the Rainbow Forest Museum.

Long Logs

Easy – (1.6 mi / 2.6 km), round trip, allow 1 hour, elev. Δ:50 ft / 15 m, trailhead at Rainbow Forest Museum parking area

Along with the Blue Mesa and Agate House, Long Logs Trail is something more of a true trail. Don't let the fact the first half of it is well paved, it allows one the ability to fully take in the views of the surrounding grasslands. This area is hard to fully describe, the land carries a forgotten loneliness to it, while at the same time sends an invitation to just walk off towards the horizon in just about any direction. It is a place that is easy to lose oneself and yet hard to get lost.

As the trail loses its pavement, the collection of petrified logs increase, both in size and quantity. This is in fact the largest concentration of petrified wood in the park. There are wonderful examples here that allow the hiker to get up close and personal with some ancient and rather larger trees.

The trail can be combined with the Agate House trail. The total round trip distance for both is 2.6 miles (4.2 km).

Blue Meas badlands

Agate House

Easy – (2.0 mi / 3.2 km), round trip, allow 1 – 2 hours, elev. Δ: 41 ft / 12 m, trailhead at Rainbow Forest Museum parking area

As the name suggests this is a very cool eight-room pueblo made entirely out of agate blocks. It is believed to have been built some 700 years ago. The ruins of this pueblo were actually rebuilt in 1933-34 by the Civilian Conservation Corps (CCC). They rebuilt parts of the pueblo and completely rebuilt "room 7", including a roof.

The inhabitants entered in through the ceiling. The Agate House today is for viewing only. Please don't climb or sit on what is now a piece of history.

Agate House

Crystal Forest

Easy – (0.75 mi / 1.2 km), round trip, allow 30 minutes, elev. Δ: 121 ft / 37 m, trailhead at Crystal Forest parking area

One of the trails that contain the petrified wood you came for, the trail is named for the many amazing crystals that are found within the logs.

This is a chance to take a close look at the colorful crystal formations within the petrified logs. Please refrain from the temptation to take even small pieces. It's for everyone to enjoy

Jasper Forest Road

Easy – (2.5 mi / 4.0 km), round trip, allow 2 hours, elev. Δ: negligible, trailhead at Jasper Forest Road parking area

There is an eroded forgotten road built in the 1930's by the CCC that makes for a wonderful hike today. Originally, a wagon path for rock hounds coming in by train, it was later transformed into a proper road with the advent of the automobile. The path allows for a great hike today amongst a large display of petrified wood that has rolled down with erosion from the bluffs above the road. Given this isn't one of the main trails; it's a great find for those that want to feel they have the park to themselves.

Blue Mesa

Easy with short steep incline– (1.0 mi / 1.6 km), round trip, allow 30 -45 minutes, elev. Δ: 97 ft / 30 m, trailhead at Blue Mesa parking area

The Blue Mesa is one of the most unique areas within the Grand Circle. First off, it's not expected. You came for the petrified wood and anticipate seeing a red rock or two. The Blue Mesa Trail takes one into a bentonite badland hills that have alternate stripes of white and blue clay. It really must be seen to be believed and is certainly a photographer's paradise. As an added bonus, there are several fossils, including the famous namesake petrified trees.

Puerco Pueblo

Easy – (0.3 mi / 0.5 km), round trip, allow 30 minutes, elev. Δ: 41 ft / 12 m, trailhead at Puerco Pueblo parking area

A paved and accessible trail with petroglyphs near the southern segment. This trail passes by the foundational remains of a hundred ancestral Puebloan site, dating back some 600 years. Aside from the ruins, there are some good views of the grasslands that are the signature of the grasslands in this part of Arizona.

The silence of light and sky

Painted Desert Rim Trail

Easy – (1.0 mi / 1.6 km), round trip, allow 30 minutes, elev. Δ: 14 ft / 4 m, trailhead at Tawa Point and Kachina Point

The Painted Desert Rim Trail sits near the park visitor center and gives expansive views of the Painted Desert badlands. This area is comprised mainly of bentonite clay formed from volcanic ash and silt deposits. The entire area is a multicolored palette of red, pink, and white hillsides that are all the more striking due the lack of vegetation due to the poor soils. While this isn't the trail for petrified wood, it is worth seeing.

Jasper Forest

Southeast Utah

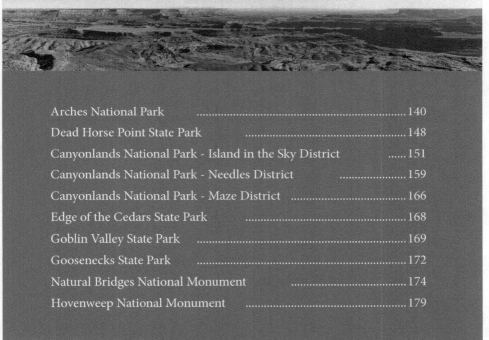

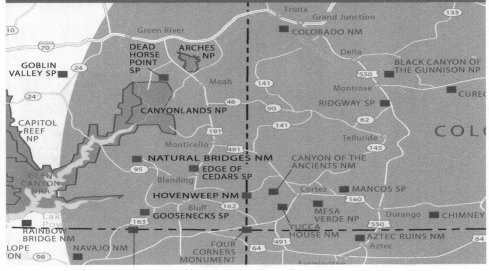

Arches National Park

Quick Facts

Official Park Website: www.nps.gov/arch

Visitor Center: (435) 719-2299

Park Accessibility:
- Okay for 2WD and RVs
- Day and Overnight Use

Experience Level:
- Family Friendly to Backcountry Hiker

Camping in Park:
- Devils Garden Campground: 50 T/RV, no water, restrooms, some pull thru sites, no hookups, all sites can be reserved and are typically full in summer. Reserve at http://www.recreation.gov/

Lodging and Dining in Park:
- None

Nearest Town with Amenities:
- Moab, UT is 5 mi / 8 km from park

Getting There:
- From Moab, UT: Take US-191 North 5 mi / 8 km to park entrance

Delicate Arch, arguably the most recognized arch in the world

What Makes Arches Special

- Contains over 2,000 natural stone arches, the highest concentration of arches in the world

- Landscape Arch, the longest arch in North America and second largest in the world

- Seeing Delicate Arch, the most photographed and recognized arch on the planet

Arches National Park contains some of the most recognized arches in the world. At the top of the list is Delicate Arch. Most everyone who visits the park takes this hike in spite of the steep incline at the front end of the trail. The hike to Delicate Arch has amazing views along the way and just at the moment the weary hiker feels they really do not want to go any further, the trail opens up and there's the arch, big as life, with the often-snow-capped La Sal Mountains in the background. You can even stand under nearby Frame Arch to capture a unique picture of the famous Delicate Arch.

Then there is Landscape Arch, the longest arch in North America, with a span of 306 feet base to base. It is an easy 1.6-mile (2.4 km) hike and baffles the imagination with its threadlike frailty. It has in fact lost a bit of itself with three decent stone slabs falling from the arch in recent years. In 1991, the trail to walking under the arch closed as a result.

There is something wonderful and even magical about stepping through an arch. For everyone who comes, the arch draws them in, invites them to stand underneath these bows of rock and step through them to see what they look like from the other side. Watch your fellow visitor. They walk up to the arch, look up underneath it, and then carry through to see it from the other side. Arches fascinate, and at Arches NP, there is a lot of fascination. Nowhere in the world is there a place quite like this park. The arches are an invitation, every one of them.

Hiking Arches National Park

Park Avenue

Easy – (2.0 mi / 3.2 km), round trip, allow 1 – 2 hours, elev. Δ: 330 ft / 101 m, trailheads at Park Avenue or North Park Avenue parking areas

Park Avenue has a small elevation change as it descends steeply into a wide canyon with amazing thin-walled fins of rock that sheer upwards hundreds of feet into the air. The scenery is best described as epic southwest, as grand as anything the Colorado Plateau has to offer. Once in the canyon, the walk is easy enough, allowing one to take in the view of the Courthouse Towers, including The Organ, a massive sandstone fin tower. Other notables are Sheep Rock, which looks like a lamb on a rock, and the Three Gossips, which resemble three figures standing around. If you are of the paranoid type, the Three Gossips are definitely talking about you! If you look to your left of Sheep Rock, you can see a newly forming arch that some have nicknamed "Baby Arch." Sheep Rock itself is thought to have once been part of a double arch. See if you can make out the remnant towers that have sparked this theory.

The area is well marked and is one of the first pull-offs as you enter the park. To get back to your car, either return the way you came or arrange for a shuttle car to pick you up at the end of the trail. The Park Service discourages hikers from walking on the park road.

ARCHES NATIONAL PARK

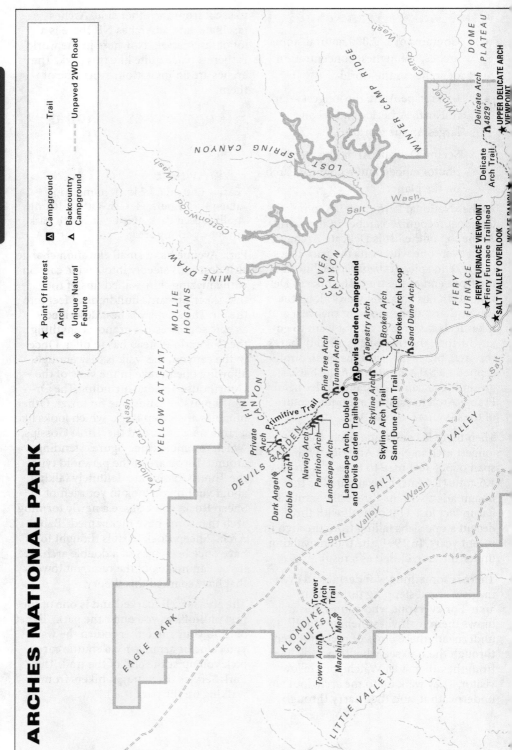

Legend:
- ★ Point Of Interest
- ⋂ Arch
- ◈ Unique Natural Feature
- 🅐 Campground
- ⛺ Backcountry Campground
- ------- Trail
- === Unpaved 2WD Road

DOME PLATEAU

Delicate Arch ⋂4829'

★ UPPER DELICATE ARCH VIEWPOINT

Delicate Arch Trail

WINTER CAMP RIDGE

Camp Wash

LOST SPRING CANYON

Salt Wash

Cottonwood Wash

MINE DRAW

MOLLIE HOGANS

YELLOW CAT FLAT

Yellow Cat Wash

Mollie

FIN CANYON

DEVILS GARDEN

Primitive Trail

Private Arch

Dark Angel ◈
Double O Arch ⋂
Partition Arch ⋂
Landscape Arch

Navajo Arch ⋂

Pine Tree Arch ⋂
Tunnel Arch ⋂

Landscape Arch, Double O and Devils Garden Trailhead

🅐 Devils Garden Campground

CLOVER CANYON

Tapestry Arch ⋂

⛺ Broken Arch
Broken Arch Loop
Sand Dune Arch ⋂

Skyline Arch ⋂

Skyline Arch Trail
Sand Dune Arch Trail

SALT VALLEY

Salt Valley Wash

FIERY FURNACE

FIERY FURNACE VIEWPOINT
Fiery Furnace Trailhead

★ SALT VALLEY OVERLOOK

Salt Wash

EAGLE PARK

KLONDIKE BLUFFS

Tower Arch Trail

Marching Men ◈

Tower Arch ⋂

LITTLE VALLEY

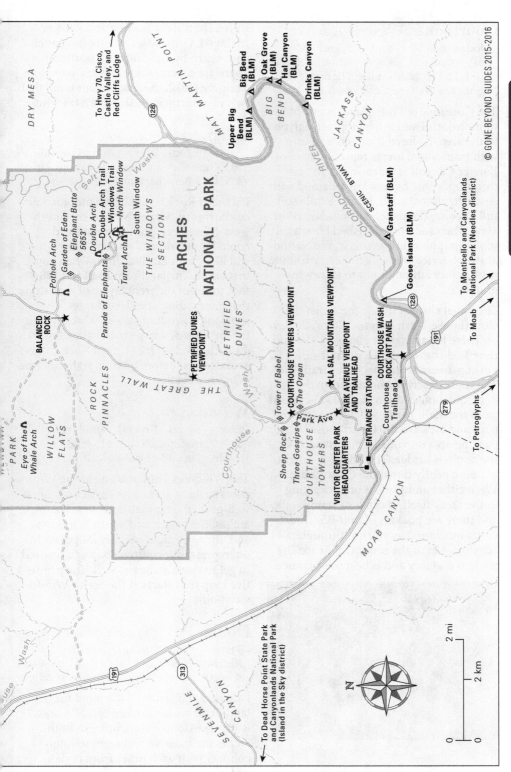

© GONE BEYOND GUIDES 2015-2016

To Hwy 70, Cisco, Castle Valley, and Red Cliffs Lodge

DRY MESA

MAT MARTIN POINT

128

BIG BEND

Upper Big Bend (BLM)

Big Bend (BLM)

Oak Grove (BLM)

Hal Canyon (BLM)

Drinks Canyon (BLM)

JACKASS CANYON

COLORADO RIVER

SCENIC BYWAY

Granstaff (BLM)

Goose Island (BLM)

128

To Monticello and Canyonlands National Park (Needles district)

To Moab

191

To Petroglyphs

279

Courthouse Wash Trailhead

COURTHOUSE WASH ROCK ART PANEL

MOAB CANYON

ENTRANCE STATION

VISITOR CENTER PARK HEADQUARTERS

Park Ave

PARK AVENUE VIEWPOINT AND TRAILHEAD

LA SAL MOUNTAINS VIEWPOINT

The Organ

COURTHOUSE TOWERS VIEWPOINT

Tower of Babel

Three Gossips

Sheep Rock

COURTHOUSE TOWERS

Courthouse Wash

PETRIFIED DUNES

PETRIFIED DUNES VIEWPOINT

THE GREAT WALL

ROCK PINNACLES

BALANCED ROCK

WILLOW FLATS

Eye of the Whale Arch

PARK

Pothole Arch

Garden of Eden

Elephant Butte 5653'

Double Arch

Double Arch Trail

Windows Trail

North Window

South Window

THE WINDOWS SECTION

Turret Arch

Parade of Elephants

Salt Valley Wash

ARCHES NATIONAL PARK

191

313

SEVENMILE CANYON

To Dead Horse Point State Park and Canyonlands National Park (Island in the Sky district)

N

2 mi

2 km

0

0

Arches

Courthouse Wash Rock Art

Moderate to Strenuous – (5.5 mi / 8.9 km), round trip, allow 6 – 8 hours, elev. Δ: 210 ft / 64 m, trailhead on Highway 191, 0.5 mi north of the Colorado River

The Courthouse Wash Panel is one of the more colorful and intriguing petroglyphs in the area. It shows humanoid figures with trapezoidal forms representative of Barrier Canyon Style rock art. The anthropomorphic figures are ordained with abstract, almost alien, heads. While still full of color, the panel was vandalized in 1980 when someone splashed bleach on it. As disappointing as this is, the National Park Service was able to perform some restoration, although not to its original grandeur.

The panel sits just inside the outlet of Courthouse Wash into the Colorado River. There is parking off Highway 191 and the panel sits less than a quarter mile (1.2 km) upstream from this lower trailhead. The route described here is from the upper Courthouse Wash Trailhead accessed from the main park road. Come into the park and look for the Courthouse Wash parking area on your right, just across the obvious bridge. The hike is a delight, winding gently down the Courthouse Wash either alongside it or by walking in the creek itself. It can be a sandy walk, and there are pockets of non-life-threatening quicksand as you cut through tall canyon walls to the lower trailhead. The route is one way and is best pre-planned

Courthouse Wash Rock Art

with a shuttle car waiting at the lower trailhead. Otherwise, admire the panel and return by walking back upstream. There are several side canyons to explore along this hike, the first encountered that cuts in a northerly fashion is a favorite.

Balanced Rock

Easy – (0.3 mi / 0.5 km), round trip, allow 30 minutes, elev. Δ: negligible, trailhead at Balanced Rock parking area

Balanced Rock is one of the more iconic landforms in Arches NP and the Southwest. It has been photographed and copied in movie sets so many times; it will likely be a familiar form when you first see it. The landform itself is a 128-foot tower of different layers of sandstone that are eroding at different rates. The capstone is eroding slower, which makes for the look of a large rock balancing on a smaller pedestal. Balanced Rock can be accessed just before turning right into the Windows Section.

Windows

Easy – (1.0 mi / 1.6 km), round trip, allow 30 – 60 minutes, elev. Δ: 115 ft / 35 m, trailhead at end of Windows Road

The Windows Trail, starting at the Windows parking area, is an easy climb up a well-graded path that leads to three huge arches, the North and South Windows and Turret Arch. A slightly longer and often pleasant primitive loop can be used to get to these arches as well. The primitive loop trail starts at the South Window viewpoint.

Double Arch

Easy – (0.5 mi / 0.8 km), round trip, allow 30 minutes, elev. Δ: 62 ft / 19 m, trailhead at north end of circle for Windows arches

Double Arch is one of the more magical landforms within Arches NP. Not only is it a true double arch, but also both arches are massive and seem to interconnect with each other from certain

Double Arch

angles. It is tough to make out the nature of this landform from the road, and it is easily overlooked by folks who just got back in their vehicle from the Windows trailhead. That said, this is not a formation you want to miss; it is one of the highlights of the park. The trail from the parking lot is sandy and flat. It is possible to scramble up into the bases of both arches.

Delicate Arch

Strenuous – (3.0 mi / 4.8 km), round trip, allow 2 – 3 hours, elev. Δ: 500 ft / 152 m, trailhead at Wolfe Ranch parking area

The hike up to Delicate Arch is not as strenuous as some will tell you. Granted, there is no shade, so bring plenty of water and wear a hat and sunscreen. There is a decent 500-foot ascent on slick rock after a half mile (0.8 km) of easy hiking. Once you summit the ascent, the trail levels out for the most part and is fairly straightforward. There is a rock ledge about 200 yards long that is navigable for two-way traffic. The nice thing about this hike is that the arch is hidden from you until you are right on it. You turn a corner and bam, there it is, Delicate Arch.

The arch is a juxtaposition of themes for the viewer, with the often-snowcapped

La Sal Mountains in the distance framing the fiery and dry sandstone in the foreground. Front and center to it all is the showpiece, the most famous arch in the world. The lighting can be nothing less than spiritual at sunset, though be prepared to share your life moment with your fellow hikers during peak season.

Devils Garden (full loop)

Strenuous – (7.2 mi / 11.6 km), round trip, allow 30 minutes, elev. Δ: 355 ft / 108 m, trailhead at Devils Garden trailhead

This is the longest maintained trail in the park and covers many of the north canyon fins and arches of Salt Valley. Expect a fair amount of scrambling and generally rugged terrain as you span farther into the canyon. The hike is worth doing, weaning out many of the visitors looking for shorter hikes and providing views of eight arches total, including the solemn Navajo Arch and the remote Private Arch.

Sand Dune Arch

Easy – (0.3 mi / 0.5 km), round trip, allow 30 minutes, elev. Δ: negligible, trailhead at Sand Dune Arch parking area

Sand Dune Arch is a secluded arch that is an easy hike along an orange red sand path. The arch is between two large fins, giving a sense of isolation within a very short hike. During windy days, be prepared to get a little sandblasting exfoliation, especially around the shins.

Broken Arch Loop

Easy – (2.0 mi / 3.2 km), round trip, allow 60 minutes, elev. Δ: negligible, trailhead at Sand Dune Arch parking area

Broken Arch is an easy loop that makes for a nice walk from Devils Garden Campground, especially in the cooler times of morning or evening. The trail ambles across a large meadow to an arch with a visible crack in the middle of it, hence the name. Clear views of the La Sal

Mountains can be seen in the distance. There is also a short spur trail to the triple arch feature called Tapestry Arch as well as a connection to Sand Dune Arch.

Skyline Arch

Easy – (0.4 mi / 0.6 km), round trip, allow 30 minutes, elev. Δ: negligible, trailhead at Skyline Arch parking area

This trail is straightforward and very short, crossing a small meadow area to Skyline Arch, which is one of the characteristically visible arches from the road. A large boulder fell out of the arch in 1940, doubling the size of the opening. This is a nice trail to take in the twilight hours for a chance to see wildlife. There are many spur trails at the end to entice the hiker for more adventure within the rock garden surroundings.

Landscape Arch

Easy – (1.6 mi / 2.6 km), round trip, allow 60 minutes, elev. Δ: 60 ft / 18 m, trailhead at Devils Garden trailhead

What makes Landscape Arch so popular is that it defies logic. It is fragile, seemingly ribbon thin in spots, yet it is the longest arch in the park and the second largest in the world. Landscape Arch is so fragile it prompted the Secretary of the Air Force to put a stop to supersonic jet flight over or even near national parks in 1972 after an outcry from local citizens. The arch measures 306 feet from base to

base and can be accessed via a fairly flat gravel trail.

This trail can be a destination in itself or the beginning of the longer hikes to Double O Arch and the Devils Garden Loop. There are nice spur trails down to the Tunnel Arch and quaint Pine Tree Arch.

Double O Arch

Strenuous – (4.0 mi / 6.4 km), round trip, allow 2 – 3 hours, elev. Δ: 277 ft / 84 m, trailhead at Devils Garden trailhead

Double O Arch is listed in case you don't want to do the more primitive loop portion of the Devils Garden Loop or some of the other spur trails to other arches. Double O is an arch on top of an arch, hence the name. It is one of the cooler landforms in the park, looking like a fin of sandstone Swiss cheese. Dark Angel, a monolithic tower of darker sandstone, is off a spur trail another 0.5 mi (0.8 km) further on.

Fiery Furnace

Strenuous – (2.0 mi / 3.2 km), round trip, allow 2 – 3 hours, elev. Δ: 250 ft / 76 m, trailhead at Fiery Furnace Viewpoint

Fiery Furnace is a special section of Arches. The area itself is a labyrinth of rock, containing no trails, and lots of scrambling, wedging, and the need for equal helpings of agility and endurance. It is best seen through the park's ranger-led programs, as this minimizes the

Landscape Arch

damage that has been caused of late through too much hiker love. You can access the area on your own, but only if you obtain a permit at the visitor center and watch a minimum impact video. The fee for a permit is $6 for each adult and $3 for children 5 through 12 and can be purchased at the visitor center. For both the permit and the ranger-led programs, children under five are not permitted.

The ranger-led tour is a tremendous amount of fun for an active family but isn't for everyone. Once you start on the hike, you are committed to completing it. The hike includes squeezing through narrow gaps, scrambling up at times, jumping over small gaps, and navigating through a maze of rock containing the usual assortment of narrow ledges, loose sandstone, and broken rocks.

This ranger-led program contains a fair number of historical and geographical descriptions from likely one of the most passionate advocates of the park you will meet. Bring good hiking shoes, plenty of water and a backpack to store everything because you will be using your hands from time to time to make your way through the terrain.

Tickets for the ranger-led program are by reservation during the peak season. They can be purchased up to six months in advance through www.recreation.gov. Like the campground in Arches, this program is quite popular and requires a bit of

planning, tenacity, and patience to get the spot you want. Tickets during November and early spring can be obtained at the visitor center. Costs are $16 for adults and $8 for children 5 through 12.

Tower Arch
Strenuous – (3.4 mi / 5.5 km), round trip, allow 2 – 3 hours, elev. Δ: 450 ft / 137 m, trailhead at Devils Garden trailhead

Fins, hoodoos, and arches, oh my! This trail is off the beaten track in the north-western Klondike Bluffs. This is a fun little area, with a bit of elevation gain to keep you in shape, but providing one sandstone oddity after the other along the way. Even the end point, Tower Arch, is unusual, giving clear sight to an arch, but with what looks like a big submarine, complete with an observation control tower on top. The "submarine" clearly overshadows the poor arch. The whole place has an M. C. Escher meets Salvador Dali element to it with fins tilted to the winds and hoodoos standing like kids getting in trouble or others that resemble little Buddhas having tea. If you are good at finding patterns in clouds, this is the place for you.

From the park map, the trail shows unpaved roads on either end. Take the Salt Valley Road and turn at the second left into the Klondike Bluffs. It is possible to enter the trail from the other end, but this is a seldom-traveled high clearance 4WD road.

Dead Horse Point State Park

Quick Facts

Official Park Website: http://stateparks.utah.gov/parks/dead-horse/

Visitor Center: (435) 259-2614

Park Accessibility:
- Okay for 2WD and RVs
- Day and Overnight Use

Experience Level:
- Family Friendly to Casual Hiker

Camping in Park:
- The Kayenta Campground: 21 T/RV + 3 yurts, hook-ups, drinking water (limited), restrooms, 4 sites are first come-first served, rest are reservable through Reserve America: (800) 322-3770 or online at www.reserveamerica.com

Lodging and Dining in Park:
- Pony Express Coffee Shop, closed in winter

Nearest Town with Amenities:
- Moab, UT is 28 mi / 45 km from park

Getting There:
- From Moab, UT: Take US-191 North to I-70 West to UT-24 West. Total distance is 101 mi / 162 km to park

Colorado River from Dead Horse Point

The iconic view from Dead Horse Point with the La Sal Mountains in the background

What Makes Dead Horse Point State Park Special

- Amazing trails for both hikers and mountain bikers

- If you love Canyonlands, you will love this park, same great location, but different views

- One of the most dramatic overlooks of the Colorado River

Dead Horse Point State Park is located adjacent to the Island in the Sky District of Canyonlands as well as the town of Moab. The state of Utah has done a great job in providing a great camping, hiking and mountain biking experience within the park's boundaries. Given the popularity of mountain biking in Moab, Dead Horse Point has become a mecca for mountain bikers, especially those that are just starting out in the sport. There is no exposure and none of the trails requires a lot of experience to enjoy them.

There are a number of trails that are designed specifically for the mountain bike, though hikers can use them too. And while this book is geared more for the hiker, there really is nothing quite like tearing through a single track, finding that satisfying center point between your bike and your body, even when the bike is outstretched to the right while your body is angled to the left.

For those hikers that aren't crazy about sharing the road at 2 - 3 miles an hour with something that can go a lot faster, there are hiking only trails too. But hopefully, with over 79 parks and hundreds of trails described, certainly dear hiker, you won't mind if the mountain biking loops are described first for this park.

Mountain Biking in Dead Horse Point State Park

All mountain bike loops in Dead Horse Point State Park can be hiked by foot as well. In some cases, the hiking and mountain biking trails parallel each other, making it easy to cross over to the hiking only trails if you are on foot.

There are three loops in the park, ranging in ease and distance traveled, from 1.4 miles to 9.0 miles round trip. Many folks do all three in one session.

Intrepid Loop

Easy – (1.4 mi / 2.3 km), round trip, allow 20 – 30 minutes for bikers, 45 minutes for hikers

This is the most laid back of the three loops and the shortest. Mostly level, with minor bits of uneven terrain. High points include the Colorado Overlook, which is easily accessible. Good for a pleasant family bike outing.

Great Pyramid Loop
Moderate – (4.2 mi / 6.8 km), round trip, allow 1 hour for bikers, 2 hours for hikers

Similar red rock terrain as Intrepid Loop, but with more elevation up and down as well as a slight increase in the amount of uneven terrain and one spot that is more slick rock than trail. For folks that only mountain bike a little, this is a fun bit of single track. The trail connects with the Colorado Overlook as well as Pyramid Canyon Overlook.

Big Chief Loop
Moderate – (9.0 mi / 14.5 km), round trip, allow 2 hours for bikers, 4 hours for hikers

The longest of the three loops. The trail starts out on the Great Pyramid Loop and then continues on to Big Chief. Both loops together make up the nine-mile loop. Big Chief Loop is similar in difficulty to Great Pyramid and in fact for much of the journey is a little easier. The highlights of this trail are Big Chief Overlook, which offers great views of the distant La Sal Mountains and added remoteness. If you want to do all three loops, allow about 2 hours 30 minutes.

Hiking Dead Horse Point State Park

Nature Trail
Easy – (0.3 mi / 0.5 km), round trip, allow 10 minutes

Pick up a brochure at the visitor center for this pleasant interpretive walk. The brochure will point out different aspects of the geology and flora at numbered locations.

Now, as you start out on this trail you will pass a snack shack and they have some tempting items, which can be a problem for this hike. There are two ways to manage the snack shack. Either a) realize you have no willpower whatsoever and completely give into temptation

before you even hit the trail under the justification that it's still a trail and you need sustenance or b) hold off until after the hike as a reward for conquering this paved quarter-mile long monster. Either way, have a little fun and get something for yourself, you deserve it!

Colorado Overlook Trail
Easy – (1.0 mi / 1.6 km), round trip, allow 30 minutes

This trail parallels the Intrepid Loop for half its length. Hike is along the rim with great views of the Colorado River.

East Rim Trail
Easy – (4.0 mi / 6.4 km), round trip, allow 2 hours

The distance listed for this trail is round trip just for East Rim plus the spur trail out to Basin Overlook. Many visitors do both the East and West Rim, which is 5.7 miles with all the overlook spur trails. This trail gives nonstop panoramic views of the canyon and surrounding area. Basin Overlook provides a glimpse of Chimney Rock and Pyramid Butte.

West Rim Trail
Easy – (6.2 mi / 10.0 km), round trip, allow 3 hours

Similar to East Rim in commanding views, West Rim mileage noted here is if the trail was done as a there and back including the spur trails to Rim, Shafer Overlook and Meander Overlooks. Again, it is a better hike overall to combine the East and West Rim trails and make it a loop.

Big Horn Overlook Trail
Easy – (3.4 mi / 5.5 km), round trip, allow 90 minutes

This trail heads cross-country through pinyon juniper woodlands to an overlook and some large pothole formations. Similar views as West Rim Trail.

Quick Facts

Official Park Website: www.nps.gov/cany

Visitor Center:
- General Information: (435) 719-2313
- Backcountry Reservation Office: (435) 259-4351
- Island in the Sky Visitor Center: (435) 259-4712

Park Accessibility:
- Okay for 2WD and RVs, 4WD in some areas
- Day and Overnight Use

Experience Level:
- Family Friendly to Backcountry Hiker

Camping in Park:
- Willow Flat Campground: 12 T/RV, no water, vault toilets, no hookups, first come-first served, open year round

Lodging and Dining in Park:
- None

Nearest Town with Amenities:
- Moab, UT is 30 mi / 48 km from park

Getting There:
- From Moab, UT: Take US-191 North and UT-313 West 30 mi / 48 km to park entrance

Canyonlands from Green River Overlook

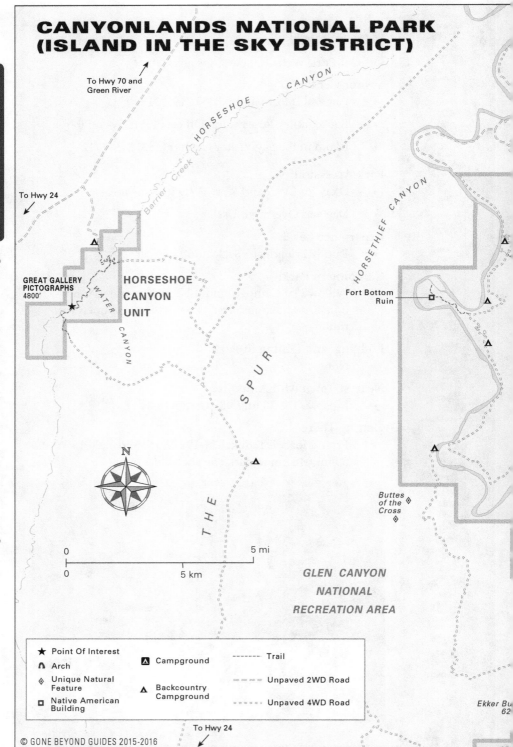

CANYONLANDS NATIONAL PARK
(ISLAND IN THE SKY DISTRICT)

To Hwy 70 and
Green River

HORSESHOE CANYON

To Hwy 24

Barrier Creek

HORSESHOE
CANYON
UNIT

HORSETHIEF CANYON

GREAT GALLERY
PICTOGRAPHS
4800'

WATER CANYON

Fort Bottom
Ruin

THE SPUR

Buttes
of the
Cross

N

GLEN CANYON
NATIONAL
RECREATION AREA

THE

| 0 | | 5 mi |
| 0 | | 5 km |

★ Point Of Interest
∩ Arch
◈ Unique Natural Feature
▫ Native American Building

▲ Campground
▲ Backcountry Campground

-------- Trail
==== Unpaved 2WD Road
====== Unpaved 4WD Road

Ekker Bu
62

To Hwy 24

© GONE BEYOND GUIDES 2015-2016

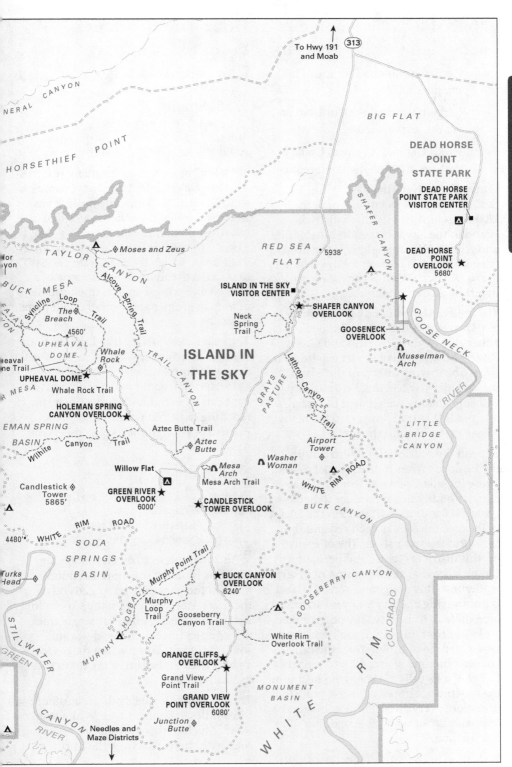

NERAL CANYON

HORSETHIEF POINT

To Hwy 191 and Moab

313

BIG FLAT

DEAD HORSE POINT STATE PARK

DEAD HORSE POINT STATE PARK VISITOR CENTER

SHAFER CANYON

RED SEA FLAT

· 5938'

DEAD HORSE POINT OVERLOOK 5680'

TAYLOR CANYON

◈ Moses and Zeus

Alcove Spring Trail

ISLAND IN THE SKY VISITOR CENTER

★ SHAFER CANYON OVERLOOK

GOOSE NECK

BUCK MESA

Syncline Loop Trail

The Breach

4560'

UPHEAVAL DOME

Whale Rock

ISLAND IN THE SKY

Neck Spring Trail

GOOSENECK OVERLOOK

Musselman Arch

GRAYS PASTURE

Lathrop Canyon

TRAIL CANYON

RIVER

eaval ne Trail

Whale Rock Trail

UPHEAVAL DOME ★

Whale Rock Trail

HOLEMAN SPRING CANYON OVERLOOK ★

LITTLE BRIDGE CANYON

EMAN SPRING

Aztec Butte Trail

Trail

Airport Tower ◈

BASIN

Wilhite Canyon Trail

Aztec Butte

Washer Woman

WHITE RIM ROAD

Willow Flat

Mesa Arch

Candlestick Tower 5865'

GREEN RIVER OVERLOOK 6000'

Mesa Arch Trail

BUCK CANYON

★ CANDLESTICK TOWER OVERLOOK

4480'·

WHITE RIM ROAD

SODA SPRINGS BASIN

Turks Head

Murphy Point Trail

★ BUCK CANYON OVERLOOK 6240'

GOOSEBERRY CANYON

MURPHY HOGBACK

Murphy Loop Trail

Gooseberry Canyon Trail

COLORADO

STILLWATER

ORANGE CLIFFS OVERLOOK ★

White Rim Overlook Trail

GREEN

Grand View Point Trail

MONUMENT BASIN

RIM

CANYON RIVER

GRAND VIEW POINT OVERLOOK 6080'

Junction Butte ◈

WHITE

Needles and Maze Districts

What Makes Canyonlands – Island in the Sky Special

- Each view holds a lifetime of hiking possibilities
- Largest National Park in Utah and yet the least visited
- Holds Cataract Canyon, Utah's biggest and most challenging rapids

Canyonlands National Park is big. In fact, it is the largest national park in Utah. It is broken into three districts. Island in the Sky is closest to Moab, UT and Arches NP. Then there is the hiker friendly Needles District followed by the Maze District, which is canyoneer and desert backcountry paradise.

The bulk of Canyonland's Island in the Sky District is a large mesa banded on either side by the Colorado and Green Rivers. Much of this District can be seen simply by driving on top of the island mesa, while 4-wheel drive enthusiasts will enjoy taking the serpent like narrow dirt roads that lead down into the many basins that surround the mesa.

Beyond the overlooks, there are more than a dozen hikes in this district as well. These include Upheaval Dome, a huge circular oddity that continues to baffle geologists as to its existence. In the Island in the Sky, the rock is deep red and the cliffs dramatic and sheer. The one word for this district is "epic" and perhaps it can be labeled as the definition of desert wilderness. It is not gentle here, the land is unforgiving and dry and yet vast and incredible in its beauty. The desert hiker looks out from the top of the Island and sees a lifetime of exploration, the canyoneer a lifetime of ascents and rappels. Canyonlands calls to those who hear it in the way the ocean calls a sailor, yearning to explore every current but knowing the impossibility of being able to doing so in one lifetime.

Hiking in the Island in the Sky District of Canyonlands NP

Neck Spring

Moderate – (5.8 mi / 9.3 km), round trip, allow 4 -5 hours, elev. Δ: 300 ft / 91 m, trailhead at Shafer Canyon Overlook

Neck Spring is popular for many reasons. It's a loop and while it does have some elevation gain and loss, the trail isn't as steep as some of the other routes that take the hiker off the mesa top. It's also close to the visitor center as well as Shafer Trail Road, which is fun to watch as 4WD cars snake their way down the side of a cliff. Neck Spring Trail has thick patches of pinyon juniper and overall much plant diversity.

The trail is very well marked, giving both views of interior canyon cliff faces as well as some panoramic views. Remains of old watering troughs and a cabin remnant can be found, indicating the historic ranching days that preceded the park. A small portion of the loop parallels the road.

Lathrop Canyon

Strenuous – (21.6 mi / 34.8 km), round trip, multi day backpacking trip, elev. Δ: 2,000 ft / 610 m, trailhead is two miles into park from visitor center

With 2,000 feet in steep elevation gain/ loss, this is one of the more strenuous hikes in the park. The trail heads off the mesa, steeply down to the Colorado River. The first 2.6 miles are single track across open low brush meadows and some slickrock. This portion makes for an easy hike to the rim of the mesa and incredible views.

The next jaunt is steeply down another three miles to connect with White Rim Road. Much of this portion is on open rock with markers. While the cairns are

Through Mesa Arch to Washer Woman

well laid out and easy to follow, the path itself is not a straight line, so be sure to have the next cairn in sight as you pass the one next to you. Backtracking your way to the marked route can be a puzzler.

The trail ultimately eases as it cuts into a sandy wash that connects with White Rim Road, your next arduous portion of the journey. Be sure to make a point to your fellow hiking companions that the "White Rim Road Segment" is about to begin and to be fully prepared for this section. After making a lot of fuss about how hard this leg will be, make a right onto this rugged and torturous 4WD drive road and walk several hundred feet and then turn left onto Lathrop Canyon Road, thus ending this leg of the journey. Before making the turn however, be sure to take a dramatic pause in gratitude to the team that this segment was completed safely, praising the group for their hard efforts. Maybe do a head count or something to make sure everyone "made it". Continue on Lathrop Canyon Road to the Colorado River. There are picnic tables and an outhouse at the river.

It is worth just doing the initial portion of this trail and turning around at the rim. For those that do the full distance, there are many spur trails to archaeological sites and old mining areas, as well as the usual assortment of arches, spires, flat boulders and all around spectacular scenery. If you are looking for a full immersion hike into Canyonlands, this will satisfy that hunger.

Mesa Arch

Easy – (0.5 mi / 0.8 km), round trip, allow 30 minutes, elev. Δ: 100 ft / 30 m, trailhead just before junction to Upheaval Dome Road

Mesa Arch is easy to find, easy to hike and has incredible views. The trail ends at Mesa Arch, which spans 50 feet and sits right on the edge of a 500-foot cliff wall. Other arches, including the well-known Washer Woman Arch, are visible. This hike is great for sunrise shots and is popular with photographers due to the ability to capture the light, views and arch all in one shot.

Aztec Butte

Moderate – (2.0 mi / 3.2 km), round trip, allow 60 - 90 minutes, elev. Δ: 200 ft / 61 m, trailhead 1 mi northwest on Upheaval Dome Road

This is a very rewarding and unique trail as it offers a lot of variety in a small package. The visitor will enjoy hiking through level, undisturbed grasslands toward the distant dome-shaped butte rising above. There is a short, steep climb to the rim of the butte where one can see ruins of Pueblo granaries. The trail loops around the top of Aztec Butte, providing inspiring views of Taylor Canyon.

Murphy Point

Moderate – (3.6 mi / 5.8 km), round trip, allow 2 hours, elev. Δ: 100 ft / 30 m, trailhead is 3 mi south on main park road from Upheaval Dome junction

See Murphy Loop for some additional elements of the trail description. The trail starts nicely across a flatland of short brush and then down a cairn marked area of slickrock to Murphy Point. Elevation gain is a modest 168 feet. Murphy Point offers an overlook to panoramic views of the many canyons that feed into the Green River. It's an immersive alternative to the drive up overlooks without having to do a steep descent off the mesa.

Murphy Loop

Strenuous – (10.8 mi / 17.4 km), round trip, allow 5 – 6 hours, elev. Δ: 1,100 ft / 335 m, trailhead at Murphy Point trailhead

Murphy Loop is similar to many of the hikes in Island in the Sky District. The hike begins well enough along a blissfully flat section of brushy flatlands, followed by an insane descent via a bunch of short switchbacks leading to the lower regions of Canyonlands. Going clockwise on this loop puts one into an epic wash before connecting briefly with White Rim Road. From here, the trail climbs up a hogback ridge and follows it back to the loop junction. Some areas of steep slickrock, exposed ledges and need for navigational skills are involved in completing this trail.

View from Aztec Butte Trail

Highlights to be found on this trail include Murphy Point which gives commanding views of Murphy Basin and down into the Green River. (See Murphy Point for details on that spur trail). The other highlight is Murphy Hogback, a mesa narrow enough to feel as if you are walking across an ancient land bridge but wide enough to give the full pleasure of walking on the flatlands of a mesa top. This thin plateau allows for amazing views on either side.

Grand View Point

Easy – (2.0 mi / 3.2 km), round trip, allow 1 hour, elev. Δ: 50 ft / 15 m, trailhead at Grand View Point

If you have been driving on the park's Grand View Point Road and on getting to the end, wish you could go just a little bit further, Grand View Point Trail is the answer. Starting at the parking lot for Grand View Point Overlook, the short little trail gets the hiker away from all those pesky cars and to very edge of Island in the Sky Mesa. This is an excellent hike for those limited on time.

Gooseberry Canyon

Strenuous – (5.4 mi / 8.6 km), round trip, allow 4 - 5 hours, elev. Δ: 1,400 ft / 427 m, trailhead at Grand View picnic area

This is one crazy steep trail that leads off the mesa top down to Gooseberry Canyon, which is an impressive draw draining into the Colorado River. The trail drops down some 1,200 feet in just 0.7 miles via a series of well-built switchbacks. Make sure whatever time it took to get down is doubled for the trip back up. The trail then follows a dry wash to White Rim Road near Gooseberry Canyon.

Gooseberry provides some great views, starting with a 200-foot cliff face on all sides of the canyon and then stretching to the canyon floor. Peering over the edge into the canyon allows for the realization that you started this hike by peering across an overlook and then hiked for miles to end at another equally impressive overlook. This hike really shows the magnitude of Canyonlands NP.

Wilhite Canyon
Strenuous – (12.2 mi / 19.6 km), round trip, allow 6 – 7 hours, elev. Δ: 1,600 ft / 488 m, trailhead on Upheaval Dome Road

Wilhite Canyon Trail starts amongst open brush flats and then descends at a very rapid rate (850 feet in 0.65 miles) dropping into Upper West Basin. From there, the trail winds around some impressive cliffs and then down a wash to West Rim Road. Highlights include great views of the Green River, Holeman Spring and Upper West Basins as well as a prominent monolith named Candlestick Tower to the southwest. This trail has some tough spots containing slickrock and talus rock combined with steep inclines. All in all, a typically strenuous trail, especially on the steep parts that reward the hiker with great views at each step. There is a cool slot canyon just over the road and it is possible to venture into it for a bit before needing canyoneering gear. Note that this canyon is easier to get down into then it is to get out of, moderate scrambling is required here.

Taylor Canyon
Strenuous – (20.0 mi / 32.2 km), round trip, multi day backpacking trip, elev. Δ: 2,000 ft / 610 m, trailhead at Trail Canyon trailhead on Upheaval Dome Road

Taylor Canyon shares a few similarities to the Lathrop Canyon trek described below. Both step off of the mesa and require long steep descents, both are incredibly scenic and worth the effort and both lead to one of the major rivers of the Southwest. In Taylor Canyon's case, the water source in question is the Green River versus the Colorado River for the Lathrop Canyon trail. As described, the trail is a nice two-day loop, which includes

Upheaval Dome and the gravity defying spires named Moses and Zeus.

Take Upheaval Dome Road to the Trail Canyon trailhead pullout and begin the steep descent into Trail Canyon. This trail does require a fair amount of skill, as there are several areas where minor scrambling and trail finding is needed. The trail makes its way to an obvious sandstone fin on the north side of the canyon, which can be used as a guide. The canyon bottom is reached after 2.1 miles.

From here, head north to a juncture where Trail Canyon merges with Taylor Canyon and the loop trail around Zeus and Moses. These two spires are quite impressive, shooting straight up, the tallest being 410 feet. Take the right trail to do the short loop around the spires and then left into Taylor Canyon. After a short distance is Taylor Campground, which is a dry camp with one pit toilet. This campsite has a lot to offer in views as it sits at the juncture of two canyons with the spires of Zeus and Moses framing the left of the camp. Good coffee, your favorite breakfast foods, and the campsite's view help make for a perfect morning moment.

Continuing on, the trail becomes a 4WD road. Travel on Taylor Canyon Road west for 5.2 miles passing humongous rocks the size of semi-trucks. At now 12 miles into the hike, you are at the Green River and Labyrinth Campground, a second choice for rolling the bag out for the night. Labyrinth does offer the lush, cooling Green River as a backdrop and is a great choice. Reservations are recommended if you plan to stay here and there is a fee of $30.

From the campground pick up White Rim Trail and continue for about a mile and then turn left at the junction into Upheaval Canyon. The trail now heads up a gorge of loose talus, making for a sluggish slow uphill stretch.

Some navigation is needed as the trail gets a little hard to follow in some spots. Keep heading up, 1,300 feet in all until the rim is once more under your feet. Check out Upheaval Dome on your way out and back to where you started.

Whale Rock

Moderate – (1.0 mi / 1.6 km), round trip, allow 60 minutes, elev. Δ: 100 ft / 30 m, trailhead just before Upheaval Dome parking area

Whale Rock Trail gives an alternative view of Upheaval Dome. There is a short climb up a large rock that indeed does look like a whale. The trail ends with a nice "big picture" view of Upheaval Dome.

Upheaval Dome

Easy – (2.0 mi / 3.2 km), round trip, allow 60 minutes, elev. Δ: 150 ft / 46 m, trailhead at Upheaval Dome parking area

Upheaval Dome as a geological feature is explained in some detail in the Canyonlands Geology section of this book. As a hike, it allows the visitor to get out and into the slick rock of the park without much fuss. It is only a mile (1.6 km) to the first overlook. It is well worth the extra effort to the second overlook, which

will take you right to the dome's edge. Be sure to follow the cairns that have been laid out to mark the way, as in some portions the trail is simply walking on slick rock with the cairns as guides.

Syncline Loop

Strenuous – (8.3 mi / 13.4 km), round trip, allow 5 - 6 hours, elev. Δ: 1,300 ft / 396 m, trailhead at Upheaval Dome parking area

For a longer hike, take this loop that circles the entirety of Upheaval Dome. There is a spur trail that leads to the center of the crater as well. Allow another 3 miles (4.8 km) for the spur trail. Another spur trail along the loop (7 mi / 11.2 km) leads to the Green River. The elevation change is about 1,300 feet. Note that this is a very rugged and strenuous trail and includes a mixture of boulder fields, steep switchbacks and plenty of slickrock. This is a fine example of a challenging hike that puts you inside one of the more remote sections of Canyonlands.

Warning: nearly all rescues in Canyonlands NP come from this trail. Route finding can be very difficult and there are many false spur trails. Also, given the various ups and downs on this loop, the actual elevation change is closer to 2900 feet. This trail is for experienced hikers only.

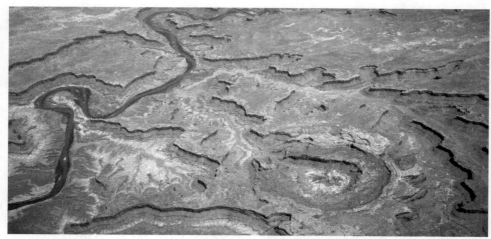

Aerial shot of Upheaval Dom and the Green River

Canyonlands National Park - Needles District

Quick Facts

Official Park Website: www.nps.gov/cany

Visitor Center:

- General Information: (435) 719-2313
- Backcountry Reservation Office: (435) 259-4351
- Needles Visitor Center: (435) 259-4711

Park Accessibility:

- Okay for 2WD and RVs, 4WD in some areas
- Day and Overnight Use

Experience Level:

- Family Friendly to Backcountry Hiker

Camping in Park:

- Squaw Flat Campground: 26 T/RV, plus 3 group campsites, drinking water, vault toilets, no hookups, first come-first served

Lodging and Dining in Park:

- None

Nearest Town with Amenities:

- Monticello, UT is 46 mi / 74 km from park

Getting There:

- From Moab, UT: Take US-191 South and UT-211 West 30 mi / 48 km to right turn onto Lark Hart road and the park's entrance

View from BLM Managed Needles Overlook

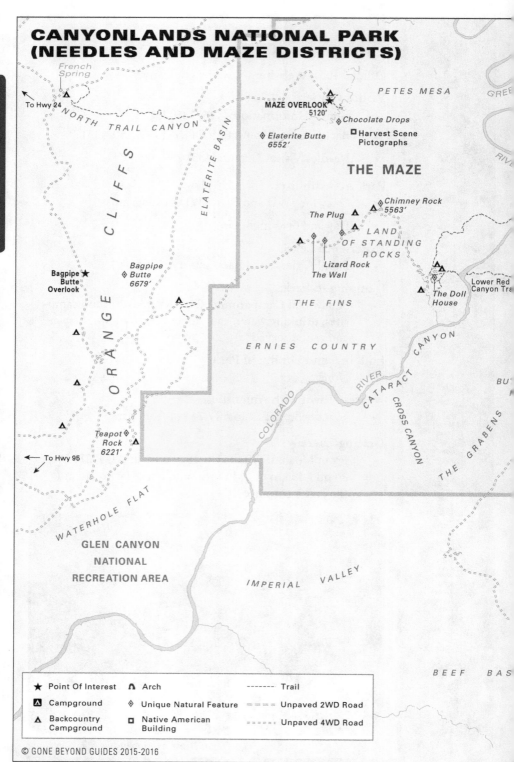

CANYONLANDS NATIONAL PARK
(NEEDLES AND MAZE DISTRICTS)

French Spring

To Hwy 24

NORTH TRAIL CANYON

ELATERITE BASIN

★ MAZE OVERLOOK 5120'

PETES MESA

GREE

RIV

◈ Chocolate Drops

◈ Elaterite Butte 6552'

◻ Harvest Scene Pictographs

THE MAZE

ORANGE CLIFFS

◈ Chimney Rock 5563'

The Plug

LAND OF STANDING ROCKS

Lizard Rock

The Wall

Bagpipe Butte Overlook ★

◈ Bagpipe Butte 6679'

⌂

▲ The Doll House

Lower Red Canyon Tra

THE FINS

ERNIES COUNTRY

RIVER

COLORADO

CATARACT CANYON

CROSS CANYON

BU

THE GRABENS

Teapot Rock 6221' ◈

To Hwy 95

WATERHOLE FLAT

GLEN CANYON
NATIONAL
RECREATION AREA

IMPERIAL VALLEY

BEEF BAS

★ Point Of Interest	⌂ Arch	------- Trail
◪ Campground	◈ Unique Natural Feature	==== Unpaved 2WD Road
▲ Backcountry Campground	◻ Native American Building	===== Unpaved 4WD Road

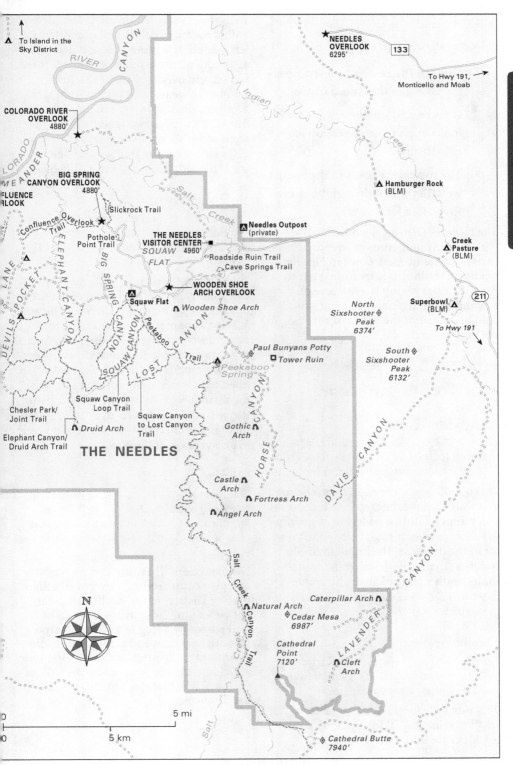

To Island in the
Sky District

**NEEDLES
OVERLOOK**
6295'

133

To Hwy 191,
Monticello and Moab

RIVER CANYON

**COLORADO RIVER
OVERLOOK**
4880'

Indian

Creek

Hamburger Rock
(BLM)

**BIG SPRING
CANYON OVERLOOK**
4880'

Salt

Creek

**FLUENCE
RLOOK**

Slickrock Trail

**Creek
Pasture**
(BLM)

Confluence Overlook Trail

Pothole
Point Trail

**THE NEEDLES
VISITOR CENTER** 4960'
*SQUAW
FLAT*

Needles Outpost
(private)

Roadside Ruin Trail
Cave Springs Trail

**WOODEN SHOE
ARCH OVERLOOK**

**North
Sixshooter
Peak**
6374'

Superbowl
(BLM)

211

Squaw Flat

Wooden Shoe Arch

To Hwy 191

ELEPHANT CANYON

BIG SPRING CANYON

DEVILS POCKET

LANE

SQUAW CANYON

Peekaboo

Trail

LOST CANYON

Paul Bunyans Potty

Tower Ruin

**Peekaboo
Spring**

HORSE CANYON

*South
Sixshooter
Peak*
6132'

Chesler Park/
Joint Trail

Squaw Canyon
Loop Trail

Druid Arch

Squaw Canyon
to Lost Canyon
Trail

*Gothic
Arch*

DAVIS CANYON

Elephant Canyon/
Druid Arch Trail

THE NEEDLES

*Castle
Arch*

Fortress Arch

Angel Arch

CANYON

Caterpillar Arch

Salt

Creek

Canyon

Trail

Natural Arch

Cedar Mesa
6987'

*Cathedral
Point*
7120'

LAVENDER CANYON

*Cleft
Arch*

N

5 mi

5 km

Salt

Cathedral Butte
7940'

What Makes Canyonlands – Needles District Special

- Some of the best and most accessible hiking in the Grand Circle

- Druid Arch, a natural arch that looks like a massive version of Stonehenge

- The two major rivers of the Southwest, the Colorado and the Green River, join forces here.

The Needles District is a hiker's paradise, with trails as numerous as they are varied in experience needed. Once in Needles, nearly all trailheads start from a paved road. Needles hiking is a mixture of fun and endurance, wonder and skill. It contains some of the best desert hiking in the Grand Circle.

Hiking in the Needles District of Canyonlands NP

Roadside Ruin

Easy – (0.3 mi / 0.5 km), round trip, allow 20 minutes, elev. Δ: negligible, trailhead is 0.4 mi from visitor center, left side of road

This quick loop starts right from the road and walks amongst desert brush and pinyon juniper within a wide valley, giving expansive views of sculptured sandstone off in the distance. The highlight of the trail is a small cylindrical granary tucked underneath a large alcove. The granary dates to 1270 to 1290 CE and is nicely preserved.

Cave Springs Trail

Easy – (0.6 mi / 1.0 km), round trip, allow 30 minutes, elev. Δ: 50 ft / 15 m, trailhead at Cave Spring trailhead

This tidy little loop leads to a series of small overhangs. Taking the loop counterclockwise leads to a historic and

well-preserved cowboy camp complete with a corral, benches, and other items left behind. It is quite a refreshing look at a more recent chapter of history. There is a second overhang that contains a number of treasures, ranging from fern grottoes, small springs, and petroglyphs. The trail includes two ladders to help up some steep slick rock that leads to some drier alcoves as the trail winds back to the trailhead. All in all, a fun little hike.

Pothole Point Trail

Easy – (0.6 mi / 1.0 km), round trip, allow 30 minutes, elev. Δ: negligible, trailhead is 6.2 mi from visitor center on Big Spring Canyon Overlook Scenic Drive

Another easy little hike with very little elevation gain. The trail is almost entirely on slickrock with cairns marking the way. While the namesake of the trail is important to note, the main reason to hike this one are the spectacular views. Along the way, look for little potholes that when filled with water, maintain an ecosystem for shrimp, who have figured out how to thrive out in the desert. At Pothole Point, there is a small spur trail south that heads to an overlook of the Needles.

Slickrock Trail

Moderate – (2.4 mi / 3.9 km), round trip, allow 90 minutes, elev. Δ: 150 ft / 46 m, trailhead is 6.2 mi from visitor center on Big Spring Canyon Overlook Scenic Drive

Slickrock has a bit of everything that Needles offers. There are four viewpoints that give commanding views of Island in the Sky District to the north and different views into the canyons below. The trail passes by a fragile arch and travels on both slickrock and actual trail. Each viewpoint is different and some offer long views into the canyons cut by the Colorado River. The Needles can also be seen in the distance.

Confluence Overlook

Strenuous – (10.0 mi / 16.1 km), round trip, 5 - 6 hours, elev. Δ: 1,250 ft / 381 m, trailhead at Big Spring Canyon Overlook

This hike for the most part covers a fair amount of open country, leaving the hiker time to take in the surroundings. Pick up the trail at the Big Spring Canyon Overlook and follow the well-marked path along the same geologic faults that helped create the needle formations. The trail ends at an overlook where one can see and hear the confluence of the Green and Colorado rivers. Depending on the weather and the resulting color of the rivers, it is possible to see the relatively green waters of the Green River mix into the Navajo Red waters of the Colorado. The water's powerful journey is heard echoing throughout the canyon, sometimes as a distant rumble, occasionally louder as the wind changes directions.

Lower Red Lake Canyon

Strenuous – (18.8 mi / 30.3 km), round trip, long day hike or multiday backpacking trip, elev. Δ: 1,000 ft / 305 m, trailhead at Elephant Hill and Squaw Flat trailheads

This hike, which heads to the Colorado River, does have some underwhelming parts. It is quite long and while it does end up at the river, the banks are pretty heavily overgrown with tamarisks, leaving the hiker more with the thought, "Is this it?" then "We made it!!" This is primarily because the trail ends at a location along the river where it flattens out, referred to as Lower Red Lake, with a flat area on the other side called Spanish Bottom. This wetland area of the river allows for plant overgrowth and isn't the raging Colorado that most folks expect to see.

The unexpected first view of the Colorado aside, there are some great aspects to this hike. The biggest is being able to see the Grabens first hand. These long valley fingers that parallel the river are a true geologic oddity. There is (or I suppose

The famous Needles

was) a sedimentary layer formed 300 million years ago named appropriately, the Paradox Layer. This layer was composed primarily of salt, which up until 10 million years ago was compressed with such pressure from the rock layers above that the salt became more liquid than solid. When the Colorado River cut through the Paradox layer, it released the pressure and the salt moved like a slow moving paste into the river. With the salt layer gone, the upper layers collapsed into the void, forming long valleys. This makes the Lower Red Canyon Trail geologically fascinating.

The trail climbs over ridges and through grabens until the river is reached. Even if only one graben is traversed, it is worth taking the trail to see some of the unique geology that Needles has to offer. By the way, if you do reach the river, it is possible to head to the confluence of the Green and Colorado Rivers, about 3.6 miles upstream. Along the way are picture perfect spots, devoid of the tamarisk. One can also walk downstream to check out Cataract Canyon, which holds some of the wildest rapids along the entire stretch of the Colorado.

Elephant Canyon / Druid Arch

Strenuous – (11.0 mi / 17.7 km), round trip, allow 5 - 6 hours, elev. Δ: 1,000 ft / 305 m, trailhead at Elephant Hill trailhead

This is arguably one of the best hikes in Needles, with incredible views along the entire trail ending at Druid Arch. A quick glance at a park map will show that there are many routes from which to choose. This description starts at the Chesler Park access trail and follows up Elephant Canyon.

The entire route is well marked and while the trail is long and it is not otherwise terribly strenuous except for the end. Once on the canyon floor you'll find it contains some sand and loose gravel, which makes hiking slower. This continues to the end of the canyon, where the last pitch is a steep climb of a quarter mile (0.4 km) involving a little scrambling up slick rock and even climbing a ladder.

Druid Arch itself is well worth the hike. The views along Elephant Canyon are spectacular and the arch is one of the more unique-looking arches, with much angularity and several keyhole windows within a fin-like blade of rock. The one thing any picture doesn't do is portray the enormity of the structure, which is humbling.

Druid Arch

Joint Trail

Moderate – (11.0 mi / 17.7 km), round trip, allow 5 - 6 hours, elev. Δ: 560 ft / 171 m, trailhead at Elephant Hill trailhead

This wonderful trail holds views of red rock monoliths amongst grassland meadows. In these sections, the sky is wide and the land holds a peaceful warmth, with inviting grasses, folding into the banded colored rocks and typically deep blue skies. This area is known as Chesler Park, surrounded all around by the famous Needles spires.

Then there is the Joint Trail itself. The trail leads to a narrow slot canyon that contains a tunnel and deep narrow crevices that require some mild scrambling to travel through. Part of what makes Joint Trail special is in the way it was formed. Unlike the water carved slot canyons typical of most of the Grand Circle, this canyon is an actual fracture in the rock just wide enough to walk through. It is a very different type of canyon and when combined with Chesler Park, the Joint Trail is a contender for one of the best hikes in the Needles District.

Squaw Canyon Loop

Strenuous – (7.5 mi / 12.1 km), round trip, allow 4 hours at Squaw Flat trailhead, elev. Δ: 700 ft / 213 m, trailhead at Squaw Flat trailhead

There are some pretty steep patches and about 500 feet in elevation gain, but gives a really nice immersion into the Needles backcountry. The trail, as described here, starts in Squaw Canyon and travels to its head. From there, it's up and over into Big Spring Canyon for the return.

At the trailhead, walk within a large desert valley to a juncture. Staying left puts you into Squaw Canyon. The canyon itself starts out wide and inviting and then narrows. Stay on the trail to Squaw Canyon, avoiding the two junctures to the left to Lost Canyon. At a well-marked juncture, the trail goes up and over some slick rock, which may look challenging but is fairly easy to navigate when dry.

Take a moment at the ridge to enjoy the views and the canyon you just walked up and then come on down the other side into Big Spring Canyon. The trip down

164

into the canyon has some steeper spots, but these are short. Note that while the slickrock offers firm holds when dry, it's a different story when wet or frozen, so use proper judgment here.

The trail ambles through Big Spring Canyon before climbing out and following closer to the Squaw Canyon side of the ridge back over and down again to the trailhead. Big Spring Canyon offers nice vegetation and great views of the Needles as you make the return.

Squaw Canyon to Lost Canyon

Strenuous – (8.7 mi / 14.0 km), round trip, allow 5 -6 hours, elev. Δ: 380 ft / 116 m, trailhead at Squaw Flat trailhead

This trail is similar to the one described above for Squaw Canyon. The hike heads up Squaw Canyon and then diverts left to Lost Canyon, traveling up that canyon and then crossing over again up and back over into Squaw. So, Squaw Canyon up, ridge climb over, Long Canyon up (if doing the canyon clockwise), ridge climb over, Squaw Canyon down and out.

There are some notable differences. This trail is a bit longer and there is reliable water to be found. The trail is marked with cairns but can be hard to follow at times, requiring a sharp eye. This hike offers a bit more challenge and skill, different views and a great hike all in all.

Peekaboo Trail

Strenuous – (10.0 mi / 16.1 km), round trip, allow 5 - 6 hours, elev. Δ: 550 ft / 112 m, trailhead at Squaw Flat trailhead

Peekaboo is an extension from Lost Canyon Trail. From the Squaw Canyon Trailhead, head up and take the first junction left towards Lost Canyon. Look for the junction again left through open country to Peekaboo Spring. The spring is situated near Salt Creek. Look for

granaries hidden away in alcoves as well as some interesting pictographs and hand symbol petroglyphs. Some scrambling is required and there are two ladders that must be climbed to complete the journey. This is a great hike for the skilled desert hiker, offering a bit of challenge in navigation with amble rewarding views, hoodoos, large meadows, and blue sky touching red rock.

Salt Creek Canyon

Strenuous – (22.5 mi / 36.2 km), round trip, long day hike or multiday backpacking trip, elev. Δ: 1,650 ft / 503 m, trailhead at end of 4WD road up Salt Creek or from Peekaboo Trail

This trail expands on the Peekaboo Trail listed above and continues along Salt Creek. As the creek holds water generally year long, this line of life holds plenty of archaeological sites, pictographs, petroglyphs, farming areas and numerous granaries. There is also an old log cabin built in the 1890's by a rancher named Rensselaer Lee Kirk showing some of the more recent history in Salt Creek Canyon.

Along the way in Elephant Canyon

Canyonlands National Park - Maze District

Quick Facts

Official Park Website: www.nps.gov/cany

Visitor Center:

- General Information: (435) 719-2313
- Backcountry Reservation Office: (435) 259-4351
- Hans Flat (Maze) Ranger Station: (435) 259-2652

Park Accessibility:

- 4WD recommended
- Primarily Overnight Use

Experience Level:

- Experienced Hiker to Backcountry Hiker

Camping in Park:

- No developed campground, backcountry camping okay with permit

Lodging and Dining in Park:

- None

Nearest Town with Amenities:

- Hanksville, UT is 61 mi / 98 km from park

Getting There:

- From Moab, UT: Take US-191 South, I-70 West and UT-24 to Lower San Rafael Road to Hans Flat Road. Total distance to Hans Flat Ranger Station is 134 mi / 216 km.

Portion of the Great Gallery

What Makes Canyonlands – Maze District Special

- The Great Gallery Petroglyphs – a 200-foot-long wall of floating ghost like figures that are so timeless that reproductions hang in the New York Museum of Modern Art

- One of the most remote places in the United States, takes a full day's drive on rough dirt roads just to get to the entrance of the park

- Only 3% of Canyonlands visitors go here, it is too remote for a day hike, thus unattainability is part of the charm.

Hiking in the Maze District of Canyonlands NP

The Maze is true desert wilderness and the trails are for the most part, more routes than actual trails. The area is remote and folks that had out this way usually plan on taking a minimum 4-5-day backpacking trip. Part of the reason is it takes nearly a full day just to get to the access points.

There is one developed trail in the Maze District and a very special one at that, Horseshoe Canyon. It is not inside the main section of the district and is an easier trip, relatively speaking. Horseshoe Canyon is definitely one of the pinnacle trails in all of the Grand Circle. To learn why, read the description below.

Horseshoe Canyon

Strenuous – (7.0 mi / 11.3 km), round trip, allow 4 -5 hours, elev. Δ: 800 ft / 244 m, trailhead described below

The one exception to this is Horseshoe Canyon. It is a protected island of land separate from the main park that was added in 1971 to protect one of the most significant examples of rock art in North America. It is arguably the best example of Barrier Canyon Style rock art. It is also one of the most recognizable. The life sized anthropomorphic figures with their unique trapezoidal shapes sit as reproductions in both the Denver Natural History Museum and the Museum of Modern Art in New York.

The centerpiece of Horseshoe Canyon is the Great Gallery. Within it is a panel of rock measuring 200 feet long (61m) and 15 feet (4.6m) high. The panel contains 20 elongated floating limbless humanoid figures, all life-sized, with one measuring over seven feet (2.1m) tall. The figures seem to float as ghosts on the rock, having no feet and distinctive trapezoidal shoulders. A visit to the Great Gallery is certainly a high-water mark for any trip.

Horseshoe Canyon is a separate unit from the main section of Canyonlands NP. It is best accessed from the west near Goblin Valley State Park at Highway 24. This road is often accessible for two-wheel drive vehicles and is okay for smaller RVs. It is graded along the 30 miles (48 km). You can also take a 47-mile (75 km) dirt road from Green River, but it has similar caveats and is longer.

Once out to the Horseshoe Canyon unit, it is an additional 7-mile (11 km) round trip hike to the Great Gallery. Allow about four hours for the hike, leaving plenty of time, water and food for the strenuous climb back out of the canyon. During the spring and fall, guided walks are held by the park's rangers. Aligning with these guided tours is an excellent way to see the petroglyphs and pictographs. The rangers do an amazing job of tying in the interesting details of what you are seeing and bringing historical context to your trip.

Go to www.discovermoab.com for a complete list of guided tours to Horseshoe Canyon and for rafting, jeep, and horseback riding tours.

Note that the roads may be closed seasonally during monsoon season. Check with the ranger station before heading out.

Edge of the Cedars State Park

Sun Sculpture at Edge of the Cedars

Official Park Website: http://stateparks.utah.gov/parks/edge-of-the-cedars//

Visitor Center:

(435) 678-2238

Park Accessibility:

- Okay for 2WD and RVs
- Day Use Only

Experience Level:

- Family Friendly

Camping in Park:

- None

Lodging and Dining in Park:

- None

Nearest Town with Amenities:

- The park is located in the town of Blanding, UT

Getting There:

- From Moab, UT: Take US-191 South to Blanding, UT. Total distance is 76 mi / 122 km to park.

What Makes Edge of the Cedars State Park Museum Special

Edge of the Cedars sits within the town of Blanding, Utah, lying south of Moab and Monticello, UT and north of the Four Corners and Mesa Verde NP. While the Ancestral Pueblo ruins are worth exploring, the highlight here is the museum, which holds a diverse selection of pottery and other artifacts. This is a great place to see the actual tools of these people and is worth seeing.

Blanding, UT is a solid little small town of about 3,500 residents. Besides being a gateway town, serving tourists on their way to the next natural park, it has economic ties within the mineral processing and agriculture industries. This is a good place to stock up on goods and grab a bite to eat.

Goblin Valley State Park

Quick Facts

Official Park Website: http://stateparks.utah.gov/parks/goblin-valley/

Visitor Center: (435) 275-4584

Park Accessibility:

- Okay for 2WD and RVs
- Day and Overnight Use

Experience Level:

- Family Friendly to Casual Hiker

Camping in Park:

- Goblin Valley Campground: 10 T/15 RV + 2 yurts, drinking water, showers, flush toilets, 4 first come-first served, rest are reservable through Reserve America: (800) 322-3770 or at www.reserveamerica.com

Lodging and Dining in Park:

- None

Nearest Town with Amenities:

- Hanksville, UT is 32 mi / 51 km from park

Getting There:

- From Moab, UT: Take US-191 North to I-70 West to UT-24 West. Total distance is 101 mi / 162 km to park

Three gregarious goblins graciously greeting guests

What Makes Goblin Valley Special

- Thousands of red-orange mushroom shaped hoodoos of varying shapes and sizes

- The nearby slot canyon within the Little Wild Horse Canyon

- Feeling like you are in the middle of nowhere on the Molly's Castle Overlook Trail

Goblin Valley is a unique place in terms of geologic formations. Here is an area that contains thousands of hoodoos. However, this is not your typical hoodoo formation. They are short and stubby toadstool shaped things, each with a unique personality. Whether you call them hoodoos or goblins, this is a fun little place.

The way these goblins were formed is even more amazing. There is evidence that the area of the park was once at the edge of a sea, where the tide ebbed and flowed. The rounded heads of the toadstools are where, for the most part, that part of the formations stayed above tidal waters while the stalks were worn down just a bit by the tidal currents.

Now for a little segment called, "name them and shame them". In October 2013, Glenn Tuck Taylor pushed over one of these ancient marvels, as his buddy and fellow Boy Scout leader, David Benjamin Hall, filmed the vandalism and then posted it on Facebook. For some reason they thought this was the right thing to do. They were stripped of their leadership roles almost immediately and then asked to leave the Boy Scouts altogether shortly thereafter. They were prosecuted and the two goblin topplers received one year of probation each. The life lesson here is don't vandalize parks. To see the actual vandalism caught on tape and more, go here: https://www.youtube.com/watch?v=3GtbSd-biCE.

Hiking Goblin Valley State Park

Valley of Goblins
Easy – distance and time varies

Most visitors just walk off the rim from the overlook and wander among the goblins. If you do come to this park, at least do this. It is cool to see these formations up close and there are some unique rock formations that you can only experience by getting down among them.

Curtis Bench Trail

Easy – (2.1 mi / 3.4 km), round trip, allow 1 hour

This is an easy trail to the Curtis Bench, which gives a nice panoramic view of the Henry Mountains and the goblins in their valley below. There are also views of Molly's Castle, Three Sisters, and Wild Horse Butte.

Entrada Canyon Trail

Easy – (2.4 mi / 3.9 km), round trip, allow 30 minutes

Another easy trail suitable for small children leading into red rock badlands. Unique and somewhat unnatural looking hoodoos in a setting that seems like you are walking in a gigantic dried mud patch.

Carmel Canyon Trail

Easy – (1.6 mi / 2.6 km), round trip, allow 1 hour

A fun and short hike that walks past Goblin Valley and into the badlands and the very short Carmel slot canyon. The trail also includes a trip to Molly's Castle Overlook. This is another good hike for kids. The slot canyon does get narrow but is never very intimating.

Little Wild Horse Canyon

Strenuous – (8.0 mi / 12.9 km), round trip, allow 4 – 5 hours

This is a great hike just outside of Goblin Valley State Park. Little Wild Horse Canyon is one of the most accessible slot canyons in the entire Grand Circle. In fact, it's so accessible, you cross the entrance to Little Wild Horse Canyon on the way into the park. The visitor center at Goblin Valley has a brochure on the hike that is worth picking up. Pick up the trailhead by backtracking about 0.25 miles from the visitor center to a maintained dirt road with a sign for Little Wild Horse Canyon. The trailhead with restrooms and a trail register is another 5.3 miles down this road.

The hike starts along a seasonal wash and after 0.3 mile heads into the spectacular slot canyon of Little Wild Horse Canyon and then left onto a connector road into the slightly wider Bell Canyon for the return. Little Wild Horse is 3.6 miles, 1.6 for the connector road and 1.8 for Bell Canyon. There are signposts marking the way but these can be hard to read and even find. Little Wild Horse is suitable for most hikers while Bell Canyon has some Class 3 scrambles to negotiate. If in doubt, return via Little Wild Horse Canyon.

There are lots of goblins at Goblin Valley State Park

Goosenecks State Park

Quick Facts

Official Park Website: http://stateparks.utah.gov/parks/goosenecks/

Visitor Center: none, contact park at (435) 678-2238

Park Accessibility:

- Okay for 2WD and RVs
- Day Use Only

Experience Level:

- Family Friendly – Experienced Hiker

Nearest Town with Amenities:

- Mexican Hat, UT is 8 mi / 13 km from park

Getting There:

- From Page, AZ: Take AZ-98 East to US-160 East to US-163 North to UT-261 North to UT-316 West. Total distance is 151 mi / 243 km to park

What Makes Goosenecks State Park Special

- Peering over the edge to see the neatly layered rock cut like artwork by the deep meander of the San Juan River

- Driving away from the general viewing area down a dusty dirt road to hike the Honaker Trail to the river's shore and becoming for a brief moment, part of this artwork

- Learning about and seeing a gooseneck

Goosenecks State Park is an easy side trip for those traveling from the Moab area parks south towards Arizona. The park has its own state highway, UT-316, which travels 3.5 miles from its juncture with UT 261 to the Goosenecks overlook and parking area. What to do once you are there is limited.

At a modest 10 acres of park, most folk's park, head to the railing and look down at the meandering San Juan River. In this section of the river, there are a number of U shaped river course ways that have been cut dramatically and deeply into the underlying strata. The view is well worth the five minutes to get there. There is also one trail that takes the more adventurous traveler down to the San Juan River shoreline.

By the way, if you are asking yourself why the river doesn't just carve a straight line, the answer has to do with the river itself. The flow of water erodes the outer banks at a faster rate, while simultaneously depositing sediment on the slower moving inner course of the river. The result of this erosional process causes a snaking pattern to form as the river cuts through the valley. Any flowing body of water can carve out a meandering course, as the principles are the same no matter the volume of the water. In the course of sandstone, this process starts very early and then essentially sets in place, eroding straight down thereafter.

Hiking Goosenecks State Park

Honaker Trail

Strenuous – (5.0 mi / 8.0 km), round trip, allow 3 - 4 hours

This is a steep route built in 1893 by prospectors during the short-lived gold rush in this territory. Honaker Trail proved too steep even for pack animals or so the legend goes, so if you do take this trail and make it the bottom, you'll have the bragging rights that you out hiked a mule. The trail is 1.5 miles northeast from the Goosenecks SP parking lot. Look for a water tank and a metal sign that says Honaker. The road travels below the first rim to the nondescript cairn-marked trailhead. From here, it's 1,000 feet over 2.5 miles to the bottom. At about 1.5 miles down, you'll notice an abundance of fossilized brachiopods (fossilized shells). It is nearly impossible to avoid walking on them in this spot. Once at the bottom, take a look up to where you came from. As a sign at the Grand Canyon reminds us hikers at times like these, "Down is optional. Up is mandatory". Keep this mind as you take the strenuous hike back up.

View from Goosenecks State Park Overlook

Natural Bridges National Monument

Quick Facts

Official Park Website: http://www.nps.gov/nabr

Visitor Center: (435) 692-1234 ext. 16

Park Accessibility:

- Okay for 2WD and RVs
- Day and Overnight Use

Experience Level:

- Family Friendly to Casual Hiker

Camping in Park:

- Natural Bridges Campground: 13 T/RV, no water, vault restrooms, no dump station, no hookups, first come-first served
- Several backcountry campgrounds

Lodging and Dining in Park:

- None

Nearest Town with Amenities:

- Blanding, UT is 44 mi / 71 km from park

Getting There:

- From Blanding, UT: Take UT-95 North to UT-275 North 44 mi / 71 km to park entrance

As above, so below. The Owachomo Bridge

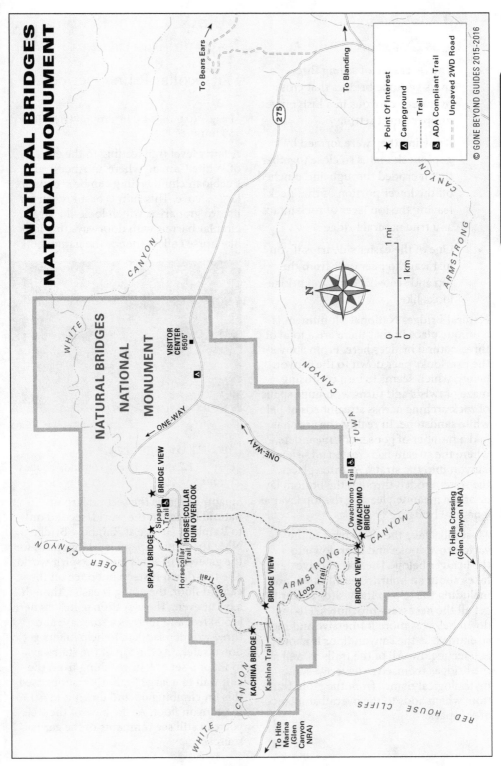

NATURAL BRIDGES
NATIONAL MONUMENT

To Bears Ears

To Blanding

275

© GONE BEYOND GUIDES 2015-2016

★ Point Of Interest
△ Campground
--- Trail
--- ADA Compliant Trail
=== Unpaved 2WD Road

N

0   1 mi
0   1 km

CANYON

ARMSTRONG

NATURAL BRIDGES

NATIONAL MONUMENT

WHITE CANYON

VISITOR
CENTER
6505'

ONE-WAY

ONE-WAY

TUWA CANYON

SIPAPU BRIDGE

Sipapu
Trail

BRIDGE VIEW

HORSECOLLAR
RUIN OVERLOOK

Horsecollar
Trail

DEER CANYON

Owachomo Trail

OWACHOMO
BRIDGE

Loop Trail

BRIDGE VIEW

ARMSTRONG

ARMSTRONG CANYON

BRIDGE VIEW

Loop Trail

To Halls Crossing
(Glen Canyon NRA)

KACHINA BRIDGE

Kachina Trail

WHITE CANYON

RED HOUSE CLIFFS

To Hite Marina (Glen
Canyon NRA)

What Makes Natural Bridges Special

- The reverence of seeing three massive stone bridges that cross over deep canyons in a lush pinyon juniper forest setting

- Knowing they were formed by a gooseneck that is so close together that it eroded through and pinched off the lower portion of the "neck", leaving the top layer of rock intact as a true natural bridge

- One of the easier side trips if you just want to peer over from the top and see what a natural bridge looks like

Natural Bridges National Monument is a unique place in that there are a total of three natural bridges here. From above, the overlooks peer down to the canyon below, which seems to be a confusing maze of twists and turns with huge spans of rock arching across streambeds of pale white sandstone. In reality, the area has had a number of gooseneck meanders, where the stream has created a U-shaped canyon into the strata. At three places, the water eroded through the bottom layer of the meander, leaving the top layer as a natural bridge.

Most folks take the short trips to the various overlooks and peer down to the bridges below. The scenic drive takes about an hour to see all three, not including the trip to the visitor center to get all the necessary brochures. Hiking down below is more immersive and more strenuous, as the canyon floor is about 500 feet below. All of the trails as well as the bridges themselves have awesome mythological names from the Hopi tradition, which adds to the overall ambiance of this park.

Hiking Natural Bridges National Monument

Horsecollar Ruin Overlook Trail

Easy – (0.6 mi / 1.0 m), round trip, allow 30 minutes

A fairly level trail leading to the edge of White Canyon where an Ancestral Puebloan cliff dwelling can be seen in a large alcove. This ruin is best known for its two granaries, which look like large circular barrels with doorways that look like horse collars (hence the name).

Horsecollar Ruins

Sipapu Bridge Trail

Easy – (1.2 mi / 1.9 km), round trip, allow 1 hour

Sipapu Bridge is the second largest natural bridge in the world, second only to Rainbow Bridge at Rainbow Bridge NM. The name Sipapu is a Hopi term for the gateway of souls into the spirit world. The trip down is steep but once on the canyon floor, the going is easier, though a bit uneven. The elevation gain/loss here is 500 feet and there is a staircase and three wooden ladders to help hikers get down safely. At the top of the stairway, look for a set of logs reaching from the cliff wall to a large fir. Early visitors used this fir, climbing up and down it to get to the canyon floor. At the base of the tree, you can still see remnants of the earlier staircase.

Kachina Bridge Trail

Easy – (1.4 mi / 2.3 km), round trip, allow 1 hour

Kachina Bridge is considered the youngest formed of the three bridges and is also the least dramatic from the overlook above due to the angle. Take switchbacks down 400 feet to the bridge.

Owachomo Bridge Trail

Easy – (0.4 mi / 0.6 km), round trip, allow 30 minutes

The easiest of the bridges to get to, Owachomo, meaning "rock mound" in the Hopi language is also the most delicate of the three bridge formation. The bridge's form suggests that it is eroding more quickly than the others. It is also considered the most pleasing to the eye, due to its thin span of rock that stretches across the sky.

Loop Trail

Strenuous – (8.6 mi / 13.8 km), round trip, allow 4 -5 hours

The Loop Trail gives the complete package of all three bridges with return options along the mesa top. At the mesa, the loop has a juncture that allows for a shorter hike. Start the hike at any of the parking areas. Starting at Sipapu gives the most flexibility if you need to return early as you pass by Sipapu and Kachina before climbing back out. If you do continue to Owachomo Bridge, follow the trail up the left side of the canyon after Kachina Bridge in order to more easily navigate past the Knickpoint pour-off, a dry fall that pours water runoff into a pool below when it rains.

Natural Bridges

Sipapu Bridge

Kachina Bridge

Hovenweep National Monument

Quick Facts

Official Park Website: http://www.nps.gov/hove

Visitor Center: (970) 562-4282 ext. 10

Park Accessibility:
- Okay for 2WD and RVs
- Day and Overnight Use

Experience Level:
- Family Friendly to Casual Hiker

Camping in Park:
- Hovenweep Campground: 31T sites, some sites will accommodate RV's, drinking water, flush toilets, no hookups, one ADA compliant site, first come-first served

Lodging and Dining in Park:
- None

Nearest Town with Amenities:
- Bluff, UT is closer by 5 miles but Cortez, CO has more amenities. Cortez is 45 mi / 72 km from the park

Getting There:
- From Cortez, CO: Take US-491 N/N Broadway and turn left onto Road Bb, which becomes County Road 10 in Utah. Total distance is 45 mi / 72 km to park entrance

The round ruins of Hovenweep

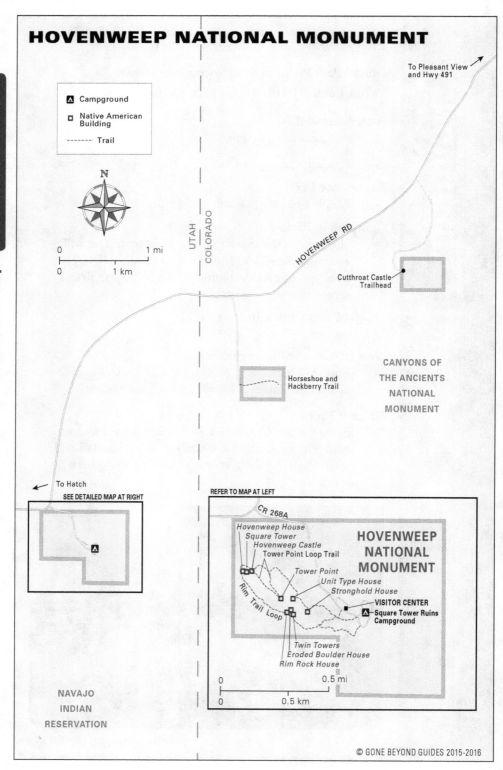

HOVENWEEP NATIONAL MONUMENT

Legend
- ▲ Campground
- ◻ Native American Building
- ------- Trail

N

0 — 1 mi
0 — 1 km

UTAH
COLORADO

HOVENWEEP RD

To Pleasant View
and Hwy 491

Cutthroat Castle
Trailhead

CANYONS OF
THE ANCIENTS
NATIONAL
MONUMENT

Horseshoe and
Hackberry Trail

To Hatch
SEE DETAILED MAP AT RIGHT

REFER TO MAP AT LEFT

CR 268A

Hovenweep House
Square Tower
Hovenweep Castle
Tower Point Loop Trail

Tower Point
Unit Type House
Stronghold House

Rim Trail Loop

VISITOR CENTER
Square Tower Ruins
Campground

HOVENWEEP
NATIONAL
MONUMENT

Twin Towers
Eroded Boulder House
Rim Rock House

0 — 0.5 mi
0 — 0.5 km

NAVAJO
INDIAN
RESERVATION

What Makes Hovenweep NM Special

The feeling of discovery as you walk from one ruin to another

Understanding the harmony of man made and natural structures under the warm glow of a late afternoon sun

The sacredness of being in the middle of nowhere

Hovenweep National Monument is a small park protecting several small villages of the Ancestral Puebloans on the borders of Utah and Colorado. What is unique here is the setting. Unlike the deep alcoves of Mesa Verde or the immensity of Chaco, Hovenweep was built in an arid flatland that at first glance would appear to have no surprises. Upon arrival however, it feels as if the visitor has stumbled upon something, the ruins feel unexpected and special. There is a sentiment of solitude that the land brings to one's visit which invokes thoughts that Hovenweep was more sanctuary than village. The harmony of the structures and their natural disposition against the frame of nature itself brings a sense of peace as one walks among these ruins. Hovenweep is a bit off the beaten path, but if any drive can lead to a place that inspires the spirit, then that is a road worth traveling on.

Hiking Hovenweep National Monument

There are six villages protected at Hovenweep. Of these, the most popular is Square Tower, which also contains the only maintained trails. The other five villages are best viewed by driving to the sites and walking amongst the ruins via short trails that are less maintained. The other five sites are Cajon, Cutthroat Castle, Holly, Horseshoe, and Hackberry and are spread out over 20 miles. A good first step in exploring Hovenweep is picking up a visitor's guide to get an understanding of the general layout of the park.

Rim Trail Loop

Easy – (1.5 mi / 2.4 km), round trip, allow 1 hour

The Rim Trail Loop is picked up just outside the visitor center and covers some of the most iconic ruin imagery in the park. Here one can see the Square Tower, Hovenweep Castle, the circular Twin Towers, and the Stronghold House, which is the first ruin found from the visitor center.

Tower Point Loop

Easy – (0.5 mi / 0.8 km), round trip, allow 20 – 30 minutes

This a quick loop that travels along a peninsular section of the mesa ending at Tower Point. The canyon drops on both sides with the ruins as a backdrop, creating a nice view of the surrounding area.

Horseshoe and Hackberry Trail

Easy – (1.0 mi / 1.6 km), round trip, allow 1 hour

This slightly more primitive trail is a nice loop covering both the Horseshoe and Hackberry sites. Highlights include the Horseshoe Tower and Horseshoe House as well as the Hackberry group, which is one of the largest ancestral population centers in the park.

Cutthroat Castle Trail

Easy – (1.4 mi / 2.3 km), round trip, allow 1 hour

This site was added to the park in 1956 and showcases typical structures of the Ancestral Puebloans. It is possible to drive right up to the site, however from the trailhead junction; the road is not maintained and is suitable only for high clearance vehicles.

Photo Attributes

Attributions and permissions given where indicated.

- All Grand Circle Maps and Park Maps copyright Gone Beyond Guides

Front Cover

- Painted Wall in Black Canyon of the Gunnison National Park, by Chris Weeler / NPS, PD US NPS

Back Cover

- All Grand Circle Maps and Park Maps copyright Gone Beyond Guides

In order of appearance.

Title Page

- Great Sand Dunes, by Phil Armitage, Copyrighted free use

Table of Contents

- Penasco Blanco, by russavia, CC-BY-SA-2.0

General Information

- All Grand Circle Maps copyright Gone Beyond Guides
- Dinosaur National Monument, by refractor, CC-By-2.0
- Kasha-Katuwe Tent Rocks, by Bureau of Land Management, CC-By-2.0
- Black Canyon, by Lorax, CC-BY-SA-3.0
- Cliff Palace, by John Fowler, CC-By-2.0

Southwest Colorado

- Cliff Palace, by Ben FrantzDale, CC-By-3.0

Yucca House NM

- Entrance, by Nationalparks, CC-BY-SA-2.5

Mesa Verde National Park

- Cliff Palace, by Tobi 87, CC-BY-3.0
- Cliff Palace, by Ben FrantzDale, CC-By-3.0
- Kiva, by Ken Lund, CC-BY-2.0
- Weatherhill Mesa, by Ken Lund, CC-BY-2.0

Mancos State Park

- Jackson Gulch and Reservoir, by McGhiever, CC-BY-3.0

Great Sand Dunes NP

- Great Sand Dunes, by Phil Armitage, PD-author
- Cliff Palace, by Footwarrior, CC-By-SA-3.0
- Great Sand Dunes, NPS, PD US NPS

Ridgway State Park

- Ridgway, by unknown, CC-BY-3.0

Black Canyon of the Gunnison National Park

- BCoftheGNP, by Jesse Varner, CC-BY-SA-2.0
- Flowers, by NPS, PD US NPS
- Painted Wall, by Jesse Varner, CC-BY-SA-2.0
- Fall foilage, by NPS, PD US NPS
- Canyon Floor, by NPS, PD US NPS
- Painted Wall, by Chris Wheeler/NPS, PD US NPS

Curecanti NRA

- Dillon Pinnacles, by unknown, CC-BY-SA-2.5

Colorado NM

- Colorado NM, by Rennett Stowe, CC-BY-2.0
- Colorado NM Panorama, by Dustin C. Gurley, CC-BY-SA-3.0
- Colorado NM, by Rennett Stowe, CC-BY-2.0
- Colorado NM, by CJ Latham, PD-User

Rifle Falls SP

- Rifle Falls SP, by unknown, CC-BY-2.0

Dinosaur NM

- Camarasaurus lentus (Marsh, 1889) sauropod dinosaur, by James St. John, CC-BY-2.0
- Confluence of the Green and Yampa Rivers , by NPS, PD US NPS

Northwest New Mexico

- Chetro Ketl, by JCTalyor, CC-BY-SA-3.0

Chaco Culture National HistoricPark

- Pueblo del Arroyo, by Greg Willis, CC-BY-SA-2.0
- Chetro Ketl, NPS, PD US NPS
- Chaco Ruins, by Steven C. Price, CC-BY-SA-3.0
- Chaco Pictograph, by Steven C. Price, CC-BY-SA-3.0
- Supernova petroglphs, by Alex Marentes, CC-BY-SA-2.0
- Pueblo del Arroyo Trail, by Greg Willis, CC-BY-SA-2.0
- Inside the Chetro Ketl Great Kiva, by SkybirdForever, CC-BY-SA-3.0
- Pueblo Bonito Doorwasy, by NPS, PS US NPS

Aztec Ruins

- Aztec Ruins Panorama, by Rationalobserver, CC-BY-SA-4.0

Heron Lakes State Park

- Heron Lake, by G. Thomas, PD-user

Bandelier National Monument

- Bandelier, by SarahStierch, CC-BY-SA-3.0
- Cliff Dwelling, by byrdiegyrl, CC-BY-SA-2.0
- Reconstructed cavate, Daniel Mayer (Mav), CC-BY-SA-3.0

Kasha-Katuwe Tent Rocks National Monument

- Tent Rocks, by BLM, CC-BY-2.0

Petroglyphs National Monument

- Petroglyph National Monument, by Angel Schatz, CC-BY-2.0
- Petroglyph National Monument, by Angel Schatz, CC-BY-2.0
- Petroglyph, by Steven C. Price, CC-BY-SA-3.0
- Petroglyph National Monument, by Angel Schatz, CC-BY-2.0

El Morro National Monument

- El Morro, by Timothy H. Sullivan, PD US Army USACE

El Malpais National Monument

- Pottery Shards, by Bob Wick, BLM California, CC-BY-2.0
- El Malpais Countryside, by Bob Wick, BLM California, CC-BY-2.0

Southeast Utah

- Dead Horse Point, by Jean-Christophe BENOIST, CC-BY-SA-2.0

Goblin Valley State Park

- Goblins, by CGP Grey, CC-BY-2.0
- Goblin Valley, by Aaron D. Gifford, CC-BY-SA-2.5

Canyonlands National Park

- Canyonlands, by Phil Armitage, PD-author
- Mesa Arch, by Michael Rissi, CC-BY-SA-3.0-migrated
- Aztec Butte Trail, by Ronnie Macdonald, CC-BY-2.0
- Upheaval Dome, by Doc Searls, CC-BY-2.0
- Needles Overlook, by Alex Proimos, CC-BY-2.0
- Needles, by Jesse Varner, CC-BY-SA-2.5
- Druid Arch, by RichieB_pics, CC-BY-2.0
- Druid Arch Trail, by RichieB_pics, CC-BY-2.0
- Great Gallery, by Scott Catron, CC-BY-3.0

Dead Horse Point State Park

- Dead Horse Point, by Clément Bardot, CC-BY-SA-3.0
- La Sals and Dead Horse Point, by Jean-Christophe BENOIST, CC-BY-SA-3.0

Arches National Park

- Delicate Arch, by National Park Service Photo, PD US NPS
- Courthouse Panel, by NPS, CC-BY-2.0
- Double Arch, by Flicka, CC-BY-2.0
- Landscape Arch, by Daniel Mayer i, CC-BY-3.0

FIND YOUR PARK

In Celebration of a Birthday

In 2016, the National Park Service will turn 100 years old. The national parks have always held a very special place in my heart. They represent some of the best of the best in terms of the natural wonders that America holds. I like the robustness that a national park offers, being fully wilderness in so many different ways, the architectural and historical significance of its buildings, and the educational aspects that the rangers play; including the junior ranger and other programs. Each park protects something that is unique to the world, continually inspiring poets, painters, and patrons every single day. They bring that amazement to all that visit them and connect in a way that we should experience more often.

There was an ask of the national park system to share something and bring a gift to this grandest of birthday celebrations. These books are my gift. Happy birthday NPS, for me you represent America at its best! Here's hoping we can continue to enjoy and protect these lands as a nation for many centuries to come.

The Grand Circle Series Project

This series of hiking guides started from a passion for the area itself. I started visiting the Grand Circle while still in diapers, coming along with my dad on fishing trips up Oak Creek Canyon in the 60's. I have lived within the Grand Circle for much of my life and have hiked many of these places multiple times and through all seasons. I have explored this land for over three decades and each time I went out on a trail or off trail; it was with the same childlike wonder. If a person can fall in love with a place, that is me. Each time I went out, I wanted to share the experience. This sharing started with my friends and then my family, but still, I continued to want to share. Therefore, in that spirit of sharing, I decided to write about my experiences.

The project started by writing my first book on the area, called *A Family Guide to the Grand Circle National Parks*. This travel guide describes a vacation around seven national parks, Zion, Bryce Canyon, Capitol Reef, Canyonlands, Arches, Mesa Verde, and the Grand Canyon. I had fun with the book. I worked with the rangers on the park descriptions and even wrote semi fictional stories to go along with each park. It was great fun sharing the Grand Circle with others.

Describing the national parks along the "main route" was awesome, but I had this larger idea. What if I described every park within the Grand Circle? I had no idea how large such a project would be or how long it would take. I simply started by writing about every park I knew of and then followed up with firsthand accounts for the ones that I hadn't. I received multiple accounts for each trail. Where I had hiked, I wrote my account, researching, and fact checking along the way. Where I hadn't hiked, I worked with others who had, incorporating firsthand accounts from a strong and amazing network of hiking experts and other folks passionate about the area. A tremendous amount of fact checking and support went into this work because while it is nearly impossible for one person to have hiked every trail in this book, I wanted to make sure every trail was described accurately and robustly.

The intent of this work is simple. The Grand Circle Series attempts at gathering every trail for every national park, national monument, national historic park, national recreation area, tribal park, and state park within the Grand Circle. I am certain that there are trails and possibly even parks yet that need to be included. The Browns Canyon National Monument is a great case in point. It was just recently added to the national park system in 2015. That said, after describing nearly 500 trails and after crossing the 100,000-word mark, I realized I was at a stopping point. (This was my 'Forest Gump at Monument Valley' moment).

When it was all done I had described 12 national parks, 31 national monuments, including national historic sites and preserves, 3 national recreation areas, 29 state parks and 4 tribal parks. These 79 parks in all cover 480 hikes and the truth is there are still hikes left to be defined, especially in the larger and more remote parks. I left out unofficial hikes within parks and also left out secret areas only known to locals, as I believe some land is so special that it should be preserved, that if it wants you to visit it, it will call you, it needs no introduction.

So what to do with all these trail descriptions? The intent originally was to put everything into one book, but then I realized that wouldn't be very useful. It would be too big to fit into a daypack and most folks would not make full use of a book covering such a large area. In the end, I decided to split the content into four guides, one each for Nevada, Utah, Arizona and finally one more collectively covering Colorado and New Mexico. These four kept everything to a manageable area of interest.

Each book spills over in its surrounding states just a bit, because that's how I would use such a book. This way if you are planning to hike Black Canyon of the Gunnison National Park using the Colorado/New Mexico trail guide, you can read on to the chapter that describes Canyonlands National Park in nearby Utah, because it's just as amazing, but in a completely different way. For the one person who buys all four books, first off, thank you! Secondly, hopefully you understand why you have four copies of the Four Corners Monument chapter.

I am always looking for feedback on improving these books and for any accuracy, misspellings, gripes, wants, and of course kudos. Please send to gonebeyondguides@gmail.com. I write, design, and publish these works myself.

Happy hiking!

Acknowledgments

First off, I want to thank MRoy Cartography for their wonderful map making, headed by Molly Roy. I came in with a request to make these the best maps out there and she fully delivered.

I am extremely thankful for the constant ebb and flow of feedback from my growing focus group, whom I used day in and day out as a sounding board for ideas, research, and pretty much for every aspect of this book. This is never a one-man shop; I couldn't do what I do without them. These include Ernie, Chris, Frank, Joel, George, Geoff, Jeff, Peggy, John, and Angela.

A special thanks to the National Park Service and its employees. There has never been a time when you weren't able to support this effort, which is remarkable given how much you all do. I truly appreciate all that you do for us as a nation and for all the help and assistance you have given me. To NPS - - Happy 100th birthday!

I also want to thank the states of Utah, Arizona, New Mexico, Colorado, and Nevada. Each of you protects some of the best and most remote lands in the United States. Each state, I commend you for your efforts here.

To my wife Angela and two boys, Everest and Bryce, thank you. The time you have given me to create these books is a true blessing, both in the adventures we have taken and in the many hours writing and editing away you have given me.

You can reach the author through our FaceBook page:

 www.facebook.com/GBG.GoneBeyondGuides

ISBN-10: 0-9971370-1-0

ISBN-13: 978-0-9971370-1-9

Eric Henze began his writing career at the age of twelve with a sci fi short titled "5:15", tackling a plot around a timepiece that could end the world. His passion for hiking started in Sedona, Arizona where he lived in his youth. It expanded to peak bagging in the Sierra Nevada Mountains and then the Andes of South America, where he lived as a Peace Corp volunteer for two years, climbing many of the peaks of Ecuador and Peru. A highlight was climbing Sangay, an active volcano that often shoots VW size rocks at climbers to maintain their attention. In his own words, "It was a delight".

His passions for writing, hiking, and adventure have led to a series of guidebooks for both the National Park Service and the California State Parks. A portion of the proceeds of all of his books will go towards directly supporting these parks.

By day, the intrepid author works for a Fortune 50 company helping large enterprises navigate towards, within and beyond the digital revolution. He is lives his family, two awesome boys, a lovely wife, and a blue-eyed merle named Sedona.

His children have noted that his last words will be while driving through the Southwest and seeing some point of interest. Those last words will be, "I'll be right back, I'm going go check that out".

Also Available Within the Grand Circle Series

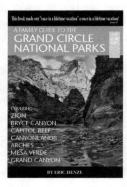

Top Trails of Utah

Top Trails of Arizona

Top Trails of Nevada

A Family Guide to the
Grand Circle National Parks

Follow us on Facebook and Twitter!

facebook.com/GBG.GoneBeyondGuides

twitter.com/GoneBeyondGuide

All titles published by Gone Beyond Guides